ADVANCE PRAISE FOR

Voices from Cape Town Classrooms

"Alan Wieder's *Voices from Cape Town Classrooms* provides a breathtaking view into a vital center of resistance during the South African nightmare known as apartheid. Schools in South Africa as elsewhere are contested spaces, arenas of hope and struggle, because schools are where we invest in our children (or not), and project a vision of the future we hope to build. During the anti-apartheid struggle, schools were a powerful center of resistance. Filled with immediacy and urgency, the struggle comes alive in these pages as vital, complex, and nuanced, something trembling and real and lived. The events around the struggle are so huge and so encompassing that they can easily be constructed into a gleaming and unproblematic icon casting a huge, seemingly impenetrable shadow across an otherwise dense and complex landscape. To Alan Wieder's eternal credit, he rescues here the reality of history as lived, paths taken before the outcome is known, difficult choices made in the dark."

Bill Ayers, University of Chicago, Illinois; Author of Fugitive Days

"Alan Wieder's book opens up new perspectives in research methodology by documenting the life histories of apartheid-era teachers in the Western Cape. Wieder's approach allows these teachers to speak for themselves and to re-create the world of apartheid education for the teacher/educator. He manages to demonstrate the tension and the excitement as well as the very real dangers of the political and the pedagogical challenges that presented themselves in Coloured schools in the 1980s and allows the reader to glimpse the realities of everyday life for activist educators. It seems that the moment was right for this work to be done and that Alan Wieder, as an outsider with unique skills, was able to persuade these teachers to share their stories with a wider public in a way that had not seemed possible earlier. This book provides a blueprint for much-needed further work on the key role that many teachers played in opposing apartheid not just as political activists or trade unionists but in the ways in which they lived their everyday lives and conducted themselves in the classroom as well as the models that they provided for the students, teachers, and parents in their communities in the dark days of racial oppression. In the present climate of demoralization of the teaching profession such work is surely essential in rebuilding a profession upon which so much of the future depends."

Peter Kallaway, University of the Western Cape;
Author of The History of Education Under Apartheid

Voices
from Cape Town Classrooms

Alan R. Sadovnik and Susan F. Semel
General Editors

Vol. 39

PETER LANG
New York • Washington, D.C./Baltimore • Bern
Frankfurt am Main • Berlin • Brussels • Vienna • Oxford

Alan Wieder

Voices
from Cape Town Classrooms

Oral Histories of Teachers
Who Fought Apartheid

Preface by Kader Asmal, South African Minister of Education

PETER LANG
New York • Washington, D.C./Baltimore • Bern
Frankfurt am Main • Berlin • Brussels • Vienna • Oxford

Library of Congress Cataloging-in-Publication Data

Wieder, Alan.
Voices from Cape Town classrooms: oral histories of teachers
who fought apartheid / Alan Wieder.
p. cm. — (History of schools and schooling: v. 39)
Includes bibliographical references.
1. Teachers—South Africa—Capetown—Political activity.
2. Anti-apartheid movements—South Africa—
Capetown. I. Title. II. Series.
LB2844.1.P6W49   371.1'0096873'55—dc21   2002155899
ISBN 0-8204-6768-5
ISSN 1089-0678

Bibliographic information published by Die Deutsche Bibliothek.
Die Deutsche Bibliothek lists this publication in the "Deutsche
Nationalbibliografie"; detailed bibliographic data is available
on the Internet at http://dnb.ddb.de/.

Cover art ©Adil Bradlow/Trace Images
AB/Protest. Cape Town. South Africa. August 1985 - Students from
High Schools in the Athlone and neighbouring coloured communities
took to the streets for a voice in a better education, they ended up
their protest outside the Alexander Sinton Secondary School

Cover design by Lisa Barfield

The paper in this book meets the guidelines for permanence and durability
of the Committee on Production Guidelines for Book Longevity
of the Council of Library Resources.

© 2003 Peter Lang Publishing, Inc., New York
275 Seventh Avenue, 28th Floor, New York, NY 10001
www.peterlangusa.com

Printed in the United States of America

Contents

ONE
Non-Racialism: Teachers' League Stories   13

Preface

In our 1997 book, *Reconciliation Through Truth*, Louise Asmal, Ronald Suresh Roberts, and I wrote about the importance of collective memory for both understanding apartheid and building democracy in the new South Africa. Alan Wieder's oral histories of teachers who fought against the apartheid regime add to this mission. He calls his work a memory book, and it provides testimony to the past and the present. The individual stories of twenty Cape Town teachers portray the horror of apartheid, and they correspond to what we wrote in 1997:

> The majority of people in South Africa lived and breathed the truths of apartheid. They suffered the indignities and humiliation of statutory inferiority. They suffered the pain of being forced out of homes and off their land; away from their loved ones. They were imprisoned and detained in the thousands. (9)

But the teachers whose voices are heard in this book joined many other South Africans who battled the apartheid regime. They believed in educational excellence, the struggle against apartheid, and a democratic South Africa. They challenged their students academically as well as politically, and they supported activism against apartheid, although in different ways. One of the strengths of these stories is that the teachers are not clones. We meet older teachers who were academic giants and strident politicians, but who shunned the activism of their younger colleagues. And these younger colleagues, some of them the children and students of the elders, believed in academia but also joined workers, parents, and students when the struggle moved to the streets. Collectively, the stories Wieder tells open windows to apartheid's crimes, but also to the courage and humanity of teachers who struggled for a democratic South Africa.

The hard work, strength, and intelligence of the teachers who speak in *Voices from Cape Town Classrooms* offer lessons for the present and the future. As we struggle to make progress in our quest for better schools for our children, we welcome examples of teachers who promote both equity and excellence. The South African teachers we meet in this book made great sacrifices for their students and for the future of all South Africans. Their lives as teachers are models for the people who teach our children today.

Kader Asmal
Minister of Education
Pretoria, South Africa

Acknowledgments

I truly cannot convey how thankful I am to the South African teachers who told me their stories. Besides the twenty whose oral histories are included in the book; and Simon Winter, Dennis Ntombela, Wendy Moult, Zozo Siyenga, Barry Liknaitzky, Polly Slingers, Dianne Gordon, Terrence Klassen, Marge Hanmer and Lionel Adriaan, who are all mentioned; I am forever grateful to Corinne Shaw, Anthony Hess, Faizel Parker, Phillip Saunders, Nat Bongo, Melken Ngcofe, Jeffrey Plam, Allan Powell, Terry Ackhurst, and Louie Roelf.

I also must acknowledge the Council for International Exchange of Scholars for supporting my work as a Fulbright Scholar in 1999, my host institution in South Africa, the University of the Western Cape, and the University of South Carolina for continuing encouragement of my research in South Africa.

There are many colleagues in both South Africa and the United States who have nurtured my work. I would like to especially thank two people. Craig Kridel, who teaches with me at the University of South Carolina, yields a very large editing pen, but most importantly he is a kind and thoughtful friend. And Peter Kallaway, my host in South Africa who suggested the oral history project with South African teachers. Those who know him admire his warmth and brilliance. I am proud to have both men as colleagues and friends.

Finally, I would like to thank the people at Peter Lang. Phyllis Korper, Chris Myers, and Lisa Dillon are kind, efficient, and make the publishing process joyful.

Calendar

1902	Formation of the African Political Organization (APO) in the Cape.
1912	Formation of South African Native Convention (becomes African National Congress—ANC—in 1923).
1943	Teachers' League of South Africa (TLSA) is taken from conservative, collaborationist educators by younger, socialist teachers.
1943	Non-European Unity Movement (NEUM) launches its Ten Point Programme.
1948	National Party wins national election and introduces apartheid.
1950	Apartheid government begins passing legislation to solidify the division of ethnic groups. Population Registration Act initiates ethnic classifications and registration. Group Areas Act segregates housing and leads to forced removals of black, Coloured, and Indian people. Immorality Act forbids sexual relations across ethnic groups. Suppression of Communism Act is soon used to oppress all dissenters.
1951	Bantu Authorities Act sets the foundation for African "homelands."
1953	Bantu Education Act initiates government control of African schools and legislates school segregation.
1956	Nelson Mandela and others are arrested and charged with treason.
1957	Declaration of the Cape as a Coloured Labor Preference Area legislating that employers are to give Coloured people preference over African people.
1959	Formation of the Pan African Congress.
1960	March 21st is the Sharpeville Massacre. Police kill 69 Africans who are protesting against being forced to carry passes. Protests are held

throughout the country and four people are killed by police in Langa, a black Cape Town township.

1961   South Africa becomes a Republic and leaves the Commonwealth. Umkhonto we Sizwe is formed as the armed wing of the ANC.

1963   Nelson Mandela and others are arrested for sabatoge. Government passes the Coloured Persons Education Act legislating school segregation of Coloured children.

1964   Nelson Mandela and seven other leaders are sentenced in the Rivonia Trial.

1965   Government passes the Indian Education Act legislating school segregation of Indian children.

1967   New laws allow indefinite imprisonment.

1970s   Under the auspices of the Group Removal Act the Government completes mass removals of Coloured, Indian, and black people from their homes and businesses.

1975   Mozambique and Angola become independent.

1976   Over a thousand students in Soweto and throughout the country are killed as they protest against general conditions and the initiation of Afrikaans, a language they don't speak and that they viewed as the language of the oppressor, as the medium of instruction.

1977   Steve Biko is killed by police while in dentention.

1980   Major boycotts of high schools by non-white students. Teachers are slow to join student protests. Throughout the eighties there are both public and school protests against the government. The state often declares States of Emergency and many people are detained, beaten, and killed.

1985   Even more intense boycotts of high schools by non-white students with much greater teacher participation than in 1980. In Cape Town the government closed schools for almost the entire second semester. WECTU is founded in Cape Town by activist teachers.

1990   President de Klerk unbans the ANC and other political organizations and frees political prisoners including Nelson Mandela, who is released February 11. Namibia becomes an independent country.

1994   Nelson Mandela is elected the first democratic president in April.

Abbreviations

ANC	African National Congress
Anti-CAD	Anti-Coloured Affairs Department
APDUSA	African Peoples Democratic Union of South Africa
APO	African Political Organization
AZAPO	Azanian Peoples Organization
BCM	Black Consciousness Movement
CAD	Coloured Affairs Department
COSAS	Congress of South African Students
COSATU	Congress of South African Trade Unions
CTPA	Cape Teachers' Professional Association
DET	Department of Education and Training
DETU	Democratic Teachers Union
MK	Umkhonto we Sizwe (Spear of the Nation)
NEUM	Non European Unity Movement
NP	National Party
NUM	New Unity Movement
PAC	Pan African Congress
PTSA	Parent, Teacher, Student Association
SABC	South African Broadcasting Corporation
SACHED	South African Committee on Higher Education
SACOS	South African Council of Sports
SADTU	South African Democratic Teachers' Union
SRC	Student Representative Council
TAC	Teachers' Action Committee
TLSA	Teachers' League of South Africa
TRC	Truth and Reconciliation Commission

UCT	University of Cape Town
UDF	United Democratic Front
UM	Unity Movement
UNISA	University of South Africa
UWC	University of the Western Cape
WECTU	Western Cape Teachers' Union

Grade Levels

Standard Ten   = Grade 12
Standard Nine   = Grade 11
Standard Eight   = Grade 10
Standard Seven = Grade 9
Standard Six   = Grade 8
Standard Five   = Grade 7
Standard Four   = Grade 6
Standard Three = Grade 5
Standard Two   = Grade 4
Standard One   = Grade 3

Oral History as Testimony: Teachers with the Fighting Spirit

This is a memory book. More specifically it portrays the memories of South African teachers who taught in their country during the apartheid era. It is a story of the recollections and reflections of people who were labeled and designated as part of a group because of the color of their skin. All of the teachers we meet in this book wed pedagogy and politics and are "teachers with the fighting spirit."

In 1999, I began working on a project with South African teachers who had fought against the apartheid regime. I began this project as the Truth and Reconciliation Commission (TRC), South Africa's attempt to allow both the victims and perpetrators of apartheid to publicly tell their stories, was holding final amnesty hearings for people who had committed apartheid travesties. At that time my colleague and friend, noted South African educational historian Peter Kallaway, suggested that I might begin interviewing South Africans who had taught during apartheid. He explained that there were few publications of teachers' stories in South Africa, and he opined that the project might become a TRC for education. As I continued to work with South African teachers in 2001 and 2002, I was constantly reminded of the power of oral history. Because for the victims of apartheid who appeared before the TRC, as well as the teachers who told me their stories, what was important was that they were testifying, that their testimony had the possibility of educating and changing the world. And it made me think of *oral history* and *testimony* as synonymous. Through people's stories we can understand the horrors of man's inhumanity to man, and we can teach "never again." But we can also celebrate the beauty of the human spirit.

The people I worked with in South Africa all testified. They spoke of the atrocities and hardships that apartheid brought teachers. Neville Alexander and Sedick Isaacs spent twelve and thirteen years respectively in Robben Island prison; many other teachers were detained for short periods; most were spied on and harassed in their jobs. All of the people I worked with suffered the treatment of their students who challenged the government because students were beaten, arrested, and sometimes killed. When Basil Snayer, who is currently the Principal of Garlandale High School, told me about police storming his home he became visibly upset as he recalled the effects on his children:

> A comrade, Anton Fransch, was cornered by police next door to my house. It was after midnight when suddenly I heard a barrage of gunfire outside. I really thought that my house was under attack. I put out the lights and soon one of my windows was shattered. And this went on for several hours that night. At three o'clock that morning, a contingent of about 10 cops stormed into my house. For years after that the effect on my children was devastating. Any little sound after that they, you know.[1]

Cape Town teachers also spoke with energy and celebration as they recalled their work—the wedding of pedagogy and politics that contributed to the changes that brought apartheid down and led to the 1994 election of Nelson Mandela as the President of South Africa.

One is very privileged to be trusted with other people's stories and thus there is great responsibility. At a 1999 meeting just north of Durban, I was criticized by a prominent historian for being a conduit for those I interviewed. A person with sharper wit than I possess would have said "Thank you." What could be a greater compliment then someone telling me that I am providing a public voice for those who are often silent? This book will portray the power of oral history as testimony through the voices of South African teachers who fought against apartheid. I am writing of oral history as testimony with two missions: (1) Human voices that portray atrocities, horror, and man's inhumanity to man can help nurture the postholocaust mantra of "never again." (2) Human voices that portray the compassion, thoughtfulness, hard work, and heroism of the human spirit can help nurture a celebration of the best of the human condition.

Apartheid and Racism in South Africa

Bigotry, racism, and white supremacy are part of the 20th-century history of South Africa. After 1948 and the coming to power of the National Party, an Afrikaner nationalist political party, racialism was increasingly formalized, and a vast array of laws were passed that set in place the building blocks of the apartheid system. Included were acts such as the Population Registration Act (1950), Group Areas Act (1950), and Immorality Act (1950) which not only classified people as African, Coloured, Indian, or white, but also designated where one was allowed to live, work, or attend school because of the color of skin. In many places African, Coloured, and Indian people were literally taken out of their family homes and forced to relocate to designated areas, often far from city centers and workplaces.

Apartheid education laws were enacted that included the Bantu Education Act (1953), the Coloured Persons Education Act (1963), and the Indian Education Act (1965). These laws were passed to guarantee that children attended school only with people of their own color. Additionally, each of the education acts sought to ensure white supremacy in South Africa. The curriculum stressed white superiority and black inferiority, and the academic curriculums for each group of people were differentiated so that schools corresponded with the occupational and economic reality of a racist South African society. In 1954, the Minister of Native Affairs and future president of the country, Hendrik Verwoerd, spoke of the non-white before the Senate:

> There is no place for him in the European community above the level of certain forms of labour. Within his own community, however, all doors are open. For that reason it is of no avail for him to receive a training which has as its aim absorption in the European community, where he cannot be absorbed. Until now he has been subjected to a school system which drew him away from his own community and misled him by showing him the green pastures of European society in which he was not allowed to graze. (Soudien, 1998, p. 9)

I spent the 1999 calendar year interviewing teachers in South Africa's Western Cape, the area that includes Cape Town and its surroundings. In 1985, a key year that connects the schools with the struggle against apartheid because students boycotted the schools and protested against the government, the population of South Africa was 64.8% African, 19.5% white, 12.1% Coloured, and 3.6% Indian (Republic of South Africa 1985 Population Census, G68A p. 1).[2] In Cape Town the demographics were very different: 57% Coloured, 27% white, 15% African, and 1% Indian. Most of the teachers I interviewed were Coloured teachers; of course, I also met with white, African, and Indian teachers. These teachers had spent most of their careers as educators in this system. All of the teachers I interviewed abhorred apartheid, but they were forced to experience the racism and hatred that were inherent in South African society.

Basil Snayer experienced racism as a child growing up in a small town called Fort Beaufort. "When I used to be sent to the shop by my parents," he said,

I would have to buy through a little window on the side of the shop. Give my money over the ledge of this window and whoever was receiving the money on the other side would fetch whatever I wanted and pass it over to me. If for any reason the change was wrong, in my opinion, it would have been my word against the white person serving me. And invariably the white person's version of that story would be right and I would be swindled out of a dime or two or whatever the case may be.

Simon Winter went to high school at Bishops, a private church-run school in the Cape Town suburbs. Because his father was an Anglican priest, he was able to attend the school for a nominal fee. He was deeply affected by racial exclusion at the school.

And I think it was in my Standard Nine year that a petition was circulated amongst the boys to open the school to all races, which we signed. I think the reason for that was that an Anglican priest called Clive McBride, who was a Coloured priest, wanted to enrol his son in the school and had been turned down purely on the grounds that he was Coloured. And it created quite a stir in the school, and I particularly felt very upset because here was I, the son of a priest, allowed in and here was the son of another priest not allowed in, purely on grounds of colour.

Helen Kies told me about her experiences as a non-white student at the University of Cape Town. "It was racist, very, very racist. You felt totally out of place as far as both the lecturers and your fellow white students were concerned. They'd just exclude you completely. There was a math lecturer whom I had to ask for advice every now and then. He'd just ignore me. He wouldn't answer any of my questions." Mandy Sanger had equally bad memories of the University of the Western Cape. "I did anthropology but then eventually we had to drop out. We dropped out because what they taught was racist anthropology. And I mean the moment you came with anything different, you were literally alienated or kicked out, it was very hostile lecturing."

Finally, Vivienne Carelse and Terrence Klassen both reflected on being forced to leave their childhood homes because of the Group Areas Act, as did Zozo Siyengo, an African teacher, who described the Cape Town reality for African people. "No, those days we were 'temporary sojourners' in Cape Town. I mean African people were seen as visitors in this area."

Although the oppression of apartheid is evident, it is difficult to define race in South Africa, just as it is in the United States. We do know that whiteness means privilege and that the apartheid government classified people because of the color of their skin and used these designations to oppress and divide non-white people. Shifting winds saw the use of the terms *Native*, *Bantu*, and *African* as official designations for black South Africans. The government provided more privileges for those deemed Coloured, but they were definitely below whites. Beginning in the eighties scholarship on South Africa included protracted caveats when discussing non-white South African people. Do you say African or black? Is it Coloured in inverted commas or "so-called Coloured" to show distaste for the term? I use the terms *African, Coloured, Indian,* and *white* because they are descriptive as apartheid racial classifications. This, of course, begs the question of the complexity of the construction of race in South Africa.

The teachers whose stories I tell believe in non-racialism in spite of the fact that they lived in a country that Bishop Tutu has described as a "pigmentocracy." When they speak of their teaching, they refer to the human race. They refer to children and not to black children, white children, Indian children, or Coloured children. Pam Hicks took issue with being described as a white teacher in a Coloured school. Like her Teachers' League of South Africa (TLSA) mentors and her Western Cape Teachers Union (WECTU) comrades, she preferred to be defined by the work she did while fighting against racism and apartheid. Mandy Sanger has addressed the issue of racial designations in recent correspondence. She was reacting to an essay where I referred to her and two colleagues as radical, Coloured, teachers.

> WE ARE NOT COLOURED! All three of us are in agreement on this! To understand you need to understand the period in which we learnt our politics and within which our sense of identity was forged, yes forged! I started high school in 1976. Black consciousness was a dominant political discourse with a popular following in high schools. From birth I was taught to reject the notions of racial classifications, particularly the misnomer "Coloured." Black is okay as a political construct. I'm black.

Being black is a political construction of racial identity for Sanger and many of the teachers I interviewed. Although they stress a foundational belief in non-racialism when it is unavoidable, they refer to themselves as black; this corresponds to their progressive stand against apartheid.

Teachers with the Fighting Spirit

In March 2000, I listened to the famous African writer Es'kia Mphahlele speak with a class of third graders in South Carolina. He was talking about the many evils of apartheid, but he also told the children that the apartheid government did not own hearts, minds, or souls. I thought of the teachers I had been privileged to meet as I worked on the oral history of apartheid era teachers. The teachers I met never surrendered. They were committed to their students both pedagogically and politically. Kevin Wildschut was an activist teacher:

> It was a very difficult time because we all hold education very dear. I think there's no teacher who will say education is not important. What we were doing, our process was some of the slogans of the day like "liberation before education." And we were saying, we're teaching liberation education. So it was a mixture of classroom academic work as well as teaching and informing learners about the need to radicalize, to change what was happening in our country and to be part of the process of change. So when learners came to me and said to me, "Sir, should I study for my exams?" my response would always be twofold. "Yes, you should because it's going to be necessary in the future. But at the same time you cannot neglect to study the real history of today, the history that you're learning today."

Politics and pedagogy continually intersected in the lives of the South African teachers I interviewed. There were different interpretations of the marriage of pedagogy and politics as the struggle against apartheid intensified in the eighties. The older TLSA group encouraged students to stay in school and taught that the placard marches and boycotts were quick fixes that wouldn't work. Helen Kies thought that activist teachers wrongfully encouraged students in these activities. "The other youngsters could predict to the month when the Nationalist government would be brought to its knees. They had all the steps and stages worked out. They thought it was just a matter, you know, of Step 1—Accomplish. Step 2—Accomplish. Step 3—Accomplish. Step 4—Revolution and Freedom." Many activist teachers joined students in the protests. Kies and her colleagues in the TLSA argued that student boycotts were unreflective and were activism for the sake of activism.

The progressive teachers viewed Kies and her colleagues as "armchair politicians"; their role was to join students in active resistance to apartheid. Glen van Harte and some of his colleagues at Gronvlei High School helped students organize marches, and he believed that the students politicized the teachers.

> I remember getting a phone call from a parent and a parent saying, "The kids are trapped in the school." They had gone to a night-time rally at the school. And so we got into our cars and went. And we didn't think about danger or anything. Because you were a teacher. That was your job. You weren't only the teacher in the classroom. You were somebody in the community. You saw yourself as a community person.

The teachers I interviewed were clear in their opposition to apartheid education. Their teaching promoted non-racialism, democracy, and the end of the apartheid system. Richard Dudley recalled the message given to teachers who interviewed for positions at Livingstone High School. "And we used to point out to them that we don't have Coloured children at this school; we don't have African children at this school; we don't have Indian children at this school; we have boys and girls." Jimmy Slingers worked to integrate his school during the struggle years.

> We said when a child applies to the school, it applies as a child and not as a black or as Coloured or as an Indian. And at the end of every term we had to submit a Quarterly Attendance Return. You had to give a breakdown of enrollment. How many whites? How many Coloureds? In fact, we didn't have whites at the time — Coloureds, Indians and blacks. We always just gave the grand total because we said, "We have children at this school. We don't have Coloured children!"

"We had to defend the children, make them understand what the rulers were trying to do, and why," said Helen Kies. "And this meant providing political education as well. Our main lesson was We Are One Human Race. There Are No Superior, No Inferior, Races." Jean September spoke about her work teaching history. "I was doing an alternative history with students. There was no way I was going to teach apartheid history . . . posters up on the wall and it's not your normal kind of posters that you have up. It's a lot of 'Down With Gutter Education,' 'The Apartheid History Curriculum Should Be Abolished.'" Pam Hicks was a white teacher who taught at Livingstone. She recalled subverting the biology syllabus in the mid-eighties. "But whenever there was a chance I would use it against itself. Like the heavy emphasis on taxonomy. I would explain how science can by used for another agenda. The use of classification here, in Nazi Germany and other racist systems." A second white teacher, Wendy Moult, spoke about her anti-apartheid responsibility in white schools. "And I often shut my door and spoke from my heart to the children because if their parents weren't doing it I actually needed to tell them what was going wrong. Because you see when you're in a cloistered environment like that, they don't realize."

Like Es'kia Mphahlele, these teachers never allowed the apartheid regime to steal their souls. The teachers whose lives are presented in this book represent a tradition described and analyzed by both Frantz Fanon (1967) and I. B. Tabata (1959). Although Fanon's work on colonialism and "slave mentality" is known throughout the world, the writings of Tabata are directly relevant to South Africa. Fanon did write about South Africa in one chapter of *Black Skin/White Masks*, but most of his writing addressed colonialism and race in France, Antilles, and Algeria. When he wrote of South Africa it was to criticize Mannoni for blaming black South Africans for their own enslavement. Fanon is especially hard and accuses Mannoni of not considering the oppressive reality of colonialism and racism. (Fanon, 1967, p. 85) Throughout *Black Skin/White Masks*, Fanon addresses the psychological enslavement that is part of colonial and capitalist oppression. He struggles with blacks trying to be white, but his analysis is within the context of colonialism and capitalism.

South African educational historian Linda Chisholm has called I. B. Tabata "arguably one of the finest black intellectuals South Africa has produced in the twentieth century" (Chisholm, 1991, p. 6). He is well known for his book *Education for Barbarism* (1959), which provides a critical analysis of the oppressive nature of Bantu education. In an article titled "Boycott as Weapon of Struggle," Tabata portrays "slave mentality" within the context of colonialism. He argues that some teachers became psychologically enslaved while others exhibited "the fighting spirit" we introduced earlier (Chisholm, 1991, p. 6). He addresses slave mentality throughout the twentieth century as colonialism used non-Europeans to enslave their brethren through education. Many of the teachers I interviewed provided examples of teachers who did their work for the apartheid regime. There are also examples in William Finnegan's book, *Crossing the Line*, which is his teaching diary of 1980 at Grassy Park High School, where June Bam, one of the teachers whose story is included below, taught in the eighties and early nineties. A powerful example of teachers' helping to enslave their students was recalled by one of the African teachers I met with, Dennis Ntombela. He spoke about protecting students from the anti-black views of other African teachers.

> Even those that had taught me who were now my colleagues held white people in high esteem. And at the same time held black people in very low esteem. And we were black and I couldn't understand. Uh, they would say something like, you know, black people are noisy, black people are lazy, black people are careless. And all those negative things would be said at pupil assemblies in the mornings as school starts.

The counterpoint for Tabata was teachers working to fight colonialism and then apartheid, and they are the teachers we will meet throughout the text. These teachers faced injustice, brutality, and overt racism during apartheid. In spite of their experiences, or maybe because of them, all of the teachers I interviewed were committed to the struggle against apartheid, and they all worked to see the election of Nelson Mandela and the birth of democracy in 1994.

Teachers' Voices

This book portrays the life stories of twenty South African teachers who taught in schools that were designated Coloured by the apartheid government. Although I also interviewed teachers who taught in African and white schools, I focus on teachers who taught in Coloured schools because of the demographic reality of Cape Town which shaped my understanding of the city and its schools. I spent a great deal of time with the teachers whose stories I tell. I asked few questions, although each interview began by setting up a timeline that noted when each person began teaching, how old one was when they started, and what the motivation was to teach. After this initial prompt teachers spoke freely and determined what was important. Methodological sustenance comes from the work of Studs Terkel, who provides important instruction because the story of the person he interviews is the stuff of his work—individuals telling personal/collective stories. He doesn't believe oral historians are interrogators: "I want them to talk about what they want to talk about in the way they want to talk about it, or not talk about it in the way they want to stay silent about it. I'll keep them to theme—age or The Depression or work or whatever—but that's all" (Parker, 1996, p. 166).

The people Studs Terkel has interviewed over the years see his interviewing as the definition of rapport. For me, the South African teachers told stories I wanted to hear and I actively listened to them speak—their stories were important. English architect Cedric Price commented on being interviewed by Terkel. "He never interrupts, which I think is very important . . . he wants to hear your point of view, and he wants you to express it first in this way and then again in that way if you feel that's a better way of putting it, and then a third time after that if you're still not happy that you've made yourself clear. A great gift, you know" (Parker, p. 117).

Methodological issues are important, but what draws me even closer to Terkel is the stories his people tell. Books like *Division Street America, Working, American Dreams Lost and Found,* and *Race* are about oral history as testimony. The people portrayed in these books speak to issues of race, class, and the human condition, as do the South African teachers I was privileged to meet. The South African teachers I worked with were eager to tell their stories. Some of my colleagues at the University of the Western Cape were initially surprised that teachers agreed to be interviewed. Might it be that the TRC hearings set the tone? Some colleagues thought that it was because I was an outsider and therefore was not threatening. I carried no South African political baggage. Others suggested that most teachers had not previously been asked to share their experiences publicly. Whatever the reason, many South African teachers told me their stories, which were unique and diverse in spite of their commitments to the academic success of their students and the end of apartheid in South Africa. Each person remembers events differently; the stories they tell are autobiographical and bring both breadth and depth to the portrayal of teachers under apartheid.

First contacting teachers by phone, I explained to them that my intention was to tell the stories of apartheid-era teachers. I told them that I was defining the lives of teachers very broadly. I was interested in their lives as teachers, and they were to decide what was important. Ivor Goodson has written extensively on the work of teachers, and his writing examines teachers' lives in and out of the classroom to provide a more complete understanding of their work. He tenders an invitation to others to write teacher life histories, and he emphasizes the importance of the task. "The proposal I am recommending is essentially one of reconceptionalising educational research so as to assure that the teacher's voice is heard, heard loudly, heard articulately" (Goodson, 1996, p 36). The importance of teachers' stories is also addressed by Bill Ayers in Craig Kridel's *Writing Educational Biography*. Ayers appropriates Mike Rose's term *Possible Lives:*

> Teacher biographies and biographical research in education can provide examples of possible lives—dynamic portraits of teachers working and making choices in an imperfect world, living in landscapes of fear and doubt, holding to a faith in the craft of teaching and in the three-dimensional humanity of their students that allows them to reach a kind of greatness against the grain. (Ayers, 1998, p. 239)

The stories of the teachers whom I interviewed are the essence of this book; they are examples of "possible lives." Their lives as teachers included "fear" and "doubt"; it is an understatement to say they taught in an "imperfect world." Each of the people I interviewed, no matter what their political stance, taught in a system that was an important part of apartheid in South Africa. No matter what their particular discipline, no matter where they taught, and no matter who they taught, their lives as teachers were affected by the apartheid system. Their lives are all informed by apartheid, but apartheid never owned them as teachers or people. Apartheid never stole their souls. It will become even more clear, as you read the teacher oral histories, that these people wed pedagogy and politics, and were "teachers with the fighting spirit."

The text is divided into three sections and a conclusion on oral history craft. Section One, Non-Racialism: Teachers' League Stories, portrays the lives of four teachers who were highly academic and political and were members of the TLSA, a group that believed in non-collaboration with the government and non-racialism, and was labeled as a Trotskyist organization. Three teachers began teaching in the 1940s and taught through the middle of the 1980s. They parallel Michele Foster's designation of elders in her work on black teachers in the United States. Although criticized by younger teachers during the struggle for being "armchair politicians," they were the teachers who taught political consciousness as they stressed academics. Pedagogy and politics were both part of their lives and classrooms, and they each paid a price for challenging the apartheid regime.

Section Two is titled "Stories from Robben Island." Robben Island was where President Mandela and other non-white political prisoners were held during apartheid. The section includes oral histories of two teachers who were imprisoned, one for twelve years and the other for thirteen years. Neville Alexander taught at Livingstone High School and Sedick Isaacs at Trafalgar High School, both highly ranked secondary schools, before they were imprisoned for anti-apartheid activities. They were each very important in transforming the prison into an educational institution where both political and common prisoners earned academic degrees and studied oppression in South Africa. Politics and pedagogy are ever present in their lives as teachers/political prisoners.

Section Three is titled "Boycotts, Marches, and Pedagogy: Teacher Struggle Stories." The section begins with six oral histories of men and women who began teaching in the 1970s before the Soweto boycotts and were teachers during the struggle years of the 1980s. Although their degree of activism varies, each of these teachers grew politically and worked closely with the younger activist teachers who came of age in the eighties. The section then includes eight oral histories of men and women who began teaching in the eighties, a time that is generally referred to as "the struggle years." Although the stories are again unique, almost all of these teachers are considered activists. They were each very concerned with both pedagogy and politics, but some leaned heavily toward "liberation before education." The teaching lives of people designated Coloured, Indian, and white are included in this section.

The book concludes with my reflections on writing oral history and the complexities of doing this work as an outsider in South Africa. The conclusion analyzes questions of "outsider" research in the context of the stories that are the heart of the book. There is a great deal of discussion and debate in South Africa on memory and history. Much of it is directly linked to the recent work and report of the Truth and Reconciliation Commission. The voices of teachers presented below, "teachers with the fighting spirit," will add to the conversation.

Notes

1. This is taken from my interview with Basil Snayer. It should be noted that Snayer testified to this before the TRC. His testimony can be read in Krog's *Country of My Skull* (pp. 50–52).
2. It should be noted that this did not include the Black African Homelands. In the Race Relations Survey, which did include the homelands, the numbers were 73.8 African, 14.8 white, 8.7 Coloured, 2.7 Indian (Race Relations Survey, Johannesburg, 1985, p. 185).

Non-Racialism: Teachers' League Stories

The main tenets of the Teachers' League of South Africa, non-racialism and non-collaboration, are the foundations of both the political ideology and the teaching of Helen Kies, Tom Hanmer, Richard Dudley, and Maureen Adriaan, longtime members of the TLSA. "Oh, the textbooks were terrible," said Adriaan. "There were many racist allegations and connotations in particular. But that was an opportunity to point out to pupils how contrary to human values those things were and that really they were just human beings like all other human beings and this whole idea of race was nonsense." South African society was divided racially before the election of the Nationalist Party and the initiation of apartheid in 1948. The apartheid regime solidified, legalized, and magnified these oppressive divisions from the time of the 1948 election until the first South African democratic election in 1994. Excluding Adriaan, the teachers whom we meet below began their teaching careers in the 1940s and were affiliated with a political organization called the Non-European Unity Movement. NEUM had a leftist ideology and was sometimes labeled as Trotskyist. The organization fought against government oppression in the economic, political, and (through the TLSA) educational arenas. It was NEUM that mandated non-racialism and non-collaboration, and the TLSA can be better understood through NEUM's "Ten Point Plan."

1. The Franchise, i.e., the right of every man and woman over the age of 21 to elect and be elected to Parliament, Provincial Councils, and all other Divisional and Municipal Councils.

2. Compulsory, free and uniform education for all children up to the age of 16, with free meals, books and school equipment for the needy.

3. Inviolability of person, of one's house and privacy.

4. Freedom of speech, press, meetings and association.

5. Freedom of movement and occupation.

6. Full equality of rights for all citizens without distinction of race, colour or sex.

7. Revision of the land question in accordance with the above.

8. Revision of the civil and criminal code in accordance with the above.

9. Revision of the system of taxation in accordance with the above.

10. Revision of the labour legislation and its application to the mines and agriculture. (Lewis, 1987, pp. 221, 222)

Although the second point has the direct effect on teachers, TLSA members campaigned for the entire plan and emphasized its tenets in their work with students, both in school and at evening and weekend meetings—meetings that many TLSA members saw as part of their responsibility as teachers. Their teachings challenged government racism and capitalism. Richard Dudley, who tells his story below, addressed the connection of class and race in the 1992 Jonas Fred Bosch Memorial Lecture:

> The class struggle and the struggle against racism are parts of one struggle. But the very dynamics of struggle, if it is nourished by the growth of class awareness, awareness of the historic duty that the workers and peasants in this country have to carry out, will promote the class struggle to its prime position in the scale of priorties of the liberation movement. (Dudley, 1992)

The story of the Teachers' League is documented in Mohamed Adhikari's book *Let Us Live for Our Children: The Teachers' League of South Africa.* (1993) Adhikari reviews the battle in the early forties, when teachers like Ben Kies, Willem Van Schoor, and Allie Fataar wrestled the TLSA away from conservative and, in their view, collaborationist members. As alluded to above, the new Teachers' League people were viewed as socialist and were referred to as the "radicals" (Adhikari, 1993, p. 70). Adhikari is not positive in his analysis of their coming to power. "The League which had been a model of 'moderation' and a paragon of 'respectability' was never to be the same again as the consensus that had sustained the organization for three decades had been shattered" (Adhikari, 1993, p. 70).

Besides the direct issues of class and race, the TLSA radicals fought with the conservative leadership because they believed that many of the old guard were government collaborators. Even before apartheid, the NEUM and TLSA analysis of the South African government was that it played divide-and-rule politics. Their older colleagues joined government commissions and task forces; this was viewed as collaboration and part of the takeover was to rid the organizations of these "traitors," referred to as "quislings" by the young "radicals" (Lewis, 1987, p. 213). The new TLSA was adamant in their contempt for those people they viewed as "quislings." "Don't have any social or personal intercourse with them. Don't greet them. Don't have any conversation with them . . . don't meet them, even if it is necessary to cross over to the other side of the street. Don't see them, even if you do come face to face with them" (Lewis, 1987, p. 214).

When apartheid began in 1948 the TLSA did not have to shift its emphasis, but the issues were magnified. Ali Fataar published an essay titled "Apartheid in Education" in the September 1948 issue of the *Educational Journal*. Throughout the fifties and sixties, articles in the journal challenged the apartheid regime from perspectives of class, race, and culture. Linda Chisholm's work offers both praise and criticism of the TLSA. Although she honestly analyzes the organization's loss of influence after Soweto in 1976 and throughout the struggle years of the eighties, her analysis of the TLSA's academic and political effect on students portrays the hearts, minds, and souls of the organization including the teachers whose stories are told below. Chisholm divides the life of the TLSA into three time periods— 1943–1963, 1963–1976, and 1976–1985. She describes the first period through the lives of teachers like Ben Kies, who was introduced earlier. Kies explained that teachers came from the working class and owed a great debt to their parents and society. For Kies that debt was political and was defined in socialist terms (Chisholm, 1991, p. 5). The TLSA constitution "bound the League to 'coordinate the struggle in the educational field with the struggle for full democratic rights' and to do this 'by cooperation or affiliation with the organisations fighting for full democratic rights for all non-Europeans'" (Chisholm, 1991, p. 8).

Sixteen TLSA teachers were banned from teaching by the early sixties, but the organization became more determined in its commitment for education to join pedagogy and politics. Teachers taught for "one" South Africa and against the class and racial separation and oppression of the apartheid state and the educational system. Chisholm cites an *Educational Journal* article titled "Scale Within Scales."

> He or she would be a traitor to education and to the profession if he or she were to teach or allow anyone to teach anything which blunted intelligence, stunted intellectual or spiritual growth, fostered provincialism or tribalism, bred intolerance of tyranny and acquiescence in social inequalities and ill-health. . . . It is no cliché to add that in that battle the teacher is among the frontline troops. (Chisholm, 1991, p. 9)

The sixties did not bring a change in TLSA ideology. Chisholm explains the marriage of academic excellence and political awareness in TLSA schools through 1976. Schools that were considered TLSA strongholds like Harold Cressy, Livingstone, Trafalgar, and South Peninsula were ranked highly as feeder schools for the

University of Cape Town. In the case of Cressy (10) and Livingstone (11), the ranking was higher than many of the elite white schools in South Africa. The schools were known for high standards and political teachings. Teachers were hired because of their academic qualifications as well as their belief in non-racialism. Bill Nasson, a student in the sixties, recalls his TLSA teachers in his essay, "The Unity Movement: Its Legacy in Historical Consciousness" (1990).

> Mostly older men of towering personality and effective educational organization, they poured out a vivid freewheeling rhetoric. . . . Above all, as socialists, they had an intuitive grasp of the primary value of "history" and of their own historical function. Whatever their specialist teaching subjects—history, literature, physics, or biology—they constituted a collective forum which molded a process of historically aware learning among pupils. (Nasson, 1990, p. 190)

Curriculum and textbooks were questioned and students were taught to think critically—challenging class disparity and racial stereotypes. "We established what we called fellowships that were actually organizations which brought together students, workers, and teachers," reflected Dudley. "We invited people of different interests to come and speak to these groups and then people who belonged to these fellowships themselves were given the task of reading up on themes. For example, we tackled the whole question of racism and racialism very seriously." Chisholm presents testimony from students praising TLSA teachers for nurturing a love for knowledge and critical thinking. She also interviewed students who found this teaching to be elitist, but even they never questioned the teachers' commitment or the quality of the education they received from TLSA teachers (Chisholm, 1991, p. 15). Nasson's opening teacher is an appropriate bridge to the stories from the Teachers' League of South Africa:

> This school has a mission to teach you history which will liberate you. We are here to make sure that you aren't contaminated by the Herrenvolk poison contained in your textbook. We as the oppressed cannot afford colonised minds. Our history, our liberation are inseparable. Because it teaches us that we should never salaam before this country's rulers. (Nasson, 1990, p. 189)

Teachers' Leaguers, including Kies, Hanmer, Dudley, and Adriaan, believed in the marriage of pedagogy and politics, and their mission, referenced in Adhikari's title, was "live for the children." Although there was great pressure from the government, they continued to teach and continued to push students both academically and politically. This mission was part of not losing their minds, hearts, and souls to the apartheid regime. Additionally, it was their duty to facilitate the same strength in the students they taught. This will become clear in the teacher stories presented below.

Helen Kies

I interviewed Helen Kies in her home in the Bo-Kaap area of Cape Town. The Bo-Kaap is the area the apartheid government named the Cape Malay district of the city, to establish apartheid on religious grounds—separating Muslim from Christian believers. Kies taught for thirty-seven years, retiring in 1985. She remains an active member of the Teachers' League of South Africa. She was married to one of the most well-known of the TLSA activists, the teacher, then lawyer, Ben Kies. Among those who don't really know her, Helen Kies has a reputation as a very tough, no-nonsense, person. Many of my colleagues were surprised that she had agreed to speak to me.

Now let me warn you that I've got a shocking historical memory. You ask me a question relating to time, I have to think. No, no, wait a minute. I started teaching in 1948, that I'm quite sure of. 1948. Now that was the year the National Party came into power. I was twenty-two. I had always wanted to become a teacher. In the years that I grew up in, women who were not white could become one of two things, a teacher or a nurse. I grew up in a very, very poor family. I think my father stopped his education at Standard Six. His father had died, so he had to go out to work to support the family. But the beautiful thing about him was that he struggled to give his children a university education.

A very interesting thing that links me to Harold Cressy High School is that Harold Cressy's brother, Norman, was one of my primary school teachers. And he took a great liking to my sister and me and always visited our family. My father had been educated at Zonnebloem. It was one of the educational institutions in these parts. Trafalgar was a fairly recent establishment, and since he had been to Zonnebloem my father intended to send me there. You see, Zonnebloem went as far as Standard Eight only, and that wouldn't have given entrance into a university. You had to have a Matriculation Certificate. And Mr. Cressy said, "No, no, no. She's going to Trafalgar, because she has to go to University." So that was Norman Cressy, brother of Harold Cressy after whom the school at which I taught for most of my life was named. He was also a great intellect. I used to love talking to him.

I asked Kies if there were other teachers who influenced her.

There was one special teacher, whom I married. He didn't teach me, fortunately. But he was at the school, at Trafalgar. He had one hell of a reputation as an activist, politico, atheist, and all sorts of things that at that time stamped one as a monster. My father told his friends that I was going to Trafalgar. They came in a deputation. "You can't send your daughter to that school. She's going to come under the influence of Ben Kies. He's an atheist, a Communist." I mean all the most shocking things you could think of, you know. And I married him.

Pupils came under his influence as far as politics was concerned. In the school there were organizations that gave us a very sound political grounding. And then from school we went into student fellowships and that sort of thing. Here our education was broadened much more extensively, spanning many fields of knowledge.

Then I went to UCT. It was racist—very, very racist. You felt totally out of place as far as both the lecturers and your fellow white students were concerned. They'd just exclude you completely. There was a math lecturer whom I had to ask for advice every now and then. He'd just ignore me. He wouldn't answer any of my questions. I decided I was there for a purpose and would get on with the job. I wouldn't allow their behavior to bother me. I attended lectures, did my work.

Kies graduated from the University of Cape Town and began teaching in 1948. She taught at Athlone High School and then decided to take a break from teaching after four years. Kies returned to the classroom in 1956 when her husband Ben was effectively fired for life from his job as a teacher. She spoke about the times and the apartheid government's banning of her husband, as well as their involvement in the TLSA.

It is necessary to give some background to the dismissal from their posts of Willem van Schoor and Ben. They were at the time the president and the editor of the TLSA. In his Presidential Address to the TLSA Annual Conference in 1952, the year in which the apartheid government had transferred education for the major section of the population to the control of the Bantu Affairs Department, van Schoor spelled out very clearly what government intentions were. Their introduction of a system of separate education was a desperate measure to set the political clock back.

You see, there had been the establishment in 1943 of a national liberation movement. Partly as a result of the work NEUM did throughout the country, people were responding, you know, to the lesson that the oppressive-exploitive policies of the United Party government affected all sections of the not-white people equally. There had been a growing unity among the oppressed by the time the National Party came to power in 1948. Well, they saw this as a threat to their rule. They had to devise a means of countering this growing unity, of destroying it. The adults had already been "tainted" by the poison of what the Nats called "foreign" (liberation) ideas. So they had to catch the children. Catch them young and start indoctrinating them from the time they entered school.

They created separate Departments of State—Bantu Affairs, Coloured Affairs, and later Indian Affairs Departments—that would control the entire lives of these sections of the population. The most diabolical, you know, vicious aspect of their activities would be their control of education. It was to be a policy of retribalizing. Of pushing the oppressed back into their separate kraals. Of getting them to accept their differentness one from the other, and that their liberation could not come from unity among them. They were, as we said, going to "Bantuise," "Colouredise," and "Indianise" the various sections. The white section was, of course, superior intellectually and morally to all the other groups.

They thought also they'd be very clever, you see, continue with their divide-and-rule strategy, set one section of the oppressed against another. So they started with transferring the control of education for the major section of the oppressed to the Bantu Affairs Department in 1952. They didn't transfer the control of education for all sections simultaneously. For this analysis of the rulers' intentions in his Presidential Address, and for warning that the "Coloured" section would be next in line for the transfer of their education to a Coloured Affairs Department, Willem van Schoor fell foul of the Education Department's "misconduct" clauses. He was charged with "creating enmity between the races." Well, Ben was similarly charged for having published the Presidential Address in the *Educational Journal*. To cut a long story, after departmental internal inquiries—verdict guilty. Appeal to the courts—appeal dismissed. Van Schoor and Ben were sacked from their teaching posts on the day the courts dismissed their appeal. Subsequent punishments were bannings and house arrest and then banning orders that barred them from membership of certain organizations—the TLSA among them.

These restrictions were very hard on people who had led such politically active lives—very hard. All interaction with people had to come to an end. They were restricted to one magisterial district and to their homes between certain hours. And of course for persons with van Schoor's and Ben's political reputations, getting jobs was the most difficult of all. So, I had to go back to work! Well, as I said, I had been strengthened, you know, by Ben. I knew the kind of life I could expect marrying him. So I was always very strong. I wasn't broken by the fact that it would be a long time before he would get a job.

Kies referred to her participation in the TLSA as her political education. She continued discussing government attempts to use education to strengthen apartheid.

Well, membership in the TLSA was an education on another level altogether. I say on another level because in the organization we were taught, we learned. That was where we got our political education. And as members of the organization, we were expected to teach not only the syllabus, but what every child in South Africa was entitled to know. Especially the oppressed child. When we went out recruiting we had to explain what the TLSA stood for, you know, what its objectives were. We did a lot of travelling throughout the country to talk at the various branches of the League and to participate in regional meetings, a combination of branches. I did quite a bit of that on my own after Ben had been sacked and banned.

In the local branch to which I belonged I did editorial work—the branch newsletter, for instance. We had very strong Parent-Teacher-Student Associations which we established when "Bantu" and "Coloured" education were introduced. They were very powerful organizations, the parents and teachers joined together to defend their children's education and their rights. We held regular monthly meetings to politicize the parents, and public meetings on specific issues. The PTSAs managed to block quite a number of the Education Department's retrogressive moves. So this was mainly organizational work, teaching and learning.

The *Educational Journal* also was educating, propagandizing. Teaching, making people aware of what was going on. Analyzing and exposing whatever came from the departments. Analyzing syllabuses and curricula. They had to prove that the white section was academically superior to the rest of the population. That these inferior groups could not therefore expect the same sort of education—would not be able to cope with it. They tried to develop a special program of intelligence testing. They were going to prove that "Bantu" or "Coloured" intelligence was inferior to "white" intelligence. The Teachers' League immediately set about sabotaging their intentions. We organized schools and parents and pupils to refuse to take part in this nonsense. Parents wrote letters to schools to say that their children should not be involved. We told the pupils that if the education officials tried to force them to do the tests they should fill the papers with nonsense. Except at schools where there were stooge principals, they had to abandon their "separate" intelligence effort.

And they weren't getting very far in their attempts to prove that the other sections of the population weren't as intelligent as the white section. Because the white lot, especially the Afrikaner group, were not making tremendous progress academically, you know. The majority were not making it even to Standard Eight, let alone to matric or the university. So they had all along to debase academic standards, make the syllabus less demanding, cut out subjects like math and science as requirements for university entrance. And when they presented the curricula for African and later "Coloured" children, the academic subjects were almost entirely eliminated. These people were never going to need academic knowledge, they said. What for? They were going to work on the farms, in the mines. They were going to do the jobs God had allotted them, their God-ordained tasks. Hygiene was a major subject for women. They had to be clean to work in the white madam's kitchen and look after her children. "Coloured" women would never rise above working in a factory so teach them needlework. It was diabolical.

Progressive teachers had a battle on this level too. Teach more than you are expected to was the injunction to TLSA members. Not just what the syllabus requires you to. Here also teachers had to exercise care and cunning. The Education Department adopted the ridiculous measure of prescribing one or two reference books for each subject. Beware the teacher who was found to be using any others!

Another very significant strategy was their gradually converting almost every school for the oppressed into an Afrikaans-medium institution. Their aim was to breed future generations that would not be sufficiently familiar with English to read books, newspapers, that would contaminate them with "foreign ideas," their term for progressive, liberatory ideas. They brought Afrikaans-speaking principals of Afrikaans-medium schools in rural areas and made them principals of urban schools. These characters were unable to stand the heat in their new posts, you know, and applied to return to their previous posts. And we had another fight against their attempts to convert classes from English to Afrikaans from first grade up. They invented the most ingenious formulas to do this. This Afrikaans-medium policy was what sparked the 1976 student unrest, as you know.

Kies connected her involvement in the TLSA to her teaching through the times of the school boycotts and her retirement in 1985.

You see, we had been giving the kids a political education—a broad political education—from the time I joined the Harold Cressy staff in 1957. When the question of establishing separate departments of education for the population groups was revealed there was quite a debate in the progressive teachers' organizations. With the transfer of education for the African section to a Bantu Affairs Department, our colleagues in the Cape African Teachers' Association had to decide whether they were going to stay on in the schools. One argument was that staying on would be tantamount to collaborating with the authorities in the debasement of the children's education and the attempts to retribalize the nation. The other, which won the day, was that leaving the schools would be abandoning the children to those teachers who would be only too willing to work with the rulers to achieve their plans. The decision was to stay on, to defend the children's education, to do everything possible to frustrate the rulers' plans, to work for the children, not for the department. But not unexpectedly, this decision resulted in the dismissal from their posts of the entire CATA body of officials, more than two hundred teachers, even banning and exile of some.

So with the transfer of "Coloured" education, we had an example to follow. Our officials made it quite clear, though, that if we were going to remain in the schools merely to give a sound academic education we might as well stay out. We had to defend the children, make them understand what the rulers were trying to do, and why. And this meant providing political education as well. To counter the rulers' main objective, retribalizing to make their divide-and-rule policy possible and easier. Our main lesson was We Are One Human Race. There Are No Superior, No Inferior, Races. Cut out all the rubbish the rulers are trying to make you believe. The Education Departments all had a very strict Code of Conduct for teachers, you see, with a series of misconduct clauses. Chief of these was a total ban on talking politics in classrooms. Unless, of course, it was pro-government politics. We would have to win the children over to our side, make them our allies. I've mentioned our work with the PTSAs.

A pupil might come along and say, "Miss, you must be careful what you say in class. Anna's father works for the CAD." Well, if there was just one Anna in each of the classes I taught of whom I had to be afraid, I mean, what would I have achieved? We just had to go ahead and take the chance. Also, the Special Branch Police knew at which schools the politically active teachers were to be found. They enlisted a group of pupil-spies at these schools. Gave them all sorts of bribes—money, clothing, offers of jobs when they left school. Gave them recorder-watches to use in certain teachers' classes. Teachers at some schools fell foul of the misconduct no politics clauses. I'd like to think that the TLSA teachers at Harold Cressy survived because we managed to win the trust of the pupils and their parents.

I taught to the end of 1985, the last month of which I spent in Pollsmoor prison. Not for what I did but because Education people thought I was instigating and encouraging unrest at the school. The one thing we TLSA teachers were determined to do was to keep the kids at school. We foresaw a collapse of schooling. We knew how hard it would be to get the children back into the schools, you know. But of course our concern to keep education going was later countered by the "liberation before education" slogan. There was another factor. Harold Cressy was right opposite the prison in Roeland Street. We were very worried about our children's safety. The police shot and killed a child at Trafalgar High School, just up the road from us. We had to try to control the kids.

I don't know why my memory of the details of the 1976 unrest is not very vivid. I sometimes wonder whether the role we played then was not the right one. Then I look at the thousands of young who fell out of schools during the three school uprisings—who didn't go back, who today are among the hardly literate unemployed of our country. It's strange, you know, that although the 1976 school boycotts started in the then Transvaal, the boycotts became concentrated in the Western Cape. It was in the Western Cape that the youngsters suffered the full force of police brutality—imprisonment, torture, shootings, killings.

It didn't matter during the 1980 and 1985 schools' unrest how powerful were any school's arguments for not repeating the 1976 experience. Every school had to be seen to be part of the boycotts, you know. Certain schools—Livingstone, Harold Cressy, South Peninsula—the "middle-class," "elite" schools as they were called, were especially watched to see that they were carrying out the instructions of the host of committees that purportedly organized and ran the boycotts.

Well, we had to try to keep our children under control, to keep them politically informed, to give them a history of what was happening. We had sessions every day, the whole school assembled in the hall, or classes combined in various venues, workshops, sometimes a little concert for a release from the strain or tension. But no formal lessons. This would have been breaking the boycott. You see, if you think of what the rulers were trying to do, indoctrinating the kids with their poison, you'll understand what happened in 1976 and after. Although the students' ideas were half-baked and their ideas of how they would bring about the "revolution" very naïve, where did the children get their ideas from, you might ask. They didn't fall from the air. Some ideas were coming from teachers in the schools, others from politically literate parents. Unfortunately, many of the younger, strongly activist teachers gave their pupils over-optimistic, quick fix expectations of "achieving the revolution." At the committee meetings there was a deliberate ganging up against certain schools. They were not elected onto committee executives, they were not given an opportunity to speak at the committee meetings. The other youngsters could predict to the month when the Nationalist government would be brought to its knees. They had all the steps and stages worked out. They thought it was just a matter, you know, of Step 1—Accomplish. Step 2—Accomplish. Step 3—Accomplish. Step 4—Revolution and Freedom. It was all so easy. Some of my politically brightest pupils laughed at the idea that there would have to be a set of political, economic, and social conditions in the country before revolution could even be thought of. Others were going to put their money on guerrilla warfare!

Well, you see, the one bonus was that throughout the country pupils were being given ideas. They knew at least that things were wrong and that things should change. Schools had been politicized to varying degrees. The main job was to see that something positive came from all this. Most of the schools thought Harold Cressy teachers very conservative for trying to keep school going, not having the children out boycotting. We were among the few schools that had almost all the pupils present every day. At other schools the teachers just gave up and the children did as they pleased. Inside and out. They formed groups going around to terrorize pupils and teachers at schools they felt were not toeing their line. Became quite scary at times. We were doing a lot more than many schools in that period. There was no education of any sort going on in them. I think the controlling hand we kept on the children while doing what we felt we had to do, I think that paid off. It gave them a certain maturity. It made them think. They had to discuss things. They had to think about why a particular strategy might work and another not, and that sort of thing. There were very many kids at the school who had never been exposed to political ideas—depending on who were their teachers. The boycotts were an eye-opener for them.

Kies spoke about being arrested and taken to prison in 1985.

I was collected from school. We were all in the hall enjoying a bit of relaxation—a month from the end of the 1985 school year. Told to hand over my keys to someone who could take the car home. The department obviously thought I was mainly responsible for the school's involvement in the boycotts. They were wrong, of course. I was one of a band of teachers who had to observe decisions taken by teachers at other schools who were orchestrating the boycotts. But in the eyes of the authorities, if there was one person responsible for what was happening at Harold Cressy it was me.

Pupils and teachers were brought in daily. More pupils than teachers. There was great camaraderie among us. Known activists were kept separate from us. One day they smuggled through a note to say they were going on a hunger strike and asking us to do so also. It was difficult because we couldn't expect the kids to go hungry. Anyway, we told them what we were going to do and that they should have their meals as usual. They refused the "meals" along with us. The warders were very worried. We demanded to see the person right at the top. We eventually got him. I was the spokesman, so I was not surprised when at the end of fourteen days—that was the period for which detainees were kept—I was told I would not be released. The food, in the meantime, had improved considerably. I must admit, with great shame, that I found being in prison a release from all the stress and tension that was the order in the schools. Our teachers were feeling sorry for me and I was feeling sorry for them. You see, it would have been different if I had a husband and children. I didn't have children outside waiting for me. I didn't have anyone in particular that I wanted to get out to be with. I think that was a major factor. They let me out on the last day of the school term. I suppose they thought, "The pupils have gone. She can't do anything now." I had been in Pollsmoor for a month. It hadn't been a month of gloom. We had had a lot of fun, given the warders some anxious moments, formed friendships. An amusing feature was the puzzlement we caused the warders, all of them Afrikaners with a minimum of education. When the teachers, all of them degreed, had to state their education qualifications, you could see the warders' minds working. "Why are these people doing what they're doing?" This was a breed of not-whites they had never encountered.

Helen Kies concluded by talking about trying to retire.

I had applied for retirement at the end of 1985. This had been granted, but my principal was sabotaging me, telling me he'd heard nothing from the department. When the 1986 term started, the person who had been put in charge of the school informed me that a letter dated October 1985 found in the principal's files granted my application for retirement. This ended thirty years of teaching at Harold Cressy—thirty wonderful years.

My story is, of course, the story of hundreds of other teachers. Not only those who like me grew up in the Teachers' League. But teachers who regarded teaching the children of the South African oppressed their human worth, what they were entitled to and how they would have to set about gaining it. Now my job is trying to continue this task, still with the cooperation of my colleagues, the young ones still in the schools and others, like me, "retired" but very busy. I make my contribution mainly through my editorship of the *Educational Journal*, a real labor of love.

Tom Hanmer

Tom Hanmer began his teaching career in 1945 after graduating from the University of Cape Town. He was twenty-two years old at the time. He became a member of the Teachers' League of South Africa early in his career and remains active at the present time. He taught at three teacher training institutions and was Principal at Wesley until he retired in 1984. His story includes insights into government-imposed racialism, schools within that system, and his work promoting non-racial education. My meetings with Tom Hanmer were in the garden of his home where he lives with his wife Marge, also a career teacher and member of the Teachers' League of South Africa. She was present during our discussions but spoke only once or twice to remind him of an event. Tom Hanmer concluded our discussions with a comment about meeting his old students. "I suppose even more appropriate is the fact that I still meet students who don't avoid me. Who come up and say Hewat 1958, Wesley 1960. I don't remember their names, I remember their faces. But they still remember the place, the institution, and they even deign to remember me."

I spent the war years at UCT preparing a general degree because I hadn't made up my mind, or my parents hadn't, whether I was going to go into teaching or not. I know they were very keen that I should, if possible, have gone into medicine. But we just weren't well off enough to be able to manage that, so I finished in '44 with a Bachelor of Education. UCT was "open" very much in inverted commas. During the time that I was there, I could belong to any of the academic societies. So, for example, a drama society, I didn't ever do that; music society, and so on and so on. But not any of the sports clubs, couldn't make use of any of the sports facilities so we couldn't play rugby or soccer or make use of the swimming pool or play tennis. Several friends of mine were doing medicine. Yes, they were permitted to do medicine at UCT. When they did their practical work, whenever a white patient was examined by the professor or lecturer as a demonstration to the class, they had to leave. They couldn't even work on a white cadaver.

So it was an "open" university and the university always boasted, over many years, about its liberal traditions, which always infuriates me because people were there on sufferance. And in my final year B.A., for example, we were in a small class. Just three students doing third course in geography, and our professor was going to take us out for a meal. And he had to tell me that it wasn't possible for me to go along because they had to go into places where only whites were permitted. So it was that sort of thing.

Hanmer spoke about his early years as a teacher when there were mostly white teach-ers in Coloured schools, but there was absolutely no student integration and there was "Coloured" curriculum.

So I completed in 1944 and in '45 I started teaching. I was twenty-two when I started. I started in Paarl at a teacher training institution, but it had a secondary school department attached to it. I went into the secondary department and I boarded in Paarl, and this was a Coloured institution. It was a church institution and all the primary school teaching training institutions were church controlled. So I went to Paarl and taught there for six months and then I was offered a post at Wesley in Cape Town, so I came and taught at Wesley from the middle of the year 1945. I was teaching geography, that was my first major, and history. Occasionally I taught English, very occasionally arithmetic, but primarily geography. And I taught at Wes-ley for a period of about four or five years, and then I was offered a post at Hewat Training College, which at the time was housed in Cape Town. It was a post-matric teacher training institution for Coloureds; it was the only one in the country.

What was interesting both at Paarl and at Wesley was the fact that a large pro-portion of the staff were white, and this had been a long tradition. And at the church institutions it was primarily a sort of missionary tradition; white teachers who taught at these church institutions were, in fact, members of the church. Well-qualified teachers, very dedicated, that was my general impression. And pro-gressively more and more not-white teachers joined the staff. The enrollment was confined very strictly in racial terms; teacher-training institutions were white or Coloured or black. There were no institutions in the pre-tertiary area which were mixed. But the staff at many of them, I'm talking about secondary and training in-stitutions, were very often mixed. One of the reasons at that time was that there were very few not-white teachers who had tertiary qualifications. So there were very few of them with degrees to qualify for appointment to these schools. A train-ing school, then, was defined as a school where students underwent training as teachers after Standard Eight.

The level of teaching, I think, was pretty good at that time. The teachers who were training students as primary school teachers were pretty well qualified.

Certainly that was my experience at Wesley. There was a high proportion of white staff members. All of them graduates. All of them with pretty sophisticated experience who were in charge of training students to do teaching. They were working within the confines of a prescribed syllabus, but I think, within that, a pretty good standard was being maintained. The department maintained this total separation because the courses, the prescribed texts, the examinations, the certificates, were all separate. So if you went to a Coloured school there was a Coloured syllabus, there were Coloured texts, and you got a Coloured certificate, a certificate issued by the department to an institution which was known to be a Coloured institution. But within that I think that the standards that were maintained were pretty high, taking into account the limitations that were imposed by the system itself and the circumstances.

Then I went to Hewat in 1951. And a friend of mine at the time, Stella Jacobs, was the first not-white teacher appointed to Hewat. I was the next one. And for the time that we were there, we were the only two not-white teachers at Hewat College which trained "Coloured teachers for Coloured schools, following a Coloured syllabus designed for a Coloured institution." You know, the degree of separation was absolute. I'm emphasizing that because they made no concessions about that. Black students couldn't attend Hewat and certainly not white students. At Hewat generally there was a pretty good staff. Students got the clear impression that Stella and I meant business. We felt that it was important to give our best. And we always tried, in spite of everything, to maintain the highest standards that were possible.

Hanmer spoke about his affiliation with the TLSA.

I joined the Teachers' League of South Africa. At the time it was primarily a Coloured teachers' organization. And because of the political upheavals of the forties and fifties, there was the same sort of upheaval in the Teachers' League. This was at the time when the government was beginning to set up the administrative machinery for the complete separate administration of the different racial groups. So within the government there was a Department of Coloured Affairs beginning. There was already a Department of Native Affairs. You know it took on different names as they tried to shy away from the term "native." So the Teachers' League took a very definite stand on non-racial politics and striving towards non-racial education. Simply that we were going to oppose in every possible way this separation, this inferiority. Because the Coloured Affairs Department matured and grew and got a separate identity. Separate syllabuses were being drawn up, and separate textbooks were being prescribed, and special textbooks were being written by Coloured teachers who were in that group. So we saw our role as being totally opposed to that. But they had the power to impose these syllabuses on the school, the textbooks, the different examinations, and so on. And we had to teach the syllabus and textbooks to which we were opposed. So we continued to oppose them, and part of our conferences, teachers' conferences, dealt with ways in which to subvert this process, dealt with ways in which to maintain quality and standards while they were attempting to reduce the level and the quality. Members of the Teachers' League of South Africa and various Parent-Teacher Associations as well as other progressive teachers remained at their posts to continue the business of education and refused to indoctrinate and debase. Their role was to defend and protect the children and to pursue real education in every way possible. The authorities sacked many teachers—officials of the TLSA, members of the executive, teachers who spoke at public meetings, teachers who were alleged to have criticized the government or its officials.

Hanmer spoke about department inspections.

While I was at Hewat they had had an inspection. By this time a panel inspection was the usual way of dealing with it. Not a single inspector but several inspectors formed a panel. So the chief inspector would be in charge and then a group of inspectors would descend upon an institution and conduct a panel inspection. It would last a few days or a week or whatever. Some of these things could become pretty rough, particularly when it was clear that there were teachers who were opposed to the syllabuses, to the methods, to the debasement, to the textbooks, and were doing their own thing. We set standards which are worthwhile standards, not just standards prescribed by the department. They would give special attention to people that they knew were members of the Teachers' League. And if they were officials of the organization they were even more closely watched. So when I was at Hewat and there was a panel inspection, I could be absolutely sure that Stella Jacobs and I would be inspected because we were members of the Teachers' League.

Hanmer returned to Wesley as Principal, and he spoke of the continuing racialism of the department. He told me about two incidents in the sixties where he challenged the system. The first was a flag-raising event and the second was I.Q. Testing.

So, while I was at Wesley the colouredization and debasement of schooling was taking place. Those were the terms the teachers used. The inspectorate became progressively Coloured. So they were not welcome, and I didn't ever make them feel welcome. They had a job to do, and I had to accept that they were there. They would come along, and very often they came under the supervision of a white senior inspector. The impression I got was they came with the intention of trying to find fault. Police would also turn up at the school in order to see that the school was not being used by a political organization, that staff or teachers weren't trying to influence children politically. The police used to turn up during the course of the Emergency[1] regularly and they would walk into the school, and I had an office near the entrance and they would barge in. Usually the officer in charge of the

Woodstock police station, which was nearby, with a couple of his juniors. And they'd want to chat to me in the office and they'd come in, and by this time I became rather rough about the way in which one handled the police. So I'd ask them to remove their caps and so on because they were inside. I was perfectly comfortable and so, you know, you started by getting them on the wrong foot, and so on. But this became a formality. They turned up; they knew nothing was going on, but this was part of the intimidation process.

So it was also the period when South Africa became a republic and schools were expected on Republic Day to have a special service and flag-raising ceremony. And the Coloured Affairs Department published a service, which would be followed in the schools. And there were many people who did it and there were some people who didn't, and we didn't. I had as a circuit inspector an Afrikaner who knew my views. I wasn't trying to hide anything. And I told him I wasn't going to have this. He said that he'd have to report it. And I think he turned up once, and he didn't turn up again. We never raised the flag.

Generally my role as a teacher in the sixties and seventies when the viciousness of the institutionalized system was really at its worst became one of being between the institution and the department. In other words, I had to protect the institution from the authorities and at the same time try to pursue what we regarded as the real aims of a school and not be cowered by the authorities. And that became increasingly difficult. One of the things that was happening was the standardization of Coloured Intelligence Tests. Up to that time they'd used sets of tests which were pretty standard for children. But they believed that there was a separate thing called Coloured Intelligence, which had to be tested and standardized with a special test. We knew that this was coming. There were several articles. I wrote a couple of them myself in the *Educational Journal* talking about intelligence testing. And on a particular morning a young chap, Afrikaner, turned up and said he'd come from the State Education Department in Pretoria and he was coming to conduct tests. And I refused on the grounds that we hadn't received any warning and I wasn't going to upset the school. And he insisted that he had the right to give the test. The real reason was that I didn't want to have the test conducted in this way. And he asked whether he could use the phone to get in touch with the local authorities. He spoke to the Superintendent General of Education in the Cape Province directly, and I was instructed to come into the office to see an official of the Education Department that afternoon and I was to arrange for this chap to conduct the tests. Now by that time the staff knew what was going on. I had an opportunity to speak to the staff and tell them what the circumstances were, and most of them were sympathetic to my view. And I asked the staff to tell the pupils who were going to be tested what my views were about the tests. I didn't tell them on that occasion to subvert the tests. I did that on subsequent occasions, but they then had the tests. I had to see this official at the department who was the Secretary for Education. And he warned me that if there was another occurrence they would interpret it as gross insubordination and I stood the chance of being dismissed. And I took that very seriously because some of my friends had been dismissed at that time.

Hanmer spoke about the school boycotts in the late seventies and early eighties and how they affected Wesley. He also spoke about his role as an educator during the struggle years.

So the school boycotts began in the seventies, went on into the eighties, and students were involved. And we were placed in a somewhat difficult position because student teachers were threatened that if they participated they would be put out of the college and that they wouldn't be able to qualify. And there were boycotts of classes. In other words, students very often used the school as a place to have meetings but no lessons. They boycotted classes. And at some places they began to act in a rather disruptive way where teachers just sat back and allowed students to rampage through the place. At Wesley we had long discussions with the students, and I refused them permission to have any meeting at which I was excluded. The faculty was not invited, and I would go to meetings and say to them as the principal of this institution I take responsibility for what goes on. And if anything happens here, parents are not going to ask the Student Representative Council. Parents are not going to ask the students why this happened. Parents are going to ask me. I take responsibility and I'm coming to the meeting. And I'm going to be here. I'm going to sit at the back. You run your meeting but I'll be here. They did. There were students who complained about that. And I didn't insist on this on every single occasion, but most often I made myself very visible. I was prepared to debate with them and I raised issues with them. Very often I was outvoted, obviously, but I raised issues with them.

You see, the position they took was that they didn't want to have classes. They were boycotting classes, but they wanted to arrange their own programs where they would have lectures, discussions, and films. But at many schools this just deteriorated into kids hanging around and going home early and walking about in groups all over the place. And I insisted that our students wouldn't do that. And we, as a staff, would assist them. We would offer to give them books. We would offer to lead discussions and answer questions. We would participate in debates, staff with students acting as the chairperson. We could do all sorts of wonderfully interesting things that students didn't imagine were possible. We didn't force them. It had to be done on a purely voluntary basis. But the students, I insisted, should be at the school. And I promised them no teacher would teach a lesson. Anybody who wanted to keep up with their work could do so privately and if they wanted to consult the staff they could do so after school. I undertook to ensure that they boycotted classes, that they did not receive any instruction. That there were no lectures, but that they would be present at school.

Police turned up in order to see that there was no disorder and that was not a difficulty. We had an incident when students from a nearby high school turned up at the college to force our students out of the college to join them in a march or something. Many of those marches just petered out into a useless sort of demonstration. And they turned up at the college. I happened to be working in the office with my jacket off. Most times I didn't wear a jacket. And I went outside and confronted them outside the college and they were quite aggressive. And I said, "Look, I can't talk to all of you, but you choose your representatives and they can come and talk to me in the office. And they can talk to representatives of the students as well." And eventually after a lot of consultation this happened, and then they agreed that the students had good reason to be at the college and they left. A day or two later one of the members of staff spoke to me and said they heard that at the high school the students reported that I turned up absolutely aggressive with my jacket off ready to fight.

By this time students outside had formed several student organizations which were pretty strong and influential. And so at the college there were representatives of different student organizations who were attempting to get the students of the college to go one way or the other. There were often pretty hot debates that took place at the college. We had a hall, so it was possible for them to have debates, discussions, and so on. It never became violent or unpleasant because I always insisted that some member of staff be present in order just to keep an eye on the proceedings.

I remember on one occasion at a meeting, one of our students who belonged to one of the radical groups was shouting fire and brimstone and condemning members of the staff and the institution and all the rest of it. And I felt persuaded to participate in the discussion from the floor. There was a great uproar when I asked for permission to speak. They finally settled it among themselves, and then they said that I would be permitted to speak once. That was an interesting situation. And I said I felt that I had to remind students that when all this was over they were going to come back to this place, they were coming back to classes. The people whom they had been talking about were going to be their lecturers. And this institution was going to be the institution which was going to mother and father them for their period at the college. And that they should keep this in mind and that they should not say and do things now which were going to act adversely in the weeks ahead. I think it brought a little bit of sanity to the discussion. But I felt very threatened by the fact that at my own institution of which I was the head, I had to occupy a place on the floor, get their permission, and permission wasn't easily granted. They had to discuss whether they could give me permission to talk! And that, I think, illustrated that there was a great deal of radical thinking towards action. Very often the thinking was not very radical in terms of an understanding of where they were going. The action was always something physically active, you know, you've got to march somewhere, you've got to get people together, you've got to get them out of their classes and any institution that gave any impression that there was work going on, you'd have to disrupt that. You'd have to go into the school and disrupt classes.

Tom Hanmer became tired as the system and the boycotts wore him down. He spoke about his decision to retire and his faith in his colleagues and his role as a teacher.

The Teachers' League was not very supportive of the more radical elements which were marching and singing and pamphleteering and all the rest of it; we didn't think that school boycotts were the way to go. We didn't think that hauling kids out of school, damaging property, disrupting the education process, boycotting examinations was the way to go. And we didn't think that this served the students well. I had reached retirement age and exhaustion. I had a rough time during a long period by being the principal at the school. I had to be on guard. I had to be fighting the department. I had to be objecting and defending all the time. There was no time when it was easy, when the school was just running along smoothly and I was sitting there watching the fruits of my labor passing. There was never a period when it was boring. Not a single period, because as soon as one became too used to something suddenly almost from nowhere a new development would happen. I got tired, exhausted, from the strain of this battle.

One of the things that sustained me in my job was the early allegiance to a progressive teachers and political organization that gave meaning to a lot of the things that I was doing, not only in the broad sense, but the day-to-day activities. In other words, when it was a battle dealing with students, staff, or the department, it was something that I was doing because I believed in what I was doing. And I think that sustained me and sustained the staff and sustained the students. We had some marvellous students who came from awful circumstances. But this devotion to quality, this devotion to doing a job properly, this devotion to being dependable was something that sustained them. And really made them into people to whom I would at any time and on any occasion take my hat off and say, "You're a great teacher."

Note

1. The apartheid government often declared states of emergency in the sixties, seventies, and eighties. For an ironic take on these times, see Jeff Cohen's oral history.

Richard Dudley

Richard Dudley taught from 1945 through 1984 at Livingstone High School. When you mention his name to teachers in Cape Town, you sense an immediate reverence. Rose Jackson, who taught at Livingstone in the early eighties, referred to his "benign spirit that promoted freedom." Linda Chisholm interviewed a Livingstone student from 1976. "When you came to Livingstone, you knew it was a political school. They kept preaching, 'We want to develop thinking people.' When a guy like Dudley addressed the assembly, he was just a cut above everybody else you knew. He never spoke like ordinary people, for example, but he spoke in a way we dreamed we'd one day be able to speak" (Chisholm, p. 14). Dudley came from a family of teachers. He wrote extensively in the Educational Journal and has published pamphlets and monographs on non-racialism and political/educational criticism throughout his years as an educator. Dudley's oral history portrays his strength, commitment, and individuality as an educator and citizen. Richard Dudley retired after teaching for thirty-nine years. He listed some of the reasons for his retirement, as it came the year before the massive school boycotts in Cape Town. There certainly was no need for explanation, as his commitment to both politics and pedagogy are very obvious—they are portrayed below.

I started teaching formally in 1945 at the school at which I had myself matriculated. I had actually done quite a lot of practice work as part of my training at the University of Cape Town at this school, so I was fairly familiar with the school. I became a full member of the staff in 1945, and when I started teaching I taught physical science, English, and Latin. Well, I think that life in South Africa at that time was almost ordained for persons like myself and many, many others. If your family had a reasonable amount of security in its income and they were able to afford to send you to the university or to any other tertiary institution, you either became a teacher or a preacher. It was as simple as that! Now in my case my father was a teacher and consequently he was amongst the poor—the poor who got a regular income of some sort. When I matriculated the burden on the family was slightly eased because I won a scholarship. I had no leanings toward becoming a preacher. The idea was to complete a Bachelors' degree, train as a teacher, and then get into a job because getting a job with an income was also a priority.

Dudley discussed his political education during his university years through an organization called the New Era Fellowship, which was a leftist group that discussed both South African and world politics.

Yes, well, look, by the time I left the university, I had been pretty well immersed in the politics of that period. Because when I was at the university in my second year, I joined the radical groups here in Cape Town which were associated with the New Era Fellowship. And as a youngster of sixteen, having been at the University of Cape Town, I was full of pretensions about what the extent of my knowledge was. My humbling and re-educative experience took place in the study groups that were established in the New Era Fellowship. I had been concentrating on mathematics and chemistry and physics up at the university. But I also read in the social science section because my attention had been drawn to this. We were given the opportunity of learning the history and politics of South Africa and we had tutors. They were people who were well versed in the literature of virtually all of the continents on which there were struggles occurring. And they drew our attention to the books that they felt we should read. And that made an enormous difference because it meant that our reading was focused. So we were introduced to what one might call the struggle literature of India, the struggle literature of the West Indies, of America, of Europe.

I'll tell you of an experience that I had in that respect because it wasn't a question of knowing, it was a question of being able to analyze, to see cause and effect, and to see how this projects into the present and future. My second year in the study group I was given the chance to speak to the study group. My task was to examine the position of Native Labour in South Africa. Now we used to sit in a horseshoe shape, you see. And the person who was due to speak would be in the center so that you faced everybody there. And so you go along there full of yourself and full of this information and so on. You feel that you've done a good job. And then the tutors start taking you apart. You go in there and you think that you're Gulliver in Lilliput. You shrink in size but you learn an important lesson, and that is analysis.

Dudley discussed the political spirit at Livingstone when he began teaching and then reflected on the banning of Teachers' League members in the fifties and sixties. Dudley was himself banned in 1961.

I would say that, for want of a better term, the general atmosphere that prevailed at the school was oppositional. But it wasn't just that. I think that an independence in the ideas within which framework people conducted their work at school was pretty well established. This school would act as a bastion against the kinds of things that the United Party had hoped to install in 1945 when they introduced the Coloured Education Ordinance. Because that actually attempted to set up the basis for a kind of segregated approach to the education of persons of colour. The independent ideas that people had developed had enriched the struggle in this sense; in that you could in fact see in advance what was being planned and then you could agitate against it. We used to get films of a suitable kind for the pupils. And then we used to have the assemblies at the school where children would be told about the aims and purposes of education, what we expected of them, you know. And then on top of that some of the major players were actually members on the staff at the school. We also had a number of organizations that catered for activities of the students outside of the school. We established what we called fellowships that were actually organizations which brought together students, workers, and teachers. We invited people of different interests to come and speak to these groups, and then people who belonged to these fellowships themselves were given the task of reading up on themes. For example, we tackled the whole question of racism and racialism very seriously.

I think that, here again, one has got to look at the political situation as it unfolded, because they started banning people in the mid-1950s. And amongst the people whom they banned were some of the leading spokespersons in the education field. In 1956, for example, the President of the Teachers' League of South Africa, Mr. Willem van Schoor, was banned and thrown out of teaching. And Mr. Ben Kies was banned. But by that time we had the alternatives worked out how we could cope with this. So the banning of those two individuals did produce shocks through the teaching profession. Livingstone became the target. They used to denigrate the school as being a sort of communist school. And they did whatever was possible to try and sabotage the work of the school. But the school itself had established a reputation for hard work and discipline, and parents sent their children to the school from all over the country.

You must remember what else had happened. Sharpeville (1960) and so on and the introduction of some of the most savage legislation. They banned nineteen of the leading professional teachers from the schools, including myself, but we won the right, actually, to teach in the Appeal Court. There were four of them who taught at Livingstone who were banned: Mr. Ali Fataar, myself, Mr. George Abrahams, and Mr. Victor Wessels. That was in 1961. It made our position very difficult because we couldn't attend the meetings where the opposition was being organized. But we had alternative ways of doing it; we used to provide the arsenal of ideas and then other people used to fire the shots outside. They granted us a special permission to continue teaching at the school, but they denied me permission to teach at the Technical College where I was also teaching. I was teaching workers who were apprenticed in different trades. So some of them used to turn up early, so that was actually a special lesson that I taught on their role as workers. And I think that those workers and I had a very good relationship, and that is why they prevented me from doing that teaching. Well, in 1963 they arrested a number of the teachers who had adopted a very radical stand. That included Neville Alexander he was on our staff at the time teaching German. My daughter was also one of his pupils at the time. They didn't arrest him at the school, but they used to pay regular visits to the school to check up on the behavior of the so-called radical troublemakers.

The government began to force the issue of Afrikaans as the medium of instruction in the sixties. This, of course, became the issue that precipitated the Soweto School Boycotts in 1976. Dudley spoke about the issue within the context of politics and culture.

Although they didn't transfer the school to the Coloured Affairs Department, they did appoint a number of inspectors. These were white inspectors. Again, pardon the term, but they were drawn from the contingent of experienced white teachers. And their task was actually to go through the schools and to see that the work was being done that was expected of the schools. But more than that, they had also to make quite sure that the majority of the people who were in the Coloured schools were being taught through the Afrikaans-Medium. Now this language initiative of theirs was central to their application of the Christian National Education Policy. Because they believed, and they still believe of course, that particular section of the Afrikaner intellectuals, that language acts as the vehicle for people's culture. And if you wanted to nourish a culture amongst the so-called Coloured section of the population which would produce an affinity with the culture of the Afrikaners, and in this way strengthen an alliance between the Coloured people and the Afrikaner people, then language was going to be one of the most important weapons.

Livingstone High School was located in a southern Cape Town suburb, Harfield Village, that was a multiracial community. Dudley and other teachers at the school made it clear that students of all races were welcome at the school. This changed when the Group Areas Act was enforced in the sixties and over one hundred and fifty thousand Coloured and black people in Cape Town were forced out of their homes and neighborhoods. Dudley spoke of the first incident when the Coloured Affairs Department ordered the school to remove African students.

Then in 1964 they transferred Coloured education to the Coloured partment because they reckoned that they had smashed all the effective position. One of the first things they did in August 1964, they sent a me the so-called Coloured schools that they were immediately to get rid of all African pupils. Now the principal who had been appointed in 1962 was one of their persons. He knew that if he made this public at the school that there would be a hell of a lot of trouble for him. So he attempted to get these children quietly off the school's premises. Make them, as it were, disappear into thin air. But he was also dead scared of the authorities. So what he did was to go around to the classes and to tell the children that he wanted to see them with their books outside. And these children were sitting on the stoep outside the office and outside the classrooms. And when our children moved from one class to another, they found some of their classmates sitting at the school. And then it became obvious as to what happened, and then these children mounted a strike. A stay-away in support of their fellow pupils and they demanded that they be reinstated, you know. Now that, of course, was something that upset the authorities. Because here were so-called Coloured pupils coming out in defense of the rights of African children. It was the very negation of what they had actually wanted. I knew the pupils who had organized the strike. They did it extremely well. They came to tell us what they had in mind. There was no way in which we could deny this, but we warned them that the Special Branch would be there. We gave them all the necessary assistance and so on. But this kind of demonstration had a tremendous impact upon the consciousness of the pupils. In the case of those African pupils, we couldn't rescue them immediately. But we managed to get as many of them back as possible to finish their course of study at the school.

Dudley spoke about his role in hiring teachers and he praised the faculty that taught at Livingstone from the sixties to the mid-eighties.

But I think that it must be said, and again here, I don't like this sort of thing, but the people whom we were able to attract at the school, black or white, they were highly civilized people and highly qualified people as well. Yes. Fortunately, I used to be invited by the principal to interview people who made application to the school. I was always invited to sit in with the principal, particularly during the 1970s because I had been appointed as the vice-principal in 1966. And we used to point out to people that, although the school now fell under the Coloured Affairs Department, the school had a set of aims, objectives, and directions which were very explicit. When I was given the opportunity of interviewing the teachers, we used to tell them what the school was all about. And we used to point out to them that we don't have Coloured children at this school; we don't have African children at this school; we don't have Indian children at this school; we have boys and girls. And if you can fit in with the program that we have, and if you feel that you have any prejudices and you can leave them outside at the gate of the school and so on, you'd be welcome.

Make no mistake about it, the cooperation that we had from the staff was tremendous. And the school was one of the success stories. I think that we had developed an ethos and a coherence in what we were doing that enabled people to get down to the business of teaching, and I think that they did a damn good job. It wasn't a one-man band that was there. I mean I used to do a lot of the work, but my job, as I saw it, apart from teaching physical science, was to enable the other people to do the work that they were capable of and they were very well-qualified people. I think they're studded with qualifications and experience, and so on. I mean, that we, in the 1950s already and 1960, we'd drawn up a reading list for the pupils, giving them a focused list of books. It wasn't a question of censorship. It was a question of broadening their choices in reading in all disciplines and from all parts of the world.

We had really top-class language teachers. Make no mistake about that. So that the children at the school had very good service in English, Afrikaans, and German. In fact, they were doing so well in German that they won all the German prizes. Which was actually the right to go and spend a month or so in Germany. When the examination results for the Standard Eight section were passed over to the department, you found that all the pupils came from Livingstone. I'm not using that to indicate that we were performing miracles, but we had damn good people there. And what is more, we had a lot of womenfolk there. I'm not a sexist and so on, but generally over that period you found that the womenfolk on the staff there were in fact the masthead of the school because of their competence and dedication.

South African students became involved in the struggle against apartheid in 1976 with the boycotts in Soweto, Johannesburg, and then Langa, Cape Town. Student boycotts were repeated in 1980 and again in 1985. The schools were politicized from 1976 through the eighties, and in 1985 many teachers joined students in school boycotts and demonstrations. One must remember, though, that one of the tenets of the Teachers' League was "education for liberation." More activist teachers went for the motto "liberation before education" and teachers were referred to as "education workers." Some of these teachers called Teachers' Leaguers "armchair politicians." It is within this context that Dudley speaks about the period from the late seventies through the time of his retirement in 1984.

So when 1976 occurred we were ready for the sort of thing that began to overflow into South Africa. I think that we were also prepared in another way; in 1973 there were lots of workers' strikes, and these were the things that we dealt with in the school medium to indicate the obligation of educated people towards those who were battling for a living in this country. This was the way to tell these people that they were privileged, that amongst the eight or ten million children who were at school, there were only about a hundred thousand of them who were in secondary schools. And I said, "The majority of the others will never be able to have the sort of privileges that you are having here. Don't regard this as being just a sort of handout. You've got to actually build upon it." I think that we had impressed upon them right from the 1950s that our struggle in education was a struggle for democracy and this was education for democracy.

So after that period they once again, of course, did a lot of banning. A large number of the students who were at Livingstone were involved in the public demonstrations in 1976. But there was difficulty because we wanted the thing to have political content. We had our program from the Unity Movement, where we had ten basic fundamental demands. And people at that time were raising banners, and we said that your banners must actually show not only that you understand what this is all about, but that you can state precisely in simple terms what your fundamental demands would be. So we used to teach the pupils that your basic and fundamental demand is for the franchise, and franchised people are the ones who can work inside a desegregated education system. And they could articulate this kind of thing. And there was very, very regular and vicious intervention by the police. We, for example, used to lock the school gates to prevent the police from just rushing into the school. And the police actually came to the school to search the school.

The students used to march around the school. What was also interesting about that is that there were some people who were opposed to the idea of having these banner marches around the school. They wanted the pupils to go out onto the street. And when the pupils themselves ventured to go out onto the street, the police really fired into them and that happened again in 1980 and 1985. And we indicated to them that there was no way they could, in a few days of struggle, achieve what they were demanding. That they would have a long career in front of them in which they would have to be involved in this sort of thing. Now that kind of education, I think, was very necessary for these pupils. Because one of the other things that they were attempting to do from outside was to get the pupils to leave the school and to join the army outside in exile. And there were bomb scares against the school, because our school was not prepared to take the pupils on these marches and so on. We did participate in certain marches, provided these things were properly organized, but not at random. What we tried to get the pupils to do was to understand that this was just part of a total political struggle. We didn't want these pupils to lose the momentum of their studies. We used to provide them with study guides that they could utilize at school and we worked together with the parents and the pupils. And then there was a reaction against this by certain pupils. You know that the revolution was around the corner.

Two incidents speak to Dudley's presence at Livingstone as well as to the Teachers' League motto, "We live for our children." The former happened in 1977 after a student demonstration. The latter refers to university and college students coming to the school for teaching practice in the early eighties.

(1)   They gathered on the playground under the supervision of the teachers— both white and black teachers. White teachers didn't stand aside. And then they were spoken to by two of the senior students. One of them was Ralph Freese. Another one was a chap by the name of Gabriel. They stood in the center of this. This is all some of the fun. I mean it's tragic fun. And the teachers were there, well, persons like myself. The police went through with their dogs. But therafter the police came to the school asking us to send them the two chaps who were speaking to the pupils in the playground. So they came to ask us to let them have these two, the ones with the Afro hairstyles. We told them, "No go!" I said, "We can look after the school here. We don't want you to interfere with this school."

(2)   We had students coming in from the teacher training colleges and from the University of the Western Cape, coming along wanting to dictate to us what should be done. I was in the office at the time, so I used to tell these people, "Look, I'm in charge here. I'm not in charge on my own. I have a staff. But I'm telling you now that we don't allow other people to tell us what we've got to do at this school. So if you've come for that purpose now, you must leave immediately."

Richard Dudley's recollections of one of the many times he was passed over for the principalship of Livingstone High School provides an appropriate conclusion.

I was the best qualified teacher then. By that time I had outgrown some of my feeble youth, and the teachers were prepared to back me up. I acted there for about two-and-a-half years. Then when it came to making the position permanent, the school committee was called in by the Superintendent General of Education, Mr. Malan. And they insisted that I should be appointed permanently. Malan told the school committee this. I think it's almost word-for-word. He said to them, "Look, we know Mr. Dudley. We know that he's qualified for the position, but we also know that he has been fighting our policies all the time, and we are not going to pay him now for opposing our school policies."

Maureen Adriaan

I interviewed Maureen and Lionel Adriaan at their home in Elsiesrivier on the north side of Cape Town. Maureen Adriaan carried the conversation. The Adriaans are junior members of the Teachers' League compared to the teachers whose stories are presented earlier in this section. Maureen Adriaan was twenty-two years old when she began teaching in 1961. The Adriaan children, Francois and Suzette, attended Cressy, and both were students in 1985, the year of the school boycotts. Interestingly, they are both teachers. Francois teaches in Cape Town and is a member of the Teachers' League of South Africa. Suzette is a speech and hearing teacher in London. As we were concluding our discussion, Maureen Adriaan spoke about the principal Harold Cressy. Those reflections portray the essence of the Teachers' League vision. "The principal at that time used to point out to new teachers on the staff: No matter what your colour or affiliations at this school we only have teachers and pupils. We don't have white pupils and black pupils, and white teachers and black teachers, only pupils and only teachers."

Well, I had good teachers who I thought made a very great impact on their pupils. And I felt that teachers had a tremendous role to play in the lives of young people. Could help to shape their outlook on life, give them a sense of values which the education system didn't, and just help people to grow as adults. And I found myself choosing teaching because there were also state bursaries available and my parents couldn't afford to pay for university education. So it was a convenient choice in that respect also. I qualified for a bursary. My father was a carpenter and my mother was just a—how can one say—a tea lady at the factory? They were working-class parents.

Anyway, the University of Cape Town had very few non-whites studying there because of the financial factor and because of state policy. Even though the University of Cape Town is a so-called liberal university, it had a quota system which we knew existed but which they denied. I think there were only two non-white teachers on the staff. The rest, they were lily white. That went for the student body by and large. A handful of people who were not white studied there. Anyway, I qualified there and then went to teach in Port Elizabeth. Just to get some experience of the rest of the country. Because once you start in Cape Town you tend to stay in Cape Town. So I went out first, and then I came back to Cape Town.

Adriaan spoke about the work of the TLSA in the context of government racism and harassment of teachers.

Oh, the textbooks were terrible. There were many racist allegations and connotations in particular. But that was an opportunity to point out to pupils how contrary to human values those things were and that really they were just human beings like all other human beings and this whole idea of race was nonsense. Even though teachers were prosecuted and persecuted. I think it's true that in any society the prevalent ideas are those of the ruling class. So you had teachers and parents and pupils who really believed what the state was doing. You know people tend to believe the "official" version of life. There were pupils who were spying on teachers. The Special Branch, that was a special unit of the South African Police Service, they were very active finding out who was obstructing, undermining, and impairing State Philosophy, State Policy. We belonged to the Teachers' League of South Africa. I was a student member because my teachers were leaders of the Teachers' League in South Africa and I thought they were worthwhile people. So I wanted to follow in their footsteps because of their position with regard to education. The state did not look kindly upon the Teachers' League of South Africa. I came from Trafalgar High School in Cape Town, where we knew about this activity because our teacher was taken away when we were in matric. He was just removed from the class. Yes that was 1956. Anyway, so in Port Elizabeth it was no different than Cape Town. There were people there, teachers, who were active in the Teachers' League of South Africa. They were visited by the Special Branch on a regular basis. And we knew that they were under surveillance, but that didn't stop us from trying to speak and to reinforce the ideas of equality amongst our pupils, amongst parents, amongst the old people not in schools anymore. Because we saw this as a mission in life to educate people to their being human beings, entitled to what any other human being was enjoying.

Oh, my sister was also a teacher. She's in Canada now. She belonged to the Teachers' League of South Africa here in Elsiesrivier. And in 1963 the Teachers' League ran a big campaign against the intentions of the state to take education for those classified as Coloured out of the general education department and establish a separate Department of Coloured Affairs. So the Teachers' League was conducting this campaign against the transfer of education to this Coloured Affairs Department, and they were issuing pamphlets and had meetings and all kinds of things. My sister was at the primary school here in Elsiesrivier. She sent a batch of pamphlets to a colleague at another school, and her principal intercepted these pamphlets. She was reported for doing subversive things and then she was charged with misconduct for undermining, obstructing, and impeding the work of the State Department/Coloured Affairs Department. And she was dismissed from teaching! And she wasn't the only one who was dismissed from teaching for opposing what the state was doing to the children. So as I say, despite the knowledge that Big Brother was watching, people carried on with what they saw as their educational task.

People were just scared to debate openly in staff meetings. You would have private meetings. You would identify people who were likely to listen to your point of view and have a meeting. But it was very seldom when there was open debate in a staff situation because of the presence of Special Branch activities. Informers, oh yes, they were all over, so people were very, very careful as to what they said in public. Except for those who didn't care a damn what other people thought. They believed what they did was right. So it was difficult to recruit, but I suppose it was exciting in a way too.

Well, I am from Cape Town, and I went down there just for the short while. Yes, just to find out what is was like teaching somewhere else and then I came back home. In that time it was no problem getting jobs. In fact, teachers didn't have to apply if you were a university graduate. Principals came to find you. You didn't find jobs. They found you. So you could pick and choose where you wanted to go. I came back to Heathfield High School because the principal of Heathfield was also a member of the Teachers' League of South Africa. I stayed there for a year and I didn't like it. It was a bit far travelling from Elsiesrivier to Heathfield. And there was a post at Harold Cressy High School; the principal was also a member of the Teachers' League of South Africa and he said, "Maureen, if ever you need a job, we've got jobs." Well that was a fact of life. Then I stayed there until I retired in 1996. Thirty-odd years.

In 1965, Maureen Adriaan and her husband, Lionel, both began their long tenure at Harold Cressy High School. Cressy is located in the city center of Cape Town and was a highly rated secondary school. Adriaan spoke about the school, the principal, her colleagues, and their connection to the TLSA.

Harold Cressy was regarded as a progressive school. Progressive in the academic and political and social sense. It had a good reputation academically. The teachers worked very, very hard. I think school commenced at something like 8:20 a.m. until 3:40 p.m. at that time. It was a long day, yes. There were extramural activities, debating societies, cultural societies. It had a rich student life too, but teachers learned very soon after arriving there that that was a place to work. No nonsense tolerated by principals. Now the previous principal was also a member of the Teachers' League. In fact he was the President of the Teachers' League, and he resigned from teaching in 1963 because of the imminent transfer of education to a Coloured Affairs Department. It was his choice. He didn't see himself teaching under a Coloured Affairs Department. Anyway, then after him Mr. Ritchie took over. Followed in more or less the same footsteps when it came to organizing the school, providing the best possible education for the children. I'm tempted to say regimenting the teachers, but I think it was more a matter of organizing effectively and making teachers understand that they had a very important role to play. That they were dealing with a valuable asset and they couldn't be allowed to neglect the children. It was as simple as that.

You were expected to be at school every day. You were expected to be there for the full duration of the day. No coming late and going home early. You stayed there for the full time; in fact we had to work after hours. And he was very, very keen on quality education. He would even walk around. We didn't like it at the time because we thought he was snooping. But afterwards one realized that he just wanted to have his finger on the pulse of the school. And you know, the children would say, "Miss, there he's going, there he's going." If he happened to overhear something, you know, the students making a noise, or he thought the teacher was not doing her job, he would sort of knock at the door and of course claim to come on another pretext, you know. He would ask a particular pupil, make some inquiry not related to what was happening in the classroom at the time, but the teacher knew he could see what was going on.

So there was a very strong Teachers' League presence at the school, and I think that helped to set the tone of the school. Well it was an intellectual, an educational and political home for young people. You were allowed to debate issues of the day. You were given advice as to how to become an effective teacher. You were given a broader vision of education, and you could relate to what was happening in the rest of the world. Because at their conferences they very often referred to what was happening in other countries to raise the level of consciousness of teachers in the schools under these depressing conditions. No, I always held out the hope that things must improve for the children of this country. And they always taught their members that you must rise above your circumstances. You must find the ways and means to circumvent what the state wanted you to do.

Everybody was conscious of what the state was doing. Everybody was very conscious of the fact that you could be pounced upon at any moment. So it made your job as a teacher so much more urgent. It was almost like a, no I don't want use the word, mission in life. It became a very important facet of your existence, that you had a job to do as quickly as possible, as effectively as possible, because you didn't know how long you would be able to perform that task. It was like that for many teachers in the Teachers' League. I'm not speaking for all because like in any organization you have different levels of commitment in people. The majority of the Teachers' League members were like that because they were taught like that. Do what you can while you can.

As we have already noted, 1976 was a watershed year in South Africa when students in Soweto protested against the imposition of Afrikaans as the language of instruction in South African schools. There were also protests in Cape Town, and Adriaan reflected on Cressy and police presence at the time.

Well, 1976 was the year of the Soweto uprising and it revolved on the issue of Afrikaans-Medium instruction. But it spread from Soweto to the entire country and Cressy became involved. The students knew what was going on elsewhere and, of course, they discussed what was on the news. Television wasn't really a big thing then, mainly newspapers. And they felt they also had to have a part of this protest movement, and they organized a march in the school grounds and, you know, protest activity. And then, that morning, it was a particular day in September, the principal told the caretakers to keep the gates locked because by then the police had been all over the peninsula, swarmed all over schools. So the gates were locked.

So the students marched outside. They were going to have a mass assembly so that the people outside could see that they were also in support of protest. They were lined up on the tarmac, that's the playing field in front of the gates, and they started talking. Anyway, the students were all assembled with their posters and placards and student leaders, SRC, holding up the banner. So the students were all assembled, they were having their meeting and then the Casspirs pulled up. Those are the police armored vehicles. Police in camouflage with their guns and they were demanding that they be allowed to enter the school because there was an illegal gathering taking place. And the principal instructed the caretakers not to open the gates. And they kept rattling the gates, and eventually the principal went up and said that the person in charge had to come and talk to him. And he said, "Well, he just wanted to explain to the assembly that this was an illegal gathering and he was just going to ask them politely to disperse." So the principal said, "I'll let you in, but you alone." And the other police were standing there fuming because they couldn't go in and bash the children with their batons and quirts and all kinds of things they used at the time. So the one man came in and he addressed the assembly and said, "This is an illegal gathering. I give you five minutes to disperse." But beforehand we had agreed that we would not listen to this commander; we would obey the principal. And very calmly and quietly, Mr. Ritchie said, "Will you please go back to your classes now?" And the school turned around and proceeded as they normally would do after an assembly. Went into the building very orderly and calmly, and the police couldn't take it.

It was agreed beforehand, you know, that protest action had to be disciplined. It was a serious business if you wanted to do it. And the Students' Representative Council were called into the office at regular intervals. And they would go out on their own and discuss problems they had. So it was good.

She continued with a discussion of the 1980 and 1985 school boycotts and the position of the TLSA.

1980 was another period of open overt political opposition. Like the schools in the rest of the country, Cressy pupils also felt they had to have part of this protest movement and they did. And there was a period when there were class boycotts, not for long though, in 1980. It was exciting for pupils to openly oppose, because you know teenagers are naturally rebellious, and here they had a cause to rebel and it was a just cause. After they felt that they had made their point, they went back to academic activities and life settled down again until 1985 came along.

Well, the students wouldn't have normal academic lessons; they wanted to have discussions, political debates. What they called Awareness Programmes— programs designed to make them aware of what was happening in the country and why it was happening. So they would have special periods, not the normal academic program, but slots for particular talks. They would get people to come and address them. They would do the preparation themselves and address their fellow students. Or they would ask teachers to address them on various issues.

But one had to restrain them, in a way, and try and divert their attention to things which were less dangerous for them. Yes it was so. They felt that they had to march down the street to Parliament, for instance. And one would say, "Do you think that's the best course of action to take? Look at all the police down there. Do you really want to be shot when you haven't even made a contribution yet?" And then get them to march in the school grounds. "If you stand behind the fence with your placards, the people will still see what your message is, but it won't have the same amount of danger for you physically." That worked, but that was because of the relationship between pupils and teachers. They listened, they said, "Okay, we'll do it this way." No, they weren't prepared just to ignore the teachers and go ahead with whatever schemes they had in mind. And then teachers would take them to combined SRC meetings at other schools. One or two teachers would actually be given the job just to see that the students are safe. So we tried to protect them as far as it was possible.

At the end of 1985 there was great controversy over whether students would take year-end exams. They had missed much of the year because of the boycott and subsequent closing of non-white schools by the government. Adriaan discussed how the event played out at Harold Cressy.

It reached its peak in 1985 and that was terrible. Because that was a protracted school boycott period. They wrote the June exam, and that was the end of the academic year.[1] Really, it was the end. Yes, for most schools in the country. Then from June until December there was no education going on in the strictly academic sense. You had gatherings and sort of sporadic attempts at education. But it didn't really work, with the result that at Cressy, for instance, when it came to September, it became very obvious that these children would not be able to write the final examination because they hadn't had any lessons. What were they prepared to write? And it became a big, big thing. Parents' meetings were called, and the parents felt that their children were not ready to do the final exam. So in September parents decided that if their pupils were not ready for the matric exam, they couldn't allow the other standards to do the final exam. Because if the matrics were not going to be able to do the National Exam, the other standards would also have to fall in line because they wouldn't be ready for their exams either. Teachers discussed what was happening, and we had regular meetings. And then the parents said, "No, the children can't write exams under these circumstances. They will have to repeat the year."

Some children left at the end of 1985. Particularly some matriculants didn't see their way clear to repeat the entire year. So they opted to do what was called the Supplementary Examination in February. Some of them decided to go to other colleges, but the vast majority of the pupils came back and repeated the year. There are other schools where they also repeated the year. Livingstone comes to mind. South Peninsula comes to mind. Where the entire school decided at the time not to write. But as a result of 1985, towards the end of the year, the authorities tried to exert influence on the school to conduct these examinations. There were numerous attempts. They called Mr. Ritchie in almost every day and they grilled him thoroughly. But he wouldn't give in because the parents had decided their children wouldn't write. Eventually inspectors came to the school. They wanted to take the teachers one by one. You know, the old policy of get them as individuals and fix them. And the staff had decided nobody will go off privately. They address the whole staff or they address nobody.

Three inspectors addressed the staff. They read the riot act to the staff, you know, "If you don't do this, you're guilty of insubordination." They warned the school that steps would be taken against them if they continued on this foolhardy course. We said, "We have no choice, the parents have decided." So, as a result, they suspended the principal and the entire senior staff of the school. It was in December 1985. We were suspended.

You couldn't be in school, you were sacked, but not officially, no. This was the step prior to being sacked. Suspended. You couldn't come to school. And then, of course, during the whole of that vacation school was in turmoil because nobody knew what was going to happen. The Parent Teacher Student Association planned strategy, and they collected signatures from the community at large, not only Cressy parents. They had petitions signed demanding the reinstatement of the teachers, and it wasn't the only school where people were suspended. And come January 1986 and the school had to start and parents were demanding that the teachers who belong there come back, and the department was sending substitute teachers. They sent someone to take charge as principal, and they sent other teachers and the parents chased them away. Yes. When schools reopened there was a massive protest gathering in support of the teachers who had been suspended. Eventually the department was forced to relent, and they withdrew the suspension and everybody was reinstated. And then there was great and triumphant rejoicing, you know.

She continued by discussing "education for liberation" versus "liberation before education."

Anyway, the students, the teachers, the parents participated in protest marches when they felt issues were relevant and it was important to show support. The school did not support just any and every march. Because by that time we became aware of forces out to make not only the country ungovernable, but to make education impossible. You know they had the slogan "liberation before education" and we couldn't agree with that. And we tried to get our students to understand that education cannot be sacrificed for what you think is going to be liberation. You can get liberation through education or you can get liberation and education, but you can't leave the one for the sake of the other. Education was a tool. Well that carried the day with most students. And of course, unfortunately, I don't want to say it, but its true, your less academically able pupils would be the first ones to want to dispense with education and claim that they were fighting for liberation, you know. It was a convenient way of getting out of doing your daily drudgery in a classroom. But it didn't carry on for long.

We would discuss, "What are your best options? How effective would the particular course of action be?" The one thing that comes to mind is the president or the chairperson of the SRC came. It was in 1985 because there was a rumor that Winnie Mandela was coming to Cressy. She was going to land by helicopter to come and give them a talking to because they weren't out on the streets. He was very, very perturbed because in those days they believed anything was possible, because you know this romantic notion of the revolution now. And then on another occasion at school somebody came to say that they're going to storm Pollsmoor today. That was Lorna Adams from Athlone. "Today the masses are going to march on Pollsmoor and we're going to release Mandela ourselves." And you'd say, "Sit down, calm down. How do you think this is going to be possible?" A march yes, but actually you know like storming the Bastille, those pupils had romantic ideas. And young people, it appealed to their sense of adventure. So, it happened on more than one occasion. And one just had to reassure them that what you're fighting for you have to do in a responsible manner.

Maureen Adriaan concluded with reflections on the Teachers' League of South Africa.

It meant a support system, first of all. It meant a place where you could go to with your problems. Not at our school but at other schools, principals were victimizing teachers. The Teachers' League could take up the cudgels on their behalf and give advice and do that kind of thing. There were infiltrations by the police and, in fact, it came out afterwards that when people were charged, informants had supplied information. It would be like a party and we would have music playing very softly in the background and there would be people on watch-out duty, watching cars and that. There would always be someone outside and if the Special Branch should come along, you'd turn the music up and it would be a party. Belonging to the Teachers' League was also risky at times, very risky at times. Because when there was heightened police activity, you could be sure that you were followed. People were watching cars and some people became quite paranoid, to be quite frank. You know, they would see a police informer behind every bush sort of thing. But we survived.

Note

1. The academic year in South Africa runs from February through November.

TWO

Stories from Robben Island

In January 1996, Robben Island was declared a National Monument. A year later, under the leadership of University of Western Cape history professor Dr. Andre Odendaal, Robben Island Museum was established. Since that time Robben Island has become quite a tourist attraction, for both South Africans and international visitors. The island has seen a number of transformations. It was a leper colony in the late nineteenth century and became an allied World War II base in the 1940s. It was established as a prison in 1961 and, as noted above, became Robben Island Museum in 1997. Its current attraction, however, is strictly connected to its being a prison for the famous and not so famous who were political prisoners during the apartheid regime. Besides Nelson Mandela, African National Congress leaders imprisoned on Robben Island included Walter Sisulu, Ahmed Kathrada, Mac Maharaj and the father of the current President, Govan Mbeki. Their stories, as well as the two teachers' oral histories presented in this section, provide an important chapter in the history of apartheid in South Africa.

Robben Island Prison was an extremely horrible place to spend one's life. Nelson Mandela, who had first been there for a very short stay in 1962, described the changes and the harshness when he returned in 1964. This was the same year that both Neville Alexander and Sedick Isaacs, the two teachers whose stories are told below, came to "The Island." Mandela writes:

> Two years later, Robben Island was without question the harshest, most iron-fisted outpost in the South African penal system. It was a hardship station not only for the prisoners but for the prison staff. Gone were the Coloured warders who had supplied cigarettes and sympathy. The warders were white and overwhelmingly Afrikaans-speaking, and they demanded a master-servant relationship. They ordered us to call them "baas," which we refused. The racial divide on Robben Island was absolute: there were no black warders, and no white prisoners. (Mandela, 1994, p. 372)

Alexander and Isaacs both became greatly involved in changing the prison through education. Mandela explains that the purpose of the prison was to break prisoners and that the prisoners fought that by supporting each other and teaching and learning. Mandela and his fellow Rivonia[1] trial-mates, Walter Sisulu and Ahmed Kathrada, each wrote about the importance of education on Robben Island. In a 1964 letter Kathrada wrote to his parents about his studies: "So when Ma or anyone at home starts worrying about me, they must just imagine that I'm not in jail but at university" (Kathrada, 1999, p. 39). Mandela described courses, debates, problems, and spreading education to common prisoners. The same topics elaborated on by Alexander and Isaacs. He also spoke in general terms:

> In the struggle, Robben Island was known as the University. This is not only because of what we learned from books, or because prisoners studied English, Afrikaans, art, geography, and mathematics, or because so many of our men, such as Billy Nair, Ahmed Kathrada, Mike Dingake, and Eddie Daniels, earned multiple degrees. Robben Island was known as the University because of what we learned from each other. We became our own faculty, with our own professors, our own curriculum, our own courses. We made a distinction between academic studies, which were official, and political studies, which were not. (Mandela, p. 467)

As Mandela tells us, both political and common prisoners studied politics and also earned formal degrees during their years on Robben Island. Eddie Daniels is used as an example, by both Mandela and Isaacs, because he completed high school and various college degrees while in prison. He used this education to become a teacher after his release. Daniels spoke about informal learning at the quarry and also described his formal educational life in Robben Island Prison.

> I arrived at jail with a Standard Six education, having not studied for some twenty-two years. I was given permission to study in July 1965, and obtained my matriculation certificate the following year. In 1967 I enrolled through Unisa for a BA degree. In March 1971 I was arbitrarily sentenced to six-month's isolation and my study rights were revoked. Three years later I was once again allowed to study and I completed my BA, majoring in Sociology and Economics. I then registered for a B. Comm (Administration), which I completed in February 1979, majoring in Business Economics, Industrial Psychology and Economics. (Daniels, 1998, p. 158)

The educational histories of Neville Alexander and Sedick Isaacs were very different from that of Daniels when they arrived at Robben Island Prison. Both men had degrees from the University of Cape Town, and Neville Alexander had received his doctorate at Tubingen University in Germany. As a prisoner Alexander wrote a document that was smuggled out of the prison to advertise the conditions of Robben Island to the world. This document, which was published in 1994, is titled *Robben Island Dossier 1964–1974*. Liberal Party Parliamentarian and anti-apartheid activist Helen Suzman wrote the foreword to the book. After listing many of the atrocities of the prison, she added education problems:

> The difficulties encountered by prisoners in pursuing studies with UNISA — censorship of books; no foreign languages permitted for study; no post graduate studies; the cursory removal of study privileges, the last of which I imagine was particularly cruel punishment since studying preserved the sanity of the prisoners." (Suzman, in Alexander, 1994, p. V)

Alexander devoted twenty pages to education and provided examples of how prison officials made study difficult. He also explained how they used education as a tool to control prisoners.

> It should be clear by now that "the swinging of the pendulum" has much bearing on whether or not work becomes a serious obstacle to studies. In bad periods prisoners can virtually be prevented from studying by being overworked during the day; in good periods prisoners may have more time and leisure than many a full-time student in the free world outside. At examination time prisoners have customarily been granted a day off from work . . . in bad periods or under vindictive regimes prisoners have often been forced to work harder at examination time. (Alexander, 1994, p. 53)

It is in this setting that Neville Alexander and Sedick Isaacs were both students and teachers. Harriet Deacon's essay, "Remembering Tragedy, Constructing Modernity: Robben Island As a National Monument," addresses issues of memory and warns against simplifying both the past and the present. She also argues that the Robben Island Museum is "a place to celebrate victory, where South Africans mark the attainment of mass democratic rule and the demise of apartheid" (Deacon, 1998, p. 164). Deacon writes briefly about education on the island and then quotes Ahmed Kathrada, who said that Robben Island is a "monument reflecting the triumph of the human spirit against the forces of evil, a triumph of freedom and human dignity over repression and humiliation" (Deacon, p. 171). Neville Alexander and Sedick Isaacs represent that human dignity.

Note

1. Rivonia was an ANC safe-house outside of Johannesburg where Mandela's colleagues were arrested by the apartheid government. The trial was thus referred to as the Rivonia Trial.

Neville Alexander

I interviewed Neville Alexander in the early morning at his office at the University of Cape Town. He is currently a leading proponent of dual-medium education in South Africa and works educationally and politically promoting African languages in school curricula. After completing his Ph.D. in Germany, he taught for two years at Livingstone High School, taught for many years as a political prisoner, and worked on alternative adult education as a director with the South African Committee on Higher Education (SACHED). Alexander is one of three interviewees in the film Robben Island: Our University. He is also the subject of an interview Linda Chisholm conducted with a Livingstone student. "At school you were encouraged to be free, and when I looked at Dr. Alexander he was completely different to anybody I had ever seen. He was, he just looked so free." (Chisholm, 1994, p. 14)

Originally I wanted to become a medical doctor because of course it was one of the status jobs and, apart from anything else, you made a lot of money and I had the talent. And then my advisor in Cradock, a primary school principal, advised me to apply to Fort Hare University in order to enroll as a medical student. Now he obviously did not know that Fort Hare University didn't have a medical faculty. Just shows you how isolated places like Cradock were at the time. Anyhow, the point is that I applied, and of course they wrote back and said, "No, there is no Medical Faculty, but you should apply to the University of Cape Town." Which I did, only to be told that I didn't have mathematics and I couldn't register as a medical student. I enrolled at UCT as a student in the Arts Faculty. At that stage, my idea was that I would prepare to become a preacher rather than a teacher.

In fact, both my grandfathers were preachers. So, you know, I was orientated in that direction, but it took exactly six months in 1953 when I came here to dispel all that. One of my mother's friends in Cradock had a friend in the TLSA in Middleburg, about 100 kilometers from Cradock, and they saw one another regularly. And this friend of his, Ronnie Brittan, was coming to UCT in 1953 in order to further his studies. He was a teacher. And he said to Ronnie, "Look there's a son of a very close friend of mine, a young man, not quite sixteen yet, and I'd like you to look after him, make friends with him. Because you know he's from the country, he's coming to a big city." So one of the very first people I met when I got here was Ronnie Brittan. And via him I was introduced to progressive ideas, ideas of atheism, militant politics. To become a teacher, then, became an obvious thing for me, you see. I really admired Ronnie and he was a teacher.

Throughout my university career I received scholarships and bursaries. My mother and father would never have been able to sustain me at university. So by '57 I wrote my Masters and I was offered this scholarship to go to Germany and decided to do a Ph.D. in German. I was offered posts in different parts of the world. I fell in love with a girl from Goa, in India. But then I had to make a crucial decision. Do I go to Goa, Portugal, or South Africa? There was no way I was going to go anywhere but South Africa. Now let me put it this way: I think that my religious convictions, when I switched to Marxism/Socialism, sort of transferred themselves and I was deeply committed. And by the time I was eighteen I had made up my mind that I wasn't going to get married. Didn't want to have a family of my own because I was very likely going to end up in prison, and I wouldn't want to raise a family which I wasn't going to look after.

Alexander returned to Cape Town and joined the Livingstone High School faculty.

I had done my practice teaching at Livingstone. That's when I got to know Mrs. Roberts and Kenny Jordaan, who were teachers at the time. And we had a wonderful time. Became close friends, all of us. I decided that I would teach at Livingstone if a post became available, and five years later in '61 it turned out to be the case. Anyhow, then I had been groomed, so to speak, for a post at Livingstone. I was the only black student who had done an advanced degree in German. And Livingstone was one of the few Coloured schools at the time that offered German as a subject at matric level and the person who was teaching German was about to retire, so I was being groomed to take her place. So, in 1962, I began teaching German and, of course, history, which was my other major.

Formally I taught for only two years at Livingstone because in '63 I was arrested. And in that two-year period not only did I make lasting friendships with teachers and students, but in my own way, together with a number of other young people, we really transformed the school, made it much more, I suppose, *avant garde*. We really got students involved in projects of a quasi-political nature. We got students looking at local history, for example, which was something out of the ordinary at the time because we had very conventional books, orthodox interpretations of

South African history. We felt that the reason why we're teaching these kids is that they should become change agents. I mean that's a word we would use nowadays. At that time we tended to think of it more like militant activists. We would choose the most controversial areas in the textbook. That was where you learned to teach in a sort of counteractive way. So, on the one hand, we were extremely conventional, in our manners, in our general demeanour, extremely conventional. We used to walk around with collar and tie. But on the other hand, we were really questioning. It was our way of operationalizing our left-wing ideology. I was never satisfied with what I considered to be a really cynical stance on the part of people like Kenny Jordaan, much as I admired him. I always thought that their critique never led anywhere. I didn't believe in blueprints at that time, you know. And I also think that's one of the reasons why children were very fond of people like myself and various others. The point is that we really gave them the freedom to explore things for themselves. You need to take them further, and creating bridges has always been one of my main interests in life, actually, to see how people discover and then develop their talent.

Generally in the Cape Province at the time the Teachers' League and the Cape African Teachers' Association were really the organizations that everybody looked up to for leadership, guidance, and analysis of what was going on in racist, apartheid education. The TLSA had a consistent, very lucid analysis of what was going on. My own view was that it was almost negative in a sense that they had a British Anglocentric view of what good education should be like. They would never admit this, by the way. They would say that they had a progressive, Marxist-influenced approach. And at a certain level that is true, but if you come down to brass tacks, it was an Anglocentric British view of good education—Oxbridge. And as a result there's no doubt that in bourgeois liberal terms they have a first-class notion of what a good student, a good scholar should be, and all of us basically followed that line. But some of us, people like myself, always felt that there's something wrong. It's too removed from the real conditions of the life of the people. Most of the people could never reach that, could never be that. You need to give people other options; there must be other options that they can explore for themselves. If you come with that sort of blueprint, that's why I made the point about blueprints, if you come with that sort of blueprint, you're actually going to demoralize people because if people can't become that, then you stymie them.

I was particularly involved in the TLSA itself, Parents Teachers Association, and there was an organization called APDUSA to which I belonged—African Peoples Democratic Union of Southern Africa. There was a lot of infighting within the Unity Movement, splits and counter-splits, the usual left-wing stuff. We formed an underground organization in 1961, which eventually got to be named the National Liberation Front. We were already very critical of the TLSA as a political organization, not from the point of view of a professional organization. We always admired them for their professionalism and their dedication to pedagogy. But their political stance was so negative. We decided to go our own way and actually made up our minds to go for armed struggle after Sharpeville. And by '61 when I got back here, I was deeply into that sort of thinking, and I was very influenced by the Algerians as well as by the Cuban Revolution. So we started organizing. And for the whole period I was at Livingstone, I was involved in underground work. I even organized some of the students as a site of our organization.

In 1964, Alexander began his prison term at Robben Island. He reflected on many aspects of his involvement in education as a political prisoner.

And then I was arrested in '63, July 12th. Somebody infiltrated. Yes. We were also very naïve and too young. We had no people with real underground experience, military experience, you know, so we were sort of really pre-programmed for failure. And despite that, I must say that most of our people were never actually arrested. But right from the word go, we were clear that if we were going to stay there we'd have to turn this place into a place of learning as opposed to a place of punishment. And our group, which was a very intellectual group in a sort of conventional sense, our group was strongly supported in that by the Rivonia group, Mandela and the rest of them. Mandela himself, particularly, was very, very strong on this issue. You know we felt very adversarial towards them and very critical of the ANC. We always thought of them as collaborators and people who would compromise with the bourgeoisie. We had very militant and very strong radical views, and it took a while for the corners to rub off and for us eventually to get to understand one another. And although we never agreed politically, we became very close friends, and Mandela supported us and in fact pushed us to take a lead in the education of prisoners. And he said, "Look, we're going to be here for a long time. You have the illusion that we're going to be here for two years and then we're out. That's an illusion. We're going to be here for a long time. And it's best for us to try to make the best of the conditions. One of the things you can do is empower people." He did not use this modern terminology, of course.

And we agreed with that, fundamentally, just as teachers. Before they allowed us to study, we set about simply organizing informal seminars and discussions, workshops, at work mainly because we didn't have much recreation time at all. So, initially it was just informal discussions, exchanging views, teaching people about what you knew, somebody would pick up a topic and then you'd make it more formal, systematic. And then later on as they let up a little bit, they sort of allowed us to study from '66 onwards, so we could register with UNISA, the University of South Africa, as well as with other correspondence colleges for pre-university studies. And people got books, paper, pens, pencils and so on. And then it became easier to organize actual systematic, formal studies. And we helped people with their studies for colleges, coached them. So they had professional classes, but then, obviously, you were all political prisoners so very quickly political study groups started.

As somebody who had advanced university training and as somebody who had some experience as a teacher and was very committed to it, I was looked up to as one of the leading educationists. In the general section, where most of the prisoners were kept, there were two or three people who had a similar stature, the main one being Sedick Isaacs. Now, people like us were called upon to organize formal curricula and to get people into groups, you know, depending on what sort of background they have in order to study certain things. We had people who couldn't read and write. And we organized literacy classes for them in their own languages, mostly Xhosa, but there were one or two Zulu speaking and Sotho speaking. And then gradually they went over to English literacy because that's what everybody wanted. And within something like two to three years illiteracy was actually wiped out. Because you must remember in the first years there were mainly PAC prisoners, most of them peasants from the rural areas who couldn't read and write anything. You had to read the letters that they got from home which had been written by the preacher or the teacher for their wives and families. But you know the sort of comradeship and the bonds between us were really very strong.

I did theory of history, philosophy of history, and so on. It became such a thing that eventually we actually formed a group, which we called "The Society for the Rewriting of South African History." I had quite a few people around me doing work on that, people who were themselves studying history, and others who were just studying other subjects. And people were really inspired. Anyhow, we organized these classes. I particularly history, German, Latin, those were the three subjects I organized. Other people like Mac Maharaj, who just retired as the Minister of Transport, organized things like economics seminars, and Mandela himself ran a little legal group. And yet others organized things like Xhosa classes, we all learned Xhosa, you see. So everybody had some expertise and we organized around that.

We taught the warders. They were supposed to, of course, rehabilitate us, in inverted commas. We said to the Commissioner of Prisoners, "Look, there's no way these chaps can rehabilitate us. In fact, what's happening is we're rehabilitating them because these are mostly unemployable white people, and that's why they're there." It was the lowest of occupations for most whites in South Africa at the time, and secondly, most of them were doing it, the younger ones, in order to dodge the draft. Instead of spending two years in the army, they could spend four years in prison service, and then at the same time they were allowed to study. And all of them were trying to upgrade their qualifications. Most of them had very low formal academic qualifications, Standard Seven, Standard Eight. So they were mostly doing Standard Eight or Standard Ten work. And when they realized how quickly we were progressing our people, some of them had the sort of humility to come and say, "Can't you chaps help us?" We taught them math, we taught them history, we taught them languages, English particularly, even Afrikaans. I taught some of them Afrikaans and they were Afrikaans speaking. So it was really fascinating. And some of them acknowledged, both in my presence and generally, that they had learned a lot from the prisoners. One of the consequences, however, was the danger of fraternization. So that they were regularly transferred and then we had to deal with a new group of people.

Alexander spoke of the commitment prisoners had to education and the reasons the authorities allowed it to occur.

But I was going to make a point that very few prisoners came out of Robben Island without having acquired some academic qualification. From matric up to like Eddie Daniels, a good example, who actually got two degrees in prison, and many, many others similarly, you see. So from that point of view I think two things. One is clearly that the spirit amongst South African prisoners and the bonds were very strong, no doubt about that. I think under other conditions in other parts of the world at other times, a prison like that with so many different political views could easily have collapsed, fallen apart. And people could have been at daggers drawn as they were in places like Zimbabwe, for example. That's the one thing. The other thing is that the Afrikaner Apartheid Regime had some sense of, I suppose, morality, in a sort of ironical, paradoxical way. They took their own Prisons Act quite seriously at a certain level. The Prisons Act enjoins the government to allow prisoners to study and to encourage them to study and to improve themselves as a means of rehabilitation. What they did is a two-edged thing because, on the one hand, they were simply carrying out their own laws. On the other hand, they knew that we would become dependent on these privileges because they are privileges not rights, or they were at the time, we'd become dependent and they would get leverage over us. They could take it away. They did, by the way. From time to time they would punish us.

Alexander explained that the educational experience in prison was preparation for his work as an adult educator after his release. He was placed under house arrest for five years, and when his banning was lifted in 1979 he began his work at SACHED stressing alternative, anti-apartheid, education.

I mean, we really did turn "The Island" into a university; there's no doubt about it. In fact, in some ways, that experience prepared me for the ethos in the world at large and even in South Africa. We had to do very unorthodox things, including unorthodox methods of teaching, and it started me off as an adult educator. No, I wasn't allowed to work in any educational institution. I was still a danger to the state as far as they were concerned. In fact, I had a case against them because I was banned under the Suppression of Communism Act. I chatted to the guy who served the banning order on me. I said, "Look I wasn't furthering the ends of Communism while I was in prison, I couldn't do so, and secondly I've never been a Communist." Yes, I wrote a book, did a lot of research, then I went back to education, SACHED, which came to be known as one of the most important adult education centers for alternative, anti-apartheid education. I was there from '79 until '86, formally, and still associated with it even afterwards when I went on a different route. I became Director of the Cape Town Centre of SACHED. We established other branches of SACHED, myself and John Samuel. We made it a national organization.

There were many programs. The main program we started was a kind of enrichment program for people who were registered with UNISA and with a few other correspondence colleges. Very similar to what we were doing in prison, in fact. That was really the main thrust of what SACHED was doing, but they had a thing called Turret Correspondence College, which produced correspondence material for people preparing for matric. Teachers or educators were hired to assist. Well, they weren't actually hired, they were voluntary. Most of them did it to get experience and to get access to people who had political consciousness. A lot of the people who came to teach at SACHED were people who wanted to get in touch with political activists. Then we started producing different kinds of programs, partly because there was a need after 1980 when the whole education thing was put in question. And we started producing things like *Upbeat Magazine*, which is a second-language English teaching tool. We started a junior secondary course for adults who had never been to school, you know, post-literacy type of situation. Eventually we started Khanya College, which was a first attempt at tertiary level academic development for students who came from a disadvantaged education background. And we had many other small local projects with community groups. We established schools here in Cape Town, a number of schools in squatter camps, illegally, I mean without permission.

Many South Africans, including the Teachers' Leaguers we met earlier, refer to the young people of the struggle years as the "lost generation." Neville Alexander disputes that analysis.

And a lot of those students are now working for NGOs and so on; that really was not just a lost generation. In some ways it is a generation that is deeply disappointed, I would say, despite the fact that they were the generation that actually made that Revolution in a sense. Because that group, that sort of layer of people throughout the country, a bit like academic guerrillas, if you wish. They weren't MK or in the armies of the Movement, but they were doing the kind of work on the ground here of organizing, of educating, forming community organizations, NGOs and so on. But they haven't inherited the earth, they haven't, you know, so a lot of them are terribly disappointed. And now when I look back I think that we should have done much more in those years to train people to get professional qualifications rather than just to open the vistas. We could have done it but it would have been very, very difficult. And it probably would have pushed us into a conservative mold which was out of sync with that time. So it's one of those contradictions historically which you couldn't actually foresee properly.

Alexander concluded our discussions by reflecting on the importance of Paulo Freire's work on education and the black consciousness movement in South Africa.

I think that I would like to stress here the significance of Paulo Freire and the black consciousness movement, through the prism of which Paulo Freire influenced South Africa. We worked very closely with the black consciousness movement, and a lot of the community programs that were started were quasi-political quite deliberately in the Freirian sense. And then we tried to indigenize what we understood of Freire at the time. And essentially I would say we really turned "Education for Liberation" into a pedagogy that had the potential of being really alternative. Not just questioning the existing hegemonies, but really looking at what are the alternative social forms that we can promote. What should a university look like, for example? What should schools look like? You know, the really fundamental things.

Sedick Isaacs

As I was conducting interviews for this book, Crain Soudien, an educational sociologist at the University of Cape Town, told me that I must interview Dickie Isaacs. He had heard Isaacs address local and international students about his experiences on Robben Island, and he said that the students were spellbound. Sedick Isaacs taught at Trafalgar High School in the early sixties. I interviewed him in his office at Groote Schuur Hospital, where he conducts and administrates medical research. There were many interruptions because students needed his help. Isaacs spent thirteen years in Robben Island prison. During that time he was both a student and a teacher, and he was often punished with solitary confinement or floggings because he fought for himself and his fellow prisoners. In August 1999, Sedick Isaacs was asked to write about some of his experiences by the Robben Island Museum. The essay, "The Key," is about him and other prisoners making a key as a means to escape the prison. When the key was found, Isaacs was treated severely. "I was dragged down to the punishment section, roughly thrown into a damp cell . . . I was bodily lifted by two warders, punched in the face and head by the others, dropped onto the floor and kicked about. Half dazed, I felt my clothes pulled off and chains put onto my legs and wrists."

Well, I first went to teach at a school out in the township areas, and that was in an area called Bishop Lavis. It was an Afrikaans-Medium school, and I taught there for nine months or so. That was in '62. I was twenty-two. And then I left and I did some work in the chemical area. I was going to work in the Durban City Council, joining the Engineering Department. They didn't know with whom they were talking to and offered me the job and paid for me to come over. And when I arrived at Durban they were embarrassed. They thought I was a white and they tried to explain various things. And then I made an application to the Zambian copper mines, and I was going to work there and I had some passport difficulties. Of course, at that time, I was also to some extent politically involved in the sense of getting people across the border, and I think that's probably why I had difficulties getting a passport. Remember at that time the only profession that was really open for those who were not white was teaching. It was the only course that gave bursaries. Any other profession you had to do on your own. I thought of going into the medical profession and I really looked at myself but I thought, no, I'd be more interested in science than in medicine as a profession.

Well, I went to Trafalgar as a teacher. And I quite enjoyed it. I was very young at that time, and I had some students and we became acutely interested in the politics of the time. I was not involved in any specific organizations at the time. Remember there were quite a number of organizations like the MK, the Unity Movement. And the Pan African Congress was very strong. The Pan Africanists had just slipped away from the African National Congress in '59, and they were more energetic, more radical. And I was also energetic and radical, and I thought that would be a good organization for me. I became very much involved with it at the time.

Well, first of all, it started with pamphleteering and getting people to various political meetings. Having some form of small study groups. And then during that phase we were passing out of the passive demonstrations to the more active demonstrations. And since I had a background in science and chemistry with a keen interest in explosives—remember I applied for the copper mines as the person who works with explosives. And during that time people needed to be trained and educated; trained in the use of explosives. I offered that and I ended up even making explosives.

I got caught doing that. We went out to the rural area to test it. We were driving back and one of my friends stopped, and just when he stopped the police picked us up. I think they were watching. I had a girlfriend who was white. The police were also watching me in terms of the Immorality Act. And I think that's partly why they might have been watching.

Isaacs began his prison term on Robben Island in 1964 and was released in 1977. He reflected on his initial resolutions and prison conditions.

When I found myself in prison I made two resolutions. One was that I will always try to escape, and the second was I'm going to try and resist the effects of imprisonment in any possible way I can. And when I arrived on the Island, when I was in detention for some time, with Eddie Daniels, we cut through the bars. You must have read it in his book. And then subsequently I wanted to make "The Island" uninhabitable. I was convinced that I was going to resist the effects of imprisonment and in order to do that I must also see whether I cannot contribute to keeping my comrades, in an unobtrusive way as healthy as possible. I came from the physical sciences, and I thought that I must now convert and become more interested in the human sciences.

It was not easy. There were a few people who had permission to do courses. One must remember that the Prison Department has a set of guidelines and rules to abide by from some world body. And one of things is they will give prisoners an opportunity for study. But at the time they did not want to do that. So they were in this type of dilemma since we always pointed out to prison officials that we wanted them to apply their regulations. In those years we had infinite problems. It had to do with the type of food they gave us, type of recreational facilities, what are rights as opposed to privileges, and also the need for education.

We staged a couple of hunger strikes in order to get those things seen to. I, unfortunately, was involved in these hunger strikes very, very deeply. Organizing it and in trying to get it published. Because a hunger strike on an isolated Robben Island will have very little effect unless we publish it. We were able to get one of the warders to take some notes out for publishing in the newspapers and organizations who were active. And I wrote many of those. It's unfortunate my writing is easily recognizable.

Isaacs spoke about solitary confinement and his experiences with criminal prisoners.

I was staying in the communal cells, the larger cells. And this warder picked me up, and I spent around nine months in solitary confinement. And they refused to give us books. No reading material, no sleeping during the day because they take your mattress out. If you talked you'd lose your food rations for the day. But Fiks Bam smuggled some *Reader's Digests* to me which I had to hide. Couldn't keep too long because they searched me but they gave me a Bible. I read that Bible from cover to cover. Every single word. And then since I'm Muslim I persuaded them to give me the Koran. I read it from cover to cover. I memorized it.

People who were in solitary confinement would sit there doing nothing. They brought in criminals. Remember there were also some gangs. But the gangs seemed to be impressed by us. I remember when I was in detention I met some of those criminals and one shouted to me across the passageway in Afrikaans, "What are you here for?" And I said, "Politics." And he said, "That's dangerous." Then I asked, "What are you in for?" He says, "Murder—attempted murder." That's not.

And this other criminal was in the cell right next to me. And I became a good friend of this criminal. He wanted to know various types of questions from me about education matters and writing matters. He wasn't very literate. He was, in fact, the leader of a prison gang called The Desperados, whose sign was the hammer and sickle! They didn't know anything about Russia. They weren't communist. They felt the hammer and sickle was a good sign of force and strength. There were times when we didn't have food for the day. He was just a sly criminal. He could get past a warder, go and steal half a drop of food off his dishes of *mielies*. He knew that well and he brought us some so we had something to eat for the morning. One day there was a shortage of water and a shortage of *mielies*, maize. I'm

giving you the Afrikaans word. You couldn't find *mielies* but he got a drum of coffee. I was out exercising, and when I came back there was a half a drum of coffee.
We had nothing to eat for that day, except we drank coffee.

*Isaacs became the Chairman of the prisoners' Education Committee. He remembered
some of the things they did to promote prisoner education. Although he did speak of his
own studies (psychology, geography, computers) and the degrees he earned while on "The
Island," he was more concerned with his work as an organizer and teacher.*

I was appointed Chairman of the Education Committee. Different organizations had their administrations, their governing bodies. The PAC and the ANC
and all the organizations worked very well together during that time. There was
an exchange of views and concepts. And the Education Committee was an
inter-organization committee. It was a very loose type of committee. We had informal meetings as needed to plan various approaches for teaching. What syllabus to pick up. What to teach. There was wide diversity from those who were
completely illiterate, to those who were in matric and those who were embark-
ing on university studies, and there were those who'd already done university
studies.

And we had to organize and even persuade teachers. We approached various
people with various skills. And some of them were doing it already. Then we could
look for materials, for writing materials. Look to see whether we can't get any
blackboards. And we found that there were old pieces of hardboards. We smuggled
them in and they became reasonable blackboards. We had to look for writing materials. A few people were already studying, and they were allowed to buy writing
materials. You must remember that anybody misusing these studies had study privileges withdrawn, and misconduct included sharing papers and pens. But we did
share. And at that time they were also building the prison so there was cement
around and the cement bags had three layers. And we were able to cut out those
three layers, clean off the brown paper and stick it together into a type of loose flat
book. And whenever possible, pencils were broken and halved or quartered and
shared out. And many of us started writing small in order to conserve space. My
writing is still extremely small.

*Besides having to scuffle for materials there were many different educational needs at
Robben Island. Sometimes education was in the open but at other times it was a covert
endeavor. Isaacs talked about the nightly schedule in good times, innovative teaching, and
education at the quarry.*

You worked yourself. You'd come back from the quarry with blisters on your
hands from pushing wheelbarrows the whole day or breaking stones, get in at 5
o'clock. By the time you've dried yourself from the shower, you can get to studies
block and you have classes from 6 o'clock to 7 o'clock. It was very formal, yes. And

then from 7 o'clock to 8 o'clock it was people who wanted to practice instruments, who studied music. And at 8 o'clock the prison bell rang and then it was quiet, sleeping time. But they allowed us to study before sleeping time. So it was very quiet study. The lights were always on. That's maximum security.

I taught mathematics and I taught physical science. And I thought one of the ways for me to make it as interesting as possible was to give them exercises. When you go to the Island, you'll see that there's a door leading to the bathroom. There were no doors at that time. You come back from work in the quarry, you're all dusty and so on and you rush to get a shower. My students who were interested in their mathematical problems came with me. I sometimes think I lived very non-conventional. Have you ever taught a class standing completely naked while you're in the shower? In the shower, having helped people with tutorials while sitting on the toilets. I had a friend in the next-door cell and he wanted to study mathematics. So, I wrote him a textbook of mathematics on toilet paper. I had a small study kit and half a ballpoint pen, which I managed to bring in. I think I got it from one of Neville's group. In any case, I wrote this textbook and he did exercises on it, but they discovered it. And then they rationed toilet paper—one sheet per day.

We needed to take care of one another, yes. In the quarry we had to produce a heap of stones for the day. They would come along and measure, and if you didn't have enough stones you were accused of laziness and sentenced to a day of solitary confinement during the weekend. And all my comrades knew that I came from the universities. And they used to make extra stones for me and bring it along and give a donation to me in order to make that pile. Well, in fact, because of my interest in science I got nicknames. I got three nicknames. One is called *Lwazi*, the *Xhosa* word for Mother of Knowledge. And then I've got a second, which was called *Kitso*, which is also the seat or the suspense of light. And then after I was flogged I was given another nickname, *Soranti*, because I had stripes on my body and it was *Xhosa*.

We decided to open classes in the quarry without the warders knowing. So we tried to organize classes. We'd send a notice to every cell, "There's a history class tomorrow on the stone-breaking section." It's fortunate the quarry was big, almost fifteen hundred prisoners there. When you came to the quarry they'd shout "Line up," and people lined up for wheelbarrows. You could choose your work. Remember in the quarry it's a work situation also, it's not easy for a teacher. So I found one of the best ways to learn is for everybody to prepare as if they're going to do the lecture or the teaching. So I told everybody, "Tomorrow's the history class but we don't know who the teacher is. You are going to draw lots and whoever gets the shortest lot is the teacher." And everybody had to prepare as thoroughly as possible where the rest would listen and then criticize and fill in and so on. I discovered that is the fastest, most effective way.

Isaacs also taught two warders.

And the warders observed us. Some of them heard that we were getting Matriculation Certificates and so on, and they wanted to join us. Ja. There were one or two warders that I helped on that Island which sticks very clearly in my mind. There was one warder by the name of De Wet. He was in charge of the kitchen, and when he was not in the kitchen he worked in the Warders' Mess. But he was a very cheeky warder. He was cheeky to everybody, even to his superiors. And he was once charged, I think, for insubordination or something, and they declared that he was not going to get any promotion. He would only get promotion if he could complete his matric. Now he saw us studying, and he came to me and said he would like to complete his matric. And I had a brief discussion with him, and one could sense that he's not very, you know, either hardly completed school or other standards. He was not quite ready for matric and I said to him, "Look, can't you persuade your superiors to make that condition instead of matric, one subject in matric." And he went back and they agreed to that, because they couldn't really suppress him. And then he came to me, and he said that the Prison Board said that he must do one subject and that's cookery. I said, "Well, that's very wonderful. When do you get to start?" He said, "I want to start with you." I said, "I don't know any cookery. I know nothing about it." He didn't believe me. He said, "With all the degrees you've got you must know cookery." And then I finally agreed and all the various committees said, "Well, it's good policy." So I started teaching him this cookery thing. I learned a lot. I stood next to the window and he sat by the other side of the window, and we discussed cookery. And then something happened, I'm not quite sure what happened? I was charged for something, and I ended up in solitary confinement for three months.

The other warder I worked with was there for seven years. He was in charge of the quarry, actually the boss of the quarry. He was one of the most malicious people I've actually seen. He encouraged people to be chained in that quarry. And I remember if you are in that hole with your head sticking out you're not given any food, nothing, for the whole day. And one political prisoner, one comrade, actually had the audacity to stand in the hole and said he was getting thirsty. And the warders came along. "Oh you're getting thirsty." And actually urinated in his face and said, "Now your thirst is gone." He was that type of man. He also was known to take his gun and threaten people, and they say he actually once shot someone in the leg. He was the one who also harassed me, persecuted me, victimized me. I always discussed with him whenever possible. I said, "That's not the way you wish to be treated. This is the political situation." I had discussions with him all the time and we'd argue sometimes. Sometimes he'd threaten me. But I noticed the arguments started becoming less and less intense, less and less emotional, until one day he came to me and said he's been a warder all his life, and he really wants to get on into the next phase and he would like to study. I said to him, "Well, what do you study?" And actually the quarry changed, gradually the quarry changed. Everybody sat in the sun and he said to the other warders, "Leave them." It physically changed, psychologically changed. People sat in the sun and had long discussions. There was no pressure for work anymore, and I was talking to him in his office, and I asked him what he wanted to study. He wanted to study Biblical Studies. Well, I'd read the Bible.

Near the end of his time in prison, Isaacs was allowed to study Library Science and he worked on building a library in the prison. In some ways it was his final act as a "teacher with the fighting spirit" at Robben Island.

The atmosphere of education became much more formal. I think that's why we all called it the University of Robben Island. I finally persuaded them to let me start studying Library Science. And then I persuaded the Prison Board to give me the opportunity to reorganize and build a Prison Library. The rest of the warders and the Head of the Prison never liked that. I was doing a degree in Library Science through the University of South Africa. I was learning about cataloguing and they allowed me to try and get a new supply of books. I read profusely. I read about a thousand library books a year of various types of literature. Then I persuaded the Board to allow me to write for a donation of books. I was amazed they actually gave me permission to write to the University of Cape Town Libraries. So I wrote a letter to the Library. They didn't like certain phraseology. They tore it up and it came back. I learned to negotiate until they finally had a letter and they posted the letter to the Chief Librarian. The Chief Librarian put up a collection of books that really amazed me. It was certain fiction but most of them were non-fiction and she sent me *Das Kapital.* It is a book which is normally banned in South Africa. That came there.

Sedick Isaacs was released from Robben Island in 1977. Upon his release he was banned. The story of his wedding illustrates the inhumanity of apartheid.

Well when I got outside, remember, I was banned. When I got married I had to get permission because my wife was not a member of the family. They wrote a letter saying I can't have a wedding reception because I'm banned, but my mother can have a reception provided I don't attend. And Mr. Kies, my lawyer, protested against it. And then it changed and I could have guests but the guests can only stay up 'til 9 o'clock, and I must keep a full list of all the guests and must clearly mark off who's a communist.

I applied for a teaching job. Of course, I had no chance of getting into a government school. But there was a private school, a church school, who offered me a job if I could get permission. And I wrote a letter. Yes, and then I had to apply since teaching was also restricted. I asked for permission. They laughed at it. They said, "No way."

Isaacs concluded with a last memory of "The Island" and his daughters' seeing his name at the South African Museum.

I was also interested in cultural matters, so I organized writing competitions, and one day I organized an art competition. We had judges and voting for prizes and it involved everybody. Remember, my basic principle was I must reduce the prison effects on prisoners. That was really what motivated me. And that's why I was involved in sport. I also was a sport organizer. I was cultural, education, all that. I had a pen and I wrote all the certificates by hand. When my children once went to the South African Museum as a school, they saw the certificate. They saw my name written on it; they actually were quite thrilled.

THREE

Boycotts, Marches, and Pedagogy: Teacher Struggle Stories

In 1910, Dr. Abdullah Abdurahman, the president of the African People's Organization, said in his presidential address, "If Europeans persist in their policy of repression, there will one day arise a solid mass of Black and Coloured humanity, whose demands will be irresistible" (Molteno, 1987, p. 6). Many South Africans believe that those "irresistible demands" began in 1976 with the Soweto uprisings and culminated in 1994 with President Mandela taking office. Peter Kallaway provided context in his 1984 book, *Apartheid and Education:*

> The crisis of the 1976–7 Soweto Riots and the school boycotts of 1980 focused attention on the youth and demonstrated the extent to which educational institutions had become sites of struggle in South Africa. The very institutions designed to propagate "education for domestication" on the Verwoerdian model, turned out to be trojan horses. The upsurge of student power—probably without historical precedent—linked to heightened community consciousness and worker organization, and accompanied by a new wave of guerilla incursions, marked the beginning of a new era of resistance to apartheid. (Kallaway, 1984, pp. 19, 20)

Besides 1976, the school boycotts of 1980 and 1985 are always emphasized as the key years that combined schools and the struggle against apartheid. Activism in the schools began with students, and teachers were slow to follow. In Soweto, a Johannesburg township, students demonstrated and boycotted because Afrikaans, a language that wasn't spoken by black students and was viewed as the language of oppression, was designated as the official language of instruction. Many students were beaten and killed, and the boycotts spread throughout the country. The struggle was particularly intense in the Langa section of Cape Town. Although teacher organizations remained silent during the 1976 uprisings in Cape Town, there were individual teachers who supported students in boycotts and marches. Many teachers were conservative and afraid of losing their livelihoods. The same was true in 1980 but teachers did become more vocal. An organization called the Teachers' Action Committee (TAC) was formed that challenged the conservative position of many teachers and worked with students on the 1980 school boycotts. Paul Kihn summarized TAC in "Players or Pawns? Professionalism and Teacher Disunity in the Western Cape 1980–1990": "It was an indication of growing teacher discomfort with the traditional professional style, and with non-involvement in the boycotts. Teachers wanted to reclaim their voice, and their legitimacy which had been shaken in 1976 and 1980. TAC was a form of teacher empowerment" (Kihn, 1993, p. 84).

Barry Liknaitzky was a teacher at Alexander Sinton Secondary, a school known for its activism at the time; he recalled that the student theme song was Pink Floyd's *The Wall*. The lyrics include "hey teacher, leave those kids alone." In the student-published *Inter-School Manual*, an article was titled "Teachers—The Stillborn Radicals."

> The article derided the "petty bourgeois attitudes" of teachers and maintained that, "Our first, our second, our final impression of teachers in general, is that they are a misfit lot condemned to the Sewage Tanks of Athlone. Their sole concerns are their checks, their bonds on houses, their cars, and a host of other interests. As a body, they could not be trusted." (Kihn, p. 84)

Between 1980 and 1985 non-white South Africans were becoming more and more politicized. Trade unions accrued more power, and there was a growing and more militant underground. Teachers were forced to take a stand. You were either part of the problem or part of the solution. Being part of the solution meant joining students who had formed Student Representative Councils to fight against school-based issues as well as the oppression of apartheid. When students nationwide boycotted schools in 1985 because of growing and more intense state violence, activist teachers joined in the struggle. They taught alternative awareness classes and marched with students to protest the apartheid regime. On September 28, 1985, progressive teachers in Cape Town launched the Western Cape Teachers Union (WECTU), a democratic, anti-apartheid organization.

> WECTU aligned itself with the broader, community-based struggle as well. According to its newsletter, "WECTU has placed itself firmly in the fold of all other

progressive organisations in this country struggling towards a S.A. free of oppression and exploitation". . . apart from political change, WECTU also broke from past "professionalism" by focussing on radical educational change. An articulated reason for the formation of WECTU was to support the students' position against apartheid education. One of WECTU's constitutional goals was, "To work towards democratic control over the education system and to militate against the propagation of oppressive education." (Kihn, p. 85)

The lives of the teachers whose stories are presented below exemplify what it meant to be an activist teacher in apartheid South Africa. They also represent individuals who, although activists, worked in their own unique ways. They were teachers who defied the teacher norm during apartheid. It must be remembered that many other teachers did not join the struggle. This was especially true when the teachers whose stories are told in the first part of this section began their careers in the 1970s. Since the TLSA had become somewhat silent because of the bannings and general oppression, it was teachers like Basil Snayer, Jimmy Slingers, and the other teachers introduced early in this section who provided a model for the activism of their younger colleagues who became teachers in the struggle years. The activist teachers we meet in this section were part of Tabata's cadre of teachers—"teachers with the fighting spirit." Each of them was politicized in a different way, but their stories portray the marriage of pedagogy and politics.

Basil Snayer

I met with Basil Snayer in his office at Garlandale High School during the autumn midterm holiday. Somehow people knew that he was at the school; the phone rang with people asking for his time. There was also a brief delay as students returned soccer nets that they had used the previous evening. His rapport with the students was immediately evident. They were comfortable with him and he liked seeing them. When I returned for a second visit, Snayer had just completed a class on Athol Fugard. His eyes were alight, and he was excited by his students' passion for Fugard's work.

I started teaching in 1972 and I was then twenty-one years old. I grew up in a rural Eastern Cape town called Fort Beaufort. It's about 120 miles inland from Port Elizabeth. I was brought up in Fort Beaufort because that's where my father taught. And being a rural town, I think, Fort Beaufort didn't offer much in terms of education. One, because it was rural, but more importantly because it was rural in the apartheid setup. The further you went from the urban centers, the worse apartheid became. So my years as a primary school pupil were spent firstly in a home that was fairly politicized, I would say. Both my father and mother were teachers, and both of them were also members of the Teachers' League of South Africa.

My mother and father belonged to the TLSA, which was vehemently opposed to the apartheid system. My father also held executive positions in that organization. He was part of a group of teachers who actively started opposing the apartheid regime as it was manifesting itself in schools. As a result of that, he wasn't, obviously, very popular with the regime at the time, although he was very popular as a community person in his own community, forging links across the so-called colour lines, especially with so-called black or African teachers. So my growing up was rich in that sense. It was an extremely difficult period for us because teachers didn't earn a lot of money. My father had too many children. There were seven and we grew up fairly restricted from many of the opportunities open to white children at the time. When I used to be sent to the shop by my parents, I would have to buy through a little window on the side of the shop. Give my money over the ledge of this window and whoever was receiving the money on the other side would fetch whatever I wanted and pass it over to me. If for any reason the change was wrong, in my opinion, it would have been my word against the white person serving me. And invariably the white person's version of that story would be right, and I would be swindled out of a dime or two or whatever the case may be.

The point I'm trying to make is that is where black people were allowed to buy from, whereas white people were allowed to go into the market and choose whatever they wanted. And, of course, the fundamental issue there was that black people were the thieves, black people were not to be trusted, and black people were not hygienic to touch things. And that, of course, had a major, major impact. So that's the sort of milieu that I grew up in as a child.

Snayer went to live with his grandmother so that he could attend high school in Port Elizabeth. He remembered some of his teachers.

Then when I passed, at that time it was Standard Six, Grade 8. That was the level at which Fort Beaufort offered education to children. And most of Fort Beaufort's children left school after that to go and work on farms, to go and work in factories, wherever they could find jobs in the urban areas and in the hinterland of Port Elizabeth and East London, and so on. I was fortunate enough to have a grandmother in Port Elizabeth, and I was sent to live with my granny to go to high school in Port Elizabeth. I attended a Roman Catholic institution called St. Thomas High School where I matriculated, and it was also there where I first became actively involved in protest politics. At the time our political consciousness was being developed in a very, very significant way by our teachers.

There were private teachers as well as nuns. There were lay teachers. There were those from the community. The nuns were very highly qualified people from Ireland and Germany who were teaching subjects in a very, very kind of dogged way. And not politicizing anything, so that most of the influences came from schools in the area, not necessarily from St. Thomas. Particularly from Southend High, which was a state school at the time. I can remember Mr. Raymond Durin very well. Raymond Durin became a top executive member of SACOS, the anti-apartheid sports body of the country, which also governed over school sports in so-called black schools. At my own school a teacher who really had an enormous effect on me was a teacher called Mother Louie-Bertram. She was second in charge of the nuns at this convent where the school was based. I think that she instilled in me a very, very good sense, firstly, of self-discipline but, secondly, of self-worth. An extremely good sense of the fact that human beings are human beings and that there was no difference between myself and whoever else in the country. And I think that that to me was very lasting.

Basil Snayer completed his two-year course in teacher training at Dower College in Uitenhage, which is just outside of Port Elizabeth. He then moved to Cape Town to take a special certificate in music and began teaching in Cape Town in 1972.

I got a post at Batswood Secondary School, which was just across the road from where I had trained. That's in Wynberg in Cape Town. I was under a man called Dan Ulster, who was the first let's call him black man or Coloured man, or what you want to call him. The first guy who had composed and was allowed to conduct the Cape Town Symphony Orchestra with his own symphony. That was 1972 when I started teaching. But Ulster had already done that a couple of years before. Brilliant, brilliant man, brilliant musician. Also one who had a profound effect on my development, not politically so much because I think we differed, very, very fundamentally, politically, but certainly musically we gelled, the two of us.

I think it was in that very first year that my involvement in anti-apartheid activities really took off. Dan Ulster was also involved in a teacher organization called the CTPA, which had been established in 1967. The CTPA was a group of teachers, or was a forum for teachers, established, I think, in the interests of advancing the "Separate Development Policy" of the apartheid regime. And it was obviously given enormous prominence by the state. Leaders in that organization were sort of pushed and groomed as educational leaders, whereas a grouping like the Teachers' League of South Africa was the opposing group of teachers. And soon the CTPA became a huge organization—hugely powerful. And in this body, Dan Ulster played a very pivotal role. He was my musical mentor. But because of my parentage, as well as my natural inclinations and my connections with teachers right from the outset, I was naturally drawn to people who were not thinking as Dan Ulster did.

And of particular significance was joining a male voice choir led by a man called Basil de Vries. He left South Africa during the heyday of apartheid, I think, probably around the Rivonia Trial period. Luckily so, because I think he would have been hounded as well. He was one of the leaders in the TLSA at the time, a brilliant musician, choral master, and teacher. Teachers' League people had enormous effect on my development as a teacher and in my political exposure and my political awareness. So my formative years as a teacher were very much aligned with the anti-apartheid movement.

I was teaching music and I was teaching English and I was teaching, I think, geography or history at the time. At that time people were really thinly spread in terms of their qualifications, and I had to teach whatever I was told to teach, but mainly, I would say, music. I think I coped very well because there was a very strong support group amongst the teachers at the school. A very strong network of experienced teachers who were quite prepared to take us new ones through the ropes in terms of doing administration, in terms of doing lesson preparation, in terms of the extramural activities and the like, and in terms of dealing with the officialdom at the time. I remember also one little incident when I came to school without a tie on. It was a very hot day and the school inspector had come to the school for a visit. He was then given the opportunity to go through the school, check out the classrooms, and he came to my class and he immediately asked me where my tie was. Now as a young upstart in the educational system, I had very little idea of regulations, you know, especially with regard to such mundane things as dress code and all those kinds of things. I was more interested in what I was going to do as a teacher and how I was going to develop children and how I was going to put on musicals. I was confronted by this bureaucrat asking me where my tie was. I considered it quite a petty issue and my retort was "Why are you wearing a jacket? Can't you see how hot it is outside?" And, of course, I was severely reprimanded for that, severely reprimanded, and told exactly how the system works. And that, of course, didn't do the apartheid system any good, because it just infuriated me more about how things were being done. And I didn't see the emphasis on dress code before I was even asked about my subject. How I found the kids, and so on. I didn't see how an inspector could walk into a school and assess my worth as a teacher within ten minutes when he comes for inspection once a year, or sometimes once every two years. What happens for the rest of the two years, when I am judged on the basis of a ten-minute discussion or a ten-minute observation of my work? So the whole issue of teacher appraisal, which now has become very prominent, that whole thing, in my mind, started then.

Snayer continues by discussing his move to Fort Beaufort because of family commitments. He talks about his first arrest and finding his father's curriculum and political papers.

At the end of 1975 I left to go back to Fort Beaufort where my mother was. The reason for that is that my father had died in the middle of 1974. My mother was having quite a bit of difficulty adjusting without my dad, him having done all the kind of finances and stuff in the family, and my mother felt quite lost. So I moved there with my wife for three years. That was '76, '77 and '78, where three of my children were born.

We both taught there for three years. She taught at the very school where I did my primary education. I was lucky, and my wife was lucky, to get a post right there. During that time, of course, the real political test began because it was in 1976, just the very year that I started, that this whole thing erupted in South Africa. The Soweto incident which spilled over into the country. That was the first time I was arrested. Ja. I was arrested because of whatever, I'm not quite sure anymore why. There were never any reasons given. They had come to my house on the pretext that they wanted to ask me some questions, and so on, and took me away and interrogated me for about an hour or two and then released me. And the questions were more or less about what I knew about the organization of the resistance in Fort Beaufort. Well, they asked me questions about certain teachers. I said, "Well, as far as I'm concerned, I don't know anything. I don't know what you're talking about."

So, I can only say that the reason for my arrest at that time was probably an investigation in Cape Town as to what kind of role I had been playing, and up to that point it was confrontation with the authorities. And anybody who had been seen to be in the slightest way in opposition to what was happening in the country, as far as the National Party was concerned, those people were targeted, and you were just picked up at random. Some people who were actually very involved started disappearing at the time, or were arrested, or they were detained without trial, and that sort of thing.

As I said, at the time I went to stay in my parents' home, and in going through some of the documentation that he had left behind I began to get a sense of what they were involved in. You know, all the alternative methods of teaching and all the alternative curricula that they were working on. Minutes of meetings and what was discussed. And one began to get a sense of where one should be going outside of school as well. And not confine your resistance to the school base on its own, but to begin to organize yourselves as a block of teachers, as a block of community workers, you know, in a far more coordinated way and in a far more goal-directed way. That was very enlightening for me.

At the same time, I must admit, I was also very scared because of the fact that I had been picked up. I wasn't very confident of forming relationships with any of the teachers there because one couldn't really trust anyone yet. And I suppose I did discuss it with one or two people, but, in the main, there was no real scope in Fort Beaufort, such a small town where everybody knew everybody else's business. I think it would have been fatal for me to start any discussion group, to start any political awareness amongst people I had just begun to get to know. So, that put a break on the kind of advances that should have taken place.

Besides that, I also was very aware that my stay in Fort Beaufort was going to be quite limited. My wife was not from the country. My wife was a city person, and I was not going to subject her nor my children to the deprivation of the rural areas. There was a kind of ambivalence about the fact that that's where I grew up. I needed to develop that community. But I also had this thing about, you know, "Where do I take my children?" There had been virtually no development in Fort Beaufort. The school where I grew up still had the very same infrastructure, if not less, and things were just not looking good. So, that and, of course, the major thing was that my wife wasn't terribly happy staying there, and you can imagine also staying with my mother. It's her mother-in-law, and all those kind of things.

The Snayers moved back to Cape Town in 1978, and he returned to Batswood. He taught in the teacher training division, and he recalled one mild student protest at the school in 1980. He also became involved in the progressive teacher organization that year.

In 1980 there was another uprising, which manifested itself also in Cape Town. And boycotts and all those kinds of things. And the college, where I was teaching, it was only for females, for women; those young women organized themselves into an anti-apartheid student group at the college. There was the wife of one of the school inspectors who taught, I think it was Afrikaans, at the college. I remember very clearly, they targeted this woman's car as a means of showing that they were dissatisfied with the system. And identified her as being the wife of one of the bureaucrats, and through that, they, I think what they did was to block the exhaust pipe at the back. Whatever they did there was a major hullabaloo about that incident. The long and the short of it is that Batswood Training College, as an institution, was now also part of the mass resistance that was flooding the country at the time. Needless to say, I was very central to the whole development of that particular awareness.

And also during that year I then became, for the first time, actively involved in starting to organize teachers. Meetings were held. I was called to a meeting at the Hewat Training College in Athlone, where the beginnings of a teachers' union was being discussed. I remember very clearly a chap called Yusuf Gabru, who is now head of the ANC's local education desk in the Western Cape. Yusuf was elected as the Chairperson of what was called the Teachers' Action Committee in 1980. And that Action Committee was the beginning of what today is called the South African Democratic Teachers' Union in the Western Cape.

That Teachers' Action Committee quickly formed into decentralized zones throughout the Western Cape. I became the Chairperson of the Wynberg/Claremont Branch of that particular organization. At this point I would call it an interim organisation because it was very badly organized. It was very primitive in its understanding of union activities and union organization but, nevertheless, it was the beginning. That spilled over into 1985 when the big resistance came—the Alan Boesak era, the UDF (United Democratic Front) era. That was, for me, the turning point of the resistance in schools.

Basil Snayer moved to Garlandale High School in 1983. He spoke of the volatile times in the context of students and the school

I was still teaching music and English, and it was very soon after '83 when the school was drawn in, whether we liked it or not, the school was drawn into protest politics. So that when the '85 period erupted, young teachers here, against the will of the older establishment at the school, had already established a Student Representative Council. This was contrary to the thinking of the principal and his management team. They wanted the old prefect system where monitors were nominated by teachers. We wanted an SRC where people were elected by their own body, their own constituency. So, that we established.

It was very volatile, extremely confrontational from the students' point of view. But then again, it was also a time when the University of the Western Cape, where I was studying for a degree part-time, had begun to produce the kind of teacher that was beginning to fundamentally question the system. And the kind of teacher that was coming out of UWC at the time was now being taken up into high schools. And they were more aligned with the thinking of students at the time and guided the thinking of students.

So the battle lines were drawn. The polarization became sharper, and sooner or later you had students coming to the offices of principals and asking them, "Where do you stand?" And that didn't auger well for the stability of students. Many principals, for want of a better word, succumbed to the demands of students, but the majority did not, and hence the confrontation on the school level. Students also began to show their dissatisfaction by attacking government institutions: post offices, other schools, telephone poles, whatever you could get. Any government car or anything connected with government was attacked. You know, burnt out, stoned, destroyed, whatever. Soon the political debate also became an economic debate. So that those who had economic power in the country were also beginning to be targeted. Because the connection between economics and politics was beginning to be explained to students, and they began to see the economic superstructures from a Marxist view.

So, that was key to the understanding of students. Government syllabi were rejected totally. Students just simply refused to write any tests, to listen to any lessons, particularly subjects like history and economics, they refused to listen to that. "Why must we learn about capitalism only and not about other alternatives to capitalism?" "Why must we learn about Van Riebeeck only, and not about Nelson Mandela?" You know what I'm saying. So those sorts of questions were beginning to be asked. Teachers were not prepared for that and those of us who were prepared to go and learn, who were prepared to go and look for alternatives, were seen to be in the camp of the students, and began to be targeted.

Snayer was arrested for the second time in 1985. He spoke about his short stay in prison where he met other political prisoners. He also reflected on what a difficult time it was, both publicly and personally.

It was in October that year when I was arrested for the second time, and this time I spent fourteen days in prison. Ja, that's one of the reasons I know that I was targeted. The other reason is that by then I had twelve, thirteen years of experience and was a senior teacher at the school. There were teachers who came here with two or three years' experience and they were immediately appointed as heads of department, over my head, even though I had applied. So, that was another reason why I thought, "Well, this is it. I'm never going to get any kind of promotion here."

I got arrested, and of course this time it was far more vicious in its character. I remember that morning; it was three o'clock in the morning when they came to my house, again on the pretext that they were looking for someone else. They asked my wife some phoney name, "Is this person staying there?" My wife said to them, "No." They asked her to go wake me up, and I came out, and they asked me to show my I.D. card. And I showed them my I.D. They looked at my face, they looked and said that they just want to make sure. Could I not come down with them to the station? And as I was ready to go, the one, there was a girl, a lady policeman with them, said to my wife, "Put in some toiletries for him." So I knew then. I was the first teacher to be picked up in the Western Cape. There were a whole range of political activists who were picked up on that same morning at the same time, and we were all dumped into the communal cell at Athlone Station. The next morning we were taken to the Victor Verster prison in Paarl, where Mandela came out after he came from "The Island." And that's where I spent the next two weeks, during which time there were daily interrogations for about two or three hours, with two people interrogating you. The one very friendly, the other one very aggressive, you know, normally the case. And, there again, it was a huge political education that I went through because I also became aware of people like Christmas Tinto and Zoli Malindi. Christmas Tinto and Zoli Malindi are two of the stalwart black activists in the Western Cape, especially Zoli Malindi, now an eighty-five-year old man. At that time he was already in his seventies, and the stories that I heard in the jail when we used to come together during lunch hours and chat; it was a real education to listen to the experiences of these people. Christmas Tinto told us about their years in the struggle. And that strengthened one, it strengthened one tremendously. Because these people had been in and out of jail and they could tell us what sort of tactics the interrogators would use. So we were psychologically being prepared for any kind of eventuality. I was still dead scared, of course, because even in the car leaving my house that morning I thought, "Well, this is it; this is my last; I'll never be seen by my family again." Because while I was driving I was sitting in between two cops in the back and both of them were playing with their rifles, or their guns, or whatever, and here I'm sitting! So it was a terrifically troubled period, traumatic period, that we went through. Yes, that period was probably the most horrific period in terms of the things that I personally went through. Always expecting the worst to happen.

Snayer spoke about being released from prison and his return to Garlandale.

"You can go home now." No explanation about why I was there, what I was arrested for, and what I was going to be charged with, or any kind of charge. Nothing, just, "You can go home now." The other thing that I really couldn't accept was the fact that when I got back to school I was told by the school principal that I had to accept the fourteen days as leave that I had applied for and that they would be subtracted from my general number of leave days. I had applied for this leave? I, of course, wrote numerous letters.

I got an enormous response, of course, from the students, an enormous response, and from most of my colleagues. Most of my colleagues were very happy to see me. But I also got a sense of a certain section, I suppose the most conservative section, being very wary of associating with me; probably being scared of things that they didn't really understand, you know. If you're too close to someone who had been in prison, you might land there yourself. I did not show a great deal of tolerance with the management of the school, because in my mind they had something to do with it. And I continued to do what I normally would have done having meetings with students about alternative programs that they can arrange, and how to arrange them, and becoming more and more involved with that layer of the school.

You must remember that in 1985 there were no official classes for about six months. Then schools re-opened. You know, the students started trickling back to school, and the principal had tried to stamp his authority back on the school to get teachers to teach. It went with great difficulty. When I came out of prison, there was a sense of normality which I didn't like, frankly. Not because I didn't think that there should be stability at school, but rather that the kind of normality that I saw was a kind of forced, almost artificial normality, that brought people back to school. And students sensed that.

The issue of 1985 matric examinations was discussed in Section One. Snayer and nine of his colleagues also refused to administer exams.

As I said, I immediately became more and more involved with students, and the examination at the end of 1985 came, the final examination. I'm sure you know that the matric exam is an external one, which is held in very, very high esteem by the community. I remember there were ten of us who refused to administer examinations at the school. I had in some way been successful to organize at least those ten teachers to refuse to administer an examination based on three months of work for the year. Our view was that it was educationally unsound. We thought that the sacrifices South Africans were making needed to be shown at ground level as well. We needed to show our solidarity with particularly the most disadvantaged groups in South Africa, that majority of black people who would not be promoted to the next standard. We needed to show that kind of solidarity and not make a sham of an examination simply to satisfy the whims and the fancies of the management, or to satisfy the desires and the expectations of parents out there, however difficult that was going to be to understand.

All ten of us had joined and established WECTU. And, of course, our names were handed in to the department and there was a disciplinary hearing. There was a confrontation between us and the principal. We refused to give our names. He just randomly handed in whatever names he wanted to. I was seen as one of the front-rankers in this move. And we refused to administer examinations. Many students refused to take the exams. In fact, the exams for all intent and purposes just didn't happen. We were blamed for that. And while we were not charged with anything, we were certainly marked. I believe I was marked. The reason I believe we were not charged was that many other teachers at other schools didn't administer exams. If we would have all been charged, it would have sparked a wave of protest throughout the schools because by now we had a fully-fledged union.

The school was less intense in 1986, but many students took the struggle against apartheid underground.

However, the resistance had taken another form. It had taken the form of underground movements in a very big way. Students, Standard Ten pupils, there were one or two from our school, had simply disappeared. Some of us knew where and others suspected. But we knew. I certainly knew that two of them had gone for military training, and that was the case in most of our schools. Ja, as I said the struggle, the resistance movement, had taken on another character. It had gone underground. The victories of the Cubans in Angola, and elsewhere, over the South African army had begun to play a significant role in the mindset of those who were part of the resistance. Particularly in the black townships where the South African army, which at that point seemed quite invincible, was now beginning to be seen as, "Well, we can conquer you; we can take you on, we can beat you." So from 1985 to about 1989 that resistance began to show itself in the various attacks on police, bombings.

And that, of course, made it even more difficult for you to operate openly at school. There was this sense that, "Well, you've been arrested and now you've been released and now you're being watched." I was drawn into a fairly clandestine operation of the resistance.

Snayer continued by discussing Anton Fransch's murder and the death of his nephew, Robert Watervitch. Both occurred in 1989. Snayers testified before the TRC on Fransch's murder. He spoke to me about both events; his memories are both powerful and horrible.

A comrade, Anton Fransch, was cornered by police next door to my house. It was after midnight when suddenly I heard a barrage of gunfire outside. I really thought that my house was under attack. I put out the lights and soon one of my windows was shattered. And this went on for several hours that night. At 3 o'clock that morning a contingent of about ten cops stormed into my house. For years after that the effect on my children was devastating. Any little sound after that they, you know. Anton kept them at bay for the entire night. It was a quarter to eight that morning when a hand grenade went off. They claimed that he had blown himself up, but I have proof that one of the cops had actually thrown in a hand grenade.

And then another huge event in my life happened in 1989. My wife's sister's son was a student at St. Columbus in Athlone, it was a Catholic School. And he came to ask my assistance in establishing a Student Representative Council at that school; the monks were opposed to the idea of an SRC. And, of course, with us having had that experience, I could quite easily assist. And they established an SRC, much to the consternation, of course, of the establishment of the school. And he, as a result of that, became very, very involved with the working of the SRC at the school and student politics. So that when he eventually went to University he joined Umkhonto we Sizwe. Ja, he had joined MK and he had gone for training. I would say he was very committed to changing this country and hence he had joined MK.

On that Friday he said that he was leaving that evening for a youth camp, church camp, and that he was returning on the Sunday. Now that's the story that he told his mother. I knew that he was not going on a church youth camp. He was actually going on some kind of mission. On the Sunday I received a phone call after we had heard the bomb going off in Athlone, near one of the public toilets in Athlone City Centre. It was about 9 o'clock that Sunday evening. Ja, 9 o'clock this Sunday evening this bomb went off. Everyone was standing in the street wondering what was going on. And at about 12 o'clock that evening, I received a visitor who came to ask me whether I was aware of where Robbie was. That's my sister-in-law's son. I said to him, "Yes, I know where Robbie was," but immediately my mind went to the bomb, and I knew why they were there. The person who came to see me introduced himself as their cell leader, the unit leader of Robbie's MK cell. And, of course, I wasn't quite aware of who this guy was, and I wasn't going to share that kind of information readily. But it appeared later that Robbie was killed in this bomb blast, and it must have been a bomb that was rigged somehow, and he and another colleague of his, Coline Williams, were blown up. It is still the belief of family members and political activists that the apartheid state murdered Robbie and his partner. I had to remove the MK paraphernalia from the ceiling of Robbie's granny's house. That was a most harrowing experience. A colleague of Robbie's assisted me. How we avoided the police/security branch was a miracle. That was in July 1989.

Snayer spoke about students, mostly Student Representative Council members, whom he admired and whom he stays in contact with today. He was going to a party at one of their houses that night. He also spoke about the activities that WECTU teachers

arranged for students that included orientations for new students and extracurricular cul-
tural activities. He closed by critically considering the present.

Well, I think that for me as a teacher things have changed dramatically. As a person in the community, very little has changed in the area where I'm staying. Very little has changed visibly. A lot of things have changed in terms of people's rights, but not a lot of things have changed in terms of people's day-to-day living in this area. I'm sometimes acutely and painfully aware of that.

Pam Hicks, Pam Dewes, Beth Mclagan

I interviewed four white women who taught together at Livingstone High School in the eighties. Rose Jackson is a quiet person, so the other three women dominated the interview. Subsequently, I did an individual interview with Rose Jackson that is included in this section. All four women spoke about Richard Dudley with reverence. Although these stories aren't as detailed as others in the book, they offer insights into the life of white women teachers in Coloured schools during the struggle years. It must be noted, however, that the women who speak in this section have had many different educational experiences. For instance, Pam Hicks was an active member of the Western Cape Teachers Union, Pam Dewes ended up teaching in the United States, and Beth Mclagan among other experiences ran her own private school after 1985. Hicks raised a concern that speaks to the mission of many South African teachers during the apartheid era: "I have some trouble in identifying myself as a white woman working in Coloured schools. It was that kind of identification that we were working to destroy. In teachers' organizations we defined ourselves functionally according to which department's schools we worked in. That was the significant thing."

Pam Hicks

I didn't have a Teachers' Training Certificate. I came out with an Honours Degree, and my idea was that I'd do a bit of teaching while I thought about what I wanted to do. I started in '74 at a school called Spes Bona, which was run by somebody who subsequently became South Africa's Ambassador to the United States. Not a happy year. My first year of teaching was very tough. It was under the

Coloured Affairs Department. It was a boys' school and it was designated a technical high school. Quite a showpiece, in fact, strangely enough. I think in other contexts technical high schools tend to be kind of, you know, not cracking it academically. I think that was part of the kind of project at the time where "Coloured" people were going to be shoved into trades and so on. So there was this kind of jewel of the department which was this technical high which was adequately equipped. It was a new school. The person running it was a kind of a tyrant. Oh, the other thing about that school was that it was different because it was a boarding school. So it was kind of exceptional. It was set up as quite a model, and overseas visitors would be brought to show how the state was supplying the "Coloureds." You know, it was that kind of thing. It was a very conservative Colouredist kind of management structure.

Then I went to Trafalgar in town, which is an old school—very different. An old District Six, long-fighting history, it had fallen on bad days because District Six had been eroded already or was being eroded—1975. And that was much happier. It was a more comfortable school politically. It wasn't reactionary; in fact on the contrary, largely thanks to the deputy principal. I had an interesting lesson at Trafs from a child who was one of my Standard Sevens. They were notoriously the worst and the Standard Sevens had seen one of their teachers come along the passage and they all just choopsed into class and were sitting there still. And I went into them and I said, "Why did you do that?" "Aah, no, Miss, that Miss, no, we're so scared of her." So I said, "Why?" I really wanted to find out her secret so I could use it! And this one boy said, "Miss, she just says something to you and you just want to die!" I said, "Like what?" He said, "One day she looked at me and she just said, 'Do you want to stand in the shop all your life?'" and he said, "I just felt so small."

But then at the end of that year I went overseas for two years. When I came back I went into a very strange environment of a school named Steenberg. Many a tale of that but very corrupt. A Cape Flats school where the principal was running the place for his own gain. We went to school one Monday morning and were suddenly informed that there would not be classes that day, and the reason for that was that his very good friend from the Swiss Embassy had brought an educational film to show to the children. The children would have to pay for the film. So the kids were frog-marched into this movie. Now to force kids to go into a movie on a school day you think wouldn't take much, but it did. They were just about forced in and forced to pay. And the film was a wonderful educational film from this hotline from the Swiss Embassy. It was called *Tarzan in Africa*. And even the kids were saying, "This is a junk movie. It's an old movie." So they were all trying to escape by jumping out of windows. But of course, needless to say, the monies collected, extorted you might say, were never accounted for and pocketed by the principal.

Hicks talked about going to Livingstone.

I went from that situation to an interview where this person was sitting there as the deputy principal and the first question he asked me, this was Mr. Dudley, I subsequently discovered. He said, "You've been teaching in so-called Coloured schools. Is there anything different that you noticed about the children?" I sort of came up with some sort of Neh neh neh story about, "No, well children are children, you know. No, there's no difference." And he said, "Well actually these children are subjected to pressures, you know, there are normal pressures in growing up, but I think there're specific pressures that they're subjected to." And it was like, you know, having come out of a madhouse into sanity. Somebody who just had a grip and was prepared to talk about the grip that he had. And was expecting me to respond. I wasn't to come out with platitudes. I was actually to speak about what my experience was and I had to start using my brain. And it was just amazing.

The context was that you could get on with your work and you were valued. Just Mr. Dudley being my Head of Department in Science, and he'd come and he'd say, "You're doing such wonderful work." And normally at most of the township schools, in a sense you were free to do what you liked because nobody cared, but you had to re-invent the wheel everyday because there was no kind of support, no infrastructure, and also things were just wild. So to teach, you really had to fight for discipline. Whereas at Livingstone it was a given, and there was a hell of a strong kind of handing over of responsibility to the students. The students ran their own affairs. There were lots and lots of extramural activities. They used to have a student day once a year where the students would run the school and all that sort of stuff. There was an SRC long before anybody else had an SRC and it was strong and it was very carefully democratically run.

Hicks spoke about some politics at the school in the mid-eighties as well as the Coloured Affairs Department throughout the apartheid years.

I think the underlying tension at the school was between the Unity Movement and the ANC. People got into big trouble because they were more ANC aligned, and people were marked. Also among the students within the student committees, Livingstone was marked, not just for being academic, but for being over-intellectual. It was a kind of a non-struggle school, really.

I mean the problem with teaching in that system was not the people we taught with, but the system out of which we taught. So departmental policy was obviously the repressive mechanism. The Department that was running Coloured Affairs was notoriously complicit with the Nationalist Government. The principals of the schools were generally kind of puppet figures. I mean it doesn't apply to everybody. But there was a certain pattern that applied certainly to Trafs and to Livingstone. The person who should have been principal, who had been, you know, in the trenches all the years, was very effective, fully competent and so on, was blacklisted for political reasons. And those of us who were classified as white were initially paid more until they brought in parity. And we were apparently paid some allowance on account of the incredible danger some bureaucrat thought we were exposed to. On the other hand, we were kept permanently temporary, very vulnerable and no promotion prospects—bad career choice. Many were fired because of political activism and had no comeback.

Hicks spoke about teaching science at Livingstone.

It took a couple of years to swing things the way I wanted them. But I developed a thing where I had my own room. Before that we had to move around from room to room and I decided I was going to stay put in my room because I was working with a lot of apparatus. The thing that I kept trying to work towards was working as practically as possible with kids, doing as much as possible and you can't do that if you're constantly mobile. So eventually I worked through to a point where I had a lab, and I lived in the lab, and that was it. And it took me a good few years to get there, but I got there. And then I was running classes more or less the way I wanted to, which was lots and lots of apparatus available, lots of animals available.

I reorganized things and I was lucky with the syllabus. I obviously worked much more closely with my syllabus than the English people did and the syllabus was great on the whole. But whenever there was a chance I would use it against itself. Like the heavy emphasis on taxonomy. I would explain how science can by used for another agenda. The use of classification here, in Nazi Germany and other racist systems. And it was cautious on evolution but we tackled it head-on. One could present it in a variety of ways. So my kids were doing a lot of group work, a lot of hands-on stuff, you know. If they were going to do the spider, I sent them out to gather spiders. Then return them whole and alive. Ja, forty-something kids. In my first registered class there were forty-eight. Ja, and we had a lot of fun. I don't want to sentimentalize but kids would be fighting to get into the class.

She spoke about white people's thinking on her teaching in a Coloured school.

When people would say to me, "And where do you work?" and I'd say, "Livingstone." This was such a pattern. "Oh, I've never heard of that school." Even though it's in Claremont. And then you'd say, "It's a so-called Coloured school." And you'd hear them say, "Ohhhhhh." I remember in the early seventies when I was at varsity and a friend of mine was looking for a job and the head of department advised him to go and work in Transkei.[1] He'd been at war with the head of department at that particular time, and somebody then said to him, "Do you realize that if you go into the Black Education system, you're going into the wasteland. You can forget an academic career." And I think it was the same principle. And I would argue it still actually applies in a sort of masked form, but, ja. The irony is that incredibly innovative and creative things were going on in that "wasteland" because of the way people responded to the system. The kids, and also fellow teachers, at Livingstone and across so many schools. Thanks to departmental policies, it's been a career disaster, but in personal terms I feel rich.

Pam Dewes

Well, I started roughly the same time. My situation was a bit different. I was married and I had a Teaching Diploma. But married teachers didn't get jobs easily in white schools at that time. Subsequently, after about four or five years I got divorced, which would have freed me to go and teach. But by then I was hooked. In fact, the first job that I got was very tough for me, and it was nothing that I was qualified for. You're going to laugh when you hear, I actually worked as a physical education teacher. They are laughing because I have no bent for that. No. And that was Oakland, which is around the corner from Livingstone. But it was possible to say it's more working class.

My first job. But it was quite fun because they were preparing for their sport. It was the first term of the year, things were very haphazard in that term. The textbooks come late and anyway they were all concentrating on getting through their sport and doing very well. I was only there for a term, and then I went on. And I even walked to school because I was living around the corner from there, which was quite nice. But anyway, I went on to Trafalgar. I taught English, which helped, and I started meeting stimulating people. But I remember discipline was a problem for us liberal white girls. Having to administer corporal punishment was tough. I had a particular incident there that I remember and it wasn't good. There was a particular kid who kept challenging me to hit her and I hit her. I'm very D. H. Lawrence, *rainbow*, I kind of identified with that tone. That's right, so it colored my view of things very badly. So you did have huge classes and difficulties asserting yourself, particularly as a white liberal woman. I stayed there about a year, and then I went on to Livingstone. Mr. Dudley was the real influence there, even though we had a principal; he was a bit of a puppet. He was a bit weak, a sweet man but ineffectual. Mr. Dudley was really the force. And he couldn't get promotion because politically he was persona non grata.

Dewes spoke about 1976 at Livingstone and especially about a student named Ralph Freese.

I remember very well though the way it all started with Ralph Freese. Ralph Freese made such a huge impression. He was in the SRC and also a very charismatic person. He was a student, but terrific and we respected him. And as I say, very charismatic. And then came the political turbulence which started elsewhere. It started in the black end and the SRC obviously had been talking about making a stand and showing solidarity and the way it was done was quite amazing. I think rather different from other schools because Ralph took the SRC with him in discussions, started off negotiating with the principal and Mr. Dudley, then the staff. The staff was not in favor of what he wanted to do. He wanted to form a placard demonstration on the grounds, and already the police were becoming quite militant, you know. They were bringing the Casspirs. So there was a fear that if the students demonstrated on the grounds and put up their placards, the kids would be at risk. And there was this confrontation. But the students won. They stood firm. I still remember one morning Ralph Freese got the kids into the quad. There was this big quad where they used to have assembly in a courtyard which was surrounded by the buildings so nobody from outside could see and the whole school gathered there. Ralph Freese got them all there. And he addressed them through the mike and he told them what he wanted them to do, which was to walk around the school grounds, which were surrounded by a chicken wire fence, to put their placards up, but to be orderly. That was a big thing. They had to be orderly. And he was amazing. He told them to sit down and listen, and they sat down and listened. And they did it all exactly as he had planned. The staff were powerless. But by the time he'd finished we were all on his side, really. And in fact, some of the staff, I think, a few of us actually walked around. I did. Walked around with him and he was actually politicizing me.

The slogan that was fostered at Livingstone was "education for liberation." And Dudley, I mean, he reminded them education first before liberation. I mean, it was quite complicated. So there were factions among the students as well as the staff.

That was again in '80 and I had to keep quiet. Actually, Livingstone started off in solidarity with the struggles. As time went by Livingstone had this anti-struggle image because they started getting more violent and became more and more political and that didn't wash.

Dewes concluded by talking about her teaching and being a white teacher at Livingstone.

Can I start off by saying that when I started about a third of the staff was white? There were a couple of Afrikaans who stuck it out to the bitter end. The one was like an Afrikaner churchman. So that was quite interesting. But as the years went on, and policies changed as well, there was a tightening up and fewer and fewer white teachers remained. I left, in fact, partly because there was this fear that white teachers would lose their jobs completely. Remember we were all impermanent, so every year our jobs had to be extended. And this was linked to the Labour Party; it was the Labour Party policy, Coloured preference. And at the very end they were holding meetings because white teachers' jobs were on the line. And that's when I left because I was afraid of losing my job.

Admittedly, I was there for a long time and I began to feel a little bit frustrated because I was temporary. And not just the temporary part of it, but because we weren't recognized in the sense of promotion. We worked really hard and we were doing very, very interesting things. We used to produce our own texts for the children, especially when African Literature came. You know, we did an enormous amount of work. Both in English and history, I taught history as well and we produced new syllabi and stuff. Ja. We felt that we actually had done quite a lot of work.

Beth Mclagan

I started teaching in 1975 after I qualified up in Natal. I was at Natal University. The first school I taught at was a white school. It was a Natal Education Department school for, call it, "educationally subnormal children." They were called that. And it was called a Practical Pre-Vocational High School. It was very long to write that out on an application form. I was there for a year. It was nice. There were kids who were doing probably academic to the equivalent of about a Standard Two, Three. It was called a Standard Six, Seven, and Eight practical. They spent half their day in workshops and half the day in class, and you had two classes. So it was very nice.

And then I left Natal and came to Cape Town and I taught handicapped kids. I taught cerebral palsied and severely mentally retarded children. I'm afraid these are all terms that we used. I was then employed by the Department of National Education. I did that for four years, then I stopped and I went back to university. And while I was doing my Masters I lectured for three years as a temporary assistant lecturer in the Education Faculty. That was a three-year contract and when I came to the end of that I didn't want to go back to teaching handicapped kids. I've never been keen on the idea of teaching white mainstream children at all. And then, actually, a student I'd lectured came to me and said there was an English job going at Livingstone and was I interested—and I was very interested.

So I went for the interview and I had a very similar experience where I was interviewed by Mr. Dudley and Mr. Evans. I assumed Mr. Dudley was the principal even though he wasn't. I had no idea. I mean I was just confused then by their names. I got very confused. They had told me and then I thought I had got it wrong. I was doing a lot of head swivelling, not knowing who to actually respond to. And, ja, suddenly Dudley was asking quite nice questions and it wasn't at all my idea of what a high school deputy principal would be like. I deliberately had chosen not to go into high school teaching because I thought it would be extremely boring. Which is why I liked working with the handicapped kids who were far more interesting.

I really enjoyed it at Livingstone. I was there for three years. You felt that Mr. Dudley valued you as a teacher. I mean, even though he was science and I was English, you had a strong sense that he wanted you to succeed. That he wanted you to be able to give your best in a relaxed kind of atmosphere. You always thought that he was very much on your side but not anti the kids. But interested in how you're doing, how are things going. I come from a very small school environment, so I was a bit overwhelmed by the sheer number of people at Livingstone. And I didn't feel at all anonymous, I felt very supported.

Not only Mr. Dudley but there was always a strong sense that somehow Mr. Dudley was behind it. I mean, Mr. Evans was also quite supportive. He once stood up against an inspector on my behalf, which really impressed me. I mean against that awful inspector. He wanted to look at some papers. He was querying the way I had marked a question. And Mr. Evans said, "No." He wasn't going to let him. And he really took my side. That impressed me enormously.

Mclagan discussed some staff racial tension during 1985 after Dudley had left Livingstone. She also talked about advising students that year.

For the first two years I wasn't aware of any splits amongst the staff. The first time I became aware was '85, my last year there. Eighty-five brought a lot of stuff out of the woodwork. Ja, incipient sort of racism against us. We had a temporary principal who was a pretty dodgy person. I don't know. We had been heard laughing apparently inappropriately at something. Which was not to do with being racist at all but was interpreted that way in the staff meetings. There were some splits as well between the Unity Movement and the ANC. And suddenly for me it was like something which had been overall warm and comforting and wonderful, started splitting a little bit. Not totally. I mean I still think the staff actually pulled together quite amazingly at certain times, like the Oakland Rally. Now again it was half the staff, maybe, who went. It wasn't all the staff. So that would mean you'd get a split between staff who were prepared to accompany students to rallies and those who weren't. So those who weren't could sit at the school and the rest of us would walk with the kids. Go to the school with the kids, sometimes get them out of situations, sometimes watch some of them being arrested, whatever.

I had some arguments with students. I remember that. I mean my one class was very political. They were Standard Eight. And there were several of them who were on SRC. We spent a lot of time discussing strategy, and I didn't get a sense that they weren't talking to me because I was white. But Oaklands was a rally which we, some of us, accompanied the kids. They had a student rally. The word came that the building had been surrounded by police. And eventually we were given permission, the kids were given permission to walk out in groups of three, and we had to escort them. And it was very scary, because there were these very Aryan-looking guys standing around with these quirts. Kind of hitting them on the ground waiting for one person to panic a bit and go into a group of four. They would have nailed these kids. I happened to be with a little group of Standard Sixes, you know, girls who were crying and very distressed and I was pretty scared. So you got some splits then where, you know, some of us had supported the kids and taken them to the rally and then you would get other staff saying we had exposed them—put them at risk.

And then there was a Heathfield rally where our Head Girl was actually arrested. I think at the time she was asking people to disperse in an orderly way. And she was beaten up. Livingstone is right near a police station, and periodically policemen would try and form some kind of bizarre alliance with us, particularly whites, actually. And you know you have to be very heavy because you'd have to quickly, obviously, distance yourself as much as possible. But they came in and they didn't really beat up kids there, I think because we were on a main road. I don't know why they didn't at that time. They did come in. And they would taunt the kids, and that sort of thing, but it never got totally as ugly as it did at other high schools—not on the school grounds, anyway.

Interestingly, Beth Mclagan went back to teach for a short time at Livingstone in 1993 and 1994.

I taught there until the end of '85 and then I taught there again in '93 for a term, and in fact for the first term of '94. So that was actually very interesting, I can't actually remember how many whites were there. But I think nearly everyone had gone and it was a very different school then. It was much bigger. There were more non-Coloured black people there. But it still retained an amazing kind of atmosphere. I mean I find my experience there very enlightening because it was like a three-year sort of political lesson for me. I mean, what had been theories for me before got some kind of real context. I really enjoyed the kids' perspective on politics and meeting someone like Mr. Dudley. And that's what I took away from it, was a sense of having worked with an amazing group of kids, particularly, and staff. I enjoyed working with a lot of them and it was nice going back and seeing the same people. I felt I was received in exactly the same way. I think the legacy of Dudley does live on in terms of non-racialism. So that was interesting for me to go back eight years later. I enjoyed it.

Note

1. The Transkei was one of the black puppet states that was set up in the Eastern Cape by the apartheid regime.

Jimmy Slingers

I met with Jimmy Slingers in my office at the University of the Western Cape as well as in his home in Pinelands, a Cape Town suburb. Slingers and his wife, who is an elementary school principal as well as a sports activist, moved to Pinelands in 1994. During apartheid times the suburb was a strictly white residential area. Besides providing recollections of apartheid education, Slingers talked about race relations and what others have referred to as the strange racial politics of the Western Cape. It should be noted that both of his parents were teachers and he counted eight other family members who were teachers. Slingers reflected on his changes as an educator and his work nurturing the admission of Africans into his schools during the late apartheid years. He begins with a quick review of his career in education.

I started teaching in 1971 and that was at a primary school in what we refer to as a sub-economic housing scheme. It's a scheme in which the people don't own their homes. They rent from the City Council, and generally they would be working-class factory workers. I was at that school for five years and then I moved on to another school on promotion to what was then known as a Senior Primary. I stayed at the school, which was also in a sub-economic housing area, for eighteen months, then I came back to university full-time for half a year to complete the BA degree because I had studied part-time. Then I went to another primary school as a vice-principal. I stayed for a year. Then I went into the next school as a deputy principal. I was there for three years and then I acted as principal. Then at the time there was an acute shortage of suitably qualified high school principals in Coloured high schools. Graduates were in a sense forced to go to high schools. I applied to what you refer to as a middle school—junior secondary school. Stayed there for four years. Then I went back to the primary school.

In the heyday of apartheid there were certain things which you couldn't do. In a small town everybody who went through high school either became nurses or teachers. In fact, none of my contemporaries ventured into law or medicine. In a sense teaching was it for us, you know. I would have loved to got into law, but it just so happened that after matric everybody went to Hewat Training College in Cape Town. I started teaching in my twentieth year because the very basic teaching qualification was matric plus two years. Because I came from a large family, the sort of understanding in the family was that you would go into the job market as soon as you possibly could because there were others who still needed to get through the schooling system.

Slingers spoke about children, teachers, and the system.

You said to the children you need to be the best you could be. And that education was really the only way in which you could make something of yourself. All the laborers in the country were from the non-white side of the community. So you always had to say to children, "Equip yourself so that you don't end up here sweeping the streets, or doing manual labor." So that is what we impressed on the children all the time. And so when I first started teaching, the first point was to say to people, "Try and get to complete Standard Eight." At that time there was a school-leaving certificate at Grade 10. So while it wasn't a Grade 12 one, which would allow you entry into a tertiary institution, it certainly would gain access to go into a trade because you couldn't go into a trade if you hadn't at least passed Grade 9 or 10.

You must also remember that in the mid-seventies, even going into the eighties, there was a breed of principal in the schools who thought that they just needed to be good principals. And being a good principal was to carry out almost to the letter of the law the instructions that came from the authorities. So principals were viewed, certainly in the seventies and into the early eighties, as collaborators with the system. So many of the principals just impressed upon you, and being a young teacher, and not as critical at that time as I would be several years later, you just needed to try and satisfy principals, you see. So, initially, not as politicized as I grew to be later on, it was almost in a sense like a robot doing what you needed to do to meet the management demands of the system. And then as things heightened in the country, especially from 1976 onwards, you also started saying, "Listen, I'm not destined to a life of servitude."

I studied at UWC from '73 to '77 on a part-time basis. So you were intensely aware of the struggle for equality. I guess people just wanted their rights. So there was an intense focus on an individual's rights. And teachers, in particular, were torn between this thing of doing a duty at the school, but also needing to be a citizen and emphasizing their rights. Then, of course, you had our parents who were conservative and I guess obedient citizens, and they'd been socialized to believe what white folk were doing was the right thing and that you needed to stay out of trouble. So you had that kind of conflict situation. "Please don't get involved in all this politics, you will just get into trouble." And you know, "Do your job and be a good boy!" So yes, there was a lot of that, and so any teacher who wanted to even, I'm not even saying mobilize, conscientize would be seen as an instigator.

He reflected on his own politicization as a teacher.

I was a teacher and the sort of heightened sense of awareness came round about '79/'80. There were demands that teachers should come out in support of labor unions. There would be calls upon the teachers to show solidarity, and teachers with government housing and subsidies, and safe salaries, wanted to retain that position. And there were often fingers pointed at the teachers saying: "You're too comfortable and don't identify with the masses." So I remember getting quite upset at the school where I was at that time a deputy principal. And saying to them, "You know, this school has a comfortable staff unity, but it is almost a pseudo-unity. Trying to just paper over cracks because there are people who feel strongly that we should get involved and identify with the workers out there." So people tried to play it safe as far as the principals are concerned. It became easier from the mid-eighties onwards because then a new breed of principals came in who were prepared to say, "I need to stand with my staff and with my community." And then the sort of label of a principal as a collaborator slowly started to disappear.

I think at the end of the day for me personally a teacher is a community worker. Can you really identify with the students and their parents and the struggles that they go through? I remember one day, in fact, getting so upset that I hit my fist on the table to say, "But the community's now asking us as a teacher core to respond and we're not coming out." Because I remember they asked at the time, "Teachers come out and show that you're part of an oppressed community." And I was trying to persuade people that it's time for us to come out and show solidarity. Because at the end of the day, while we're a little more comfortable than a worker in the street, we're suffering the same oppression that they suffered, every black person in the country has suffered. Apartheid had so successfully divided us into pockets that you believed you were a Coloured and you almost believed that because you were a Coloured you were better than a black.

Slingers spoke briefly about the political differences for teachers in primary and secondary schools. He also spoke about the place of teachers in the Coloured community.

The bulk of my teaching experience is in primary schools and elementary schools. It makes for quite a different experience. Primary school teachers will tell you that for primary school teachers it was more difficult to come out in support of community issues than it was for high school teachers. With the high schools there was a fairly highly conscientized student, or learner, population. Although they might not necessarily have understood it, they were willing to show solidarity and come out in blind support of any community issues. So that high school students were in fact protagonists.

Yes. We primary school teachers believed that. You just needed one very vocal and articulate high school teacher to conscientize pupils. Thereafter the teachers could just sit back and say, "But it's the students." Whereas in the primary school, the teachers had to come out as teachers because you're dealing with seven to thirteen year olds, you know, who want to be children. So in the primary schools where there was that level of involvement and concern for emancipation, it needed to come from the teachers themselves.

The principal where I was wanted to run a little English school. Maybe remnants of colonization. So it was very strict and he boasted often about how he got his ideas from English education magazines. But we respected him because he was a hard worker. At that particular school there was a system of parent/teacher contacts. Every teacher was required to visit at least one family per week and submit a report on Monday morning. So we had good contact with them.

We enjoyed the esteem we got from them because we're talking about a time when many parents had just gone through the first year of high school and then were going into the labor market. So the teacher was seen as a very important figure in the community. And, in fact, in most cases didn't come from that particular community. So it was somebody important. We enjoyed quite a bit of this esteem.

Jimmy Slingers spoke briefly about the relationship of Coloureds and Africans.

You must just remember that in a sense Coloureds were always sandwiched between whites and blacks. Right? So, while they had less than the whites, they had more than the blacks, and it's still a perception that "I don't want to be a black." Or there's an inspiration towards being white and living like the white and having the comforts that whites have. In the Coloured schools there was always "Okay, I'm better off than the blacks." So people were in a sense resigned to almost their lot in life. Certainly within the circles that I moved in. In the teaching fraternity or in some other profession, so people would be satisfied with what they had. You still find amongst black communities, African communities, that there's a certain level of distrust towards Coloureds. Because Coloureds wanted to be like whites.

Slingers was at a middle school in the eighties. He recalled some of the dynamics during the student boycotts.

You would go to school and do your job. So things were comfortable and you got your pay. Then I landed at a school which was situated within about a mile of two of the oldest schools in Cape Town, Trafalgar High School and Harold Cressy High School. Trafalgar had a reputation as a site of political conscientizing. So while the students at my school were only Grades 8 and 9, the password in the eighties was "solidarity." So, if the high school Grade 11 and 12s had gotten together and decided that they needed to take on certain social issues, our school students decided they needed to show solidarity. Ja, ja. So I remember many frustrating Monday mornings, and every morning, for that matter, especially in the second and third school terms of 1985 when for months on end there was no formal schooling in the high schools. The primary schools, by and large, carried on as normal. Our students just showed solidarity. I remember at the end of that year out of about 240 children who were at the school only eleven came to write the final examination because of this whole issue of solidarity. While on the one hand you were saying to the children, "Education is the thing that's going to get you ready for when freedom comes, and we need to have people who have the qualifications to take up those positions that had been denied them through apartheid." Here you were faced with children just saying, "No, I'm prepared to make this sacrifice once in my life for whatever I could gain in the future." So that was a very intense year.

I remember next to the school where I taught at that time, they had just started building five mansions for the members of the executive committees of the Coloured Parliament. So obviously we were in the spotlight, because those houses also became, or the sites, because it was just a construction site, became the targets of the pupils and the community's animosity and resistance. And I remember one day when the students from quite a number of the neighborhood high schools, Harold Cressy, Trafalgar, Windermere High, Salt River High, Kensington, had come in buses to our school because they wanted to ceremonially "bury the system." And they had a coffin there. I don't know whether people have told you about these symbolic burials? Then pupils had gone over next door onto the site where they had started preparing for the houses and had thrown sand into the graders that had come there to level the sites. And the police came, a whole army of them, with shields and batons and guns. The children retreated into the school grounds to strategize. And this captain came and said to me. "Have you got control over the situation here? It seems you've lost control." You know, pointing as if I was to blame for the entire system. And saying, "I'm giving you five minutes to get all those students to leave." There were students from about half a dozen schools there as militant as ever. And I thank God to this day that I was able to address them. Because you must remember, there had also been adults who were involved in the struggle who had somehow infiltrated the students and were using them. Because it was an effective psycho-struggle. You know, because schools at the end of the day are communities, and if you destabilize the high schools you had, in fact, created instability in the community. And the schools are perfect sites for launching that kind of civil disobedience. And he said then, "We will come in and we will disperse the students." And I dreaded to think what would happen, because they would just assault students. I fortunately have a strong voice when I need to address a group of students. So I then addressed these children and said, "Look, I would hate for any of you to be assaulted here today. The police have given a couple of minutes for you to disperse quietly, otherwise they will come in, and you know what the consequences are, because it's happened at other schools." Now that school has a lovely building which makes a natural quad inside, so it was easy for the police to surround the entire area with everybody trapped inside. There's no way you can physically take on the police, and I mean they were ruthless in those days. And fortunately my students listened to me and went to their classes. And then some of the girls from the others said that "No, they don't want to be assaulted." So I said, "Well, then we have Hobson's Choice. You go out in two's and then go to your busses and not be injured." And fortunately that's the way the day was saved at that particular moment.

Slingers concluded with a discussion of his role integrating schools.

You know, the current mayor of Cape Town, Nomaindia Mfeketo, her children were at our school in the eighties when she was in prison for political activities. The school recently had a fiftieth anniversary Thanksgiving service and she spoke there. I realized again how important a role the principal and teachers are. She said that at that time when she was in prison how much it meant that I had come to their home when her son was killed in a car accident. And how that school, long before other schools had done it, had opened its door to African children. That is why she feels she can come to the school Thanksgiving service and speak because she believes the school played a very significant role in desegregating school children. It was good to hear that.

This school, I believe, played a very significant role. You must remember when a school wanted to admit children of another race group they needed to apply to the department for permission, stating reasons. So our school had just refused. We said when a child applies to the school, it applies as a child and not as a black or as Coloured or as an Indian. And at the end of every term we had to submit a Quarterly Attendance Return. You also had to give a breakdown of enrollment. How many whites. How many Coloureds. In fact, we didn't have whites at the time—Coloureds, Indians and blacks. We always just gave the grand total because we said, "We have children at this school. We don't have Coloured children!"

Up to 15% were black, which was a lot, bearing in mind that those children would have to organize special transport to travel 15 miles to get to the school. I think, you know, there was a time when there were slow relaxations. I think what happened was my predecessor had allowed a black child into the school. I don't know the reason. I think it may have been a mixed couple, but they lived in a black township. And then when I was acting principal I admitted more of them, but whereas she had applied for permission, I didn't apply for permission and just admitted. So word got around, you know.

I think as a so-called Coloured, at the time, I believe that I could have and I should have done more to be less discriminating towards black people. And that we should have done far more while we were also suffering discrimination at the hands of whites. There were and still are many Coloured persons, teachers also, who could have done far more to open and integrate Coloured, black relationships. It's still an issue.

Rose Jackson

Rose Jackson graduated from Rhodes University in 1964 and then trained as a teacher at the Institute for Education in London. Her studies with David Holbrook and his book, English for the Rejected, had a lasting influence on her work as a teacher. She reflected on her teaching in England, and at Coloured, white, and black schools in South Africa. She is currently on the faculty of Western Cape Teachers College in Bellville.

My mother was a teacher. And she said that girls should become teachers so that they have the holidays and the afternoons to be with their children. And I didn't know if I wanted to teach but I wanted to study in England. That's how I got into teaching. It was an excuse to be doing something meaningful overseas because in those days girls were not supposed to wander aimlessly around Europe. I started off in England doing my training in 1965 at the Institute of Education. That's in London. It was progressive, certainly as I understood then one of the most left-wing universities at the time. David Holbrook was our sort of guru in the English Department. He wrote this book called *English for the Rejected*. So I got sold on English and language as sort of therapeutic stuff for working-class kids. I did a teaching prac at a secondary school, and I liked the modern approach that we were to use. Which at the time I suppose was humanistic and counterculture stuff. No formal grammar, just getting children to write. I suppose I got a kind of feel for *English for the Rejected*. I taught in England on and off for a year. There was a lot of freedom. Schools seemed to have complete autonomy and teachers in the classroom seemed to have complete autonomy. And the kind of message I'd come away from the Institute with I had a lot of conviction about. You plugged into where children were and you used materials related to their experience. And I had a lot of conviction about those methods. I kind of stumbled into jobs. I got a job at a little private school, an independent school for girls which was chaotic. I mean I didn't see my future in England and I wanted to see England and this job had a lot of freedom. They were privileged children.

And then I taught for two years in Johannesburg. It was quite a thing to get a job because my diploma was looked at with suspicion because I wasn't locally trained. So for the first year the only job I could get was as a school librarian. Then I got a job in a high school, a very conservative girls' high school in the British tradition. And the teaching I enjoyed most there was with the rejected, the school leavers. Because I could do a lot of drama and poetry and stuff in the classroom. I suppose I had an arrogant rightness of my conviction of the methods I brought back with me, and I ran into a lot of trouble with the headmistress and the more conservative teachers. It was a middle-class government school. The students I had were seen as the rejects of the school. So that really was doing "English for the Rejected." They had real low self-esteem, and I think they realized that most of the teachers were just waiting for them to turn sixteen so that they could get out of the system. But I found that I related very well to them and my aim was to give them a sense of worth. So we did plays, and they wrote about themselves, and I took them outside to write from their experience, and I got in a lot of trouble for that. They saw me as sort of subverting the system.

Rose Jackson taught at the University of Witswatersand and then moved with her husband to Cape Town in 1976. She spoke about teaching at a Coloured night school and at SACHED, the adult education program that Neville Alexander administrated after his release from prison.

He came to do a Masters in Surveying at UCT and I had a baby. So I used to teach at night school in '76 and it abruptly came to an end. June '76 happened, so I couldn't go out there anymore because the schools were sort of trashed. This was in Bridgetown out sort of Athlone way. They were adults and it was quite difficult because there seemed to be about three light bulbs in the whole school. So there would be no light and we would have to go around the school looking for a light bulb that worked. It was quite a struggle. I used to photocopy because I wanted to use material to tie into the interests and experience of the students. I was always looking for materials that would be relevant to the life experiences of students. Once the Soweto language thing spread to the Cape, I think I kept on going and my husband would accompany me because we weren't sure it was safe. And he used to sit in the car. And then one time we went out and there was nobody there. The school was trashed. They had burned down the library and there was graffiti all over the walls. It must have been about July, the beginning of the third term. Ja, there was graffiti about Vorster and Kruger all over the walls. The principal had been detained and the whole thing just disintegrated.

And then I went and taught at SACHED. I taught English II. That was at night as well. It was in Mowbray. I taught there for about a year. It was for those who couldn't get into white universities and didn't want to study at bush universities. The only alternative was SACHED and this was to make up the deficit. You know, what they couldn't get through UNISA, which was tutorials. So we did seminars around the texts that they were studying for UNISA. I think I helped them with their essays.

In 1977, Jackson's husband took a faculty position at Fort Hare University and she moved with him to the Eastern Cape. She received an education on the disparity that existed in South Africa as she worked in the schools.

Then we went to Alice in the Eastern Cape. I had hoped to get a teaching job but Alice was oversupplied with academics' wives. But there weren't any jobs for a while and then we got labeled radicals or Communists because we had a bumper sticker. That was a time when the apartheid state was at its most repressive. A friend of ours gave us a bumper sticker that said, "Innocent Until Proven Guilty— Charge or Release the Detainees." And we just put it on our car in a naïve sort of way and we got harassed quite a lot for that. I mean, Jay had sort of tenure but they tried to ban the car from campus and he refused to remove the bumper sticker. They said that it was inciting students and detrimental to staff relations. This was Fort Hare. It was Broederbond[1] run at that time. When we got there in '77 there had actually been some burning. No staff had ever been threatened or anything but students had burned down part of the university. I got a job at Lovedale,[2] and then they said, "No, we will let you know." And then I found out they had checked on me and decided I would be inciting or whatever. I would be a bad influence and too radical. Which if it had been true I would have been flattered, but I saw myself as a moderate kind of liberal. Jay was kind of outspoken but not too much. He was kind of seen as a student sympathizer as a "native lover," you know, "kaffir lover." But because surveyors with a masters degree were few and far between, he was needed. But I was sort of persona non grata. We made some friends and they got me a job part-time in the Education Department of Fort Hare. And that's where I first got into some black teacher training. So this was part-time work and I was supposed to do language to improve their proficiency. But I said I want to go and visit schools so I could see what they were doing in their curriculum so I could structure my course. So that was my first introduction to black schools, to Department of Education and Training schools, to rural schools. And it was quite a shock and I've never actually recovered from it. The shock of going into DET schools, to see how really under resourced and in a state of disrepair they are. But it was extremely interesting. It was a kind of culture shock, but that's when I started to think about the implications of teachers being forced to teach in those conditions and the damage. This was a kind of built-in learning disability and an extreme disadvantage. The children were trying to learn in a language that was not their mother tongue. So I started to try and find ways to teach through a non-mother-tongue language in the least detrimental way. I tried to get teachers to teach in a way that related to children's experience outside the classroom. I mean, even today I go to evaluate teachers in township schools and they teach as though students don't have a life outside the classroom. And knowledge has nothing to do with what goes on in their everyday lives. They were educated to take subservient roles, so to me it was a desperately inferior education. But I just realized the size of the disadvantage under which they labored. So that was all "English for the Rejected" in another form.

Jackson moved back to Cape Town and taught in Coloured schools in the mid-eighties.

I decided to leave Alice and leave my marriage. And the night before I left, the principal of one of the schools in the area came to me. He had heard that I was leaving and I had said that one of the reasons I was leaving was because I couldn't get a job. I was unemployable and I suppose I didn't have any optimism or faith that the system was going to change. Because it was very dark days—the time of Biko's murder and so on. Especially in the Eastern Cape there was a lot of aggression and persecution. And this guy came and said, "Please don't leave. I begged the Department to allow them to let me employ you in my school, and I promised them I would keep an eye on you so that you won't be active politically." I said that it was too late and I had already planned to go. It was like a dead end. I was never going to get a proper job there.

My parents were in Cape Town and I knew people from the years we had spent there before. I had quite a few friends here. That was '81. Through the network I got a job at Spes Bona. It was run by a sort of mafia called the CTPA, the more collaborationist grouping. It was unique in that it was a single sex school. Had a kind of status, I think it saw itself as in the top four along with Livingstone, Trafalgar, and Harold Cressy. And it was a boarding school and had people from up country and it was unique because there was a technical section. The guys who taught in this technical section were barbaric. I remember this one guy saying, "You have to beat these guys." He was saying it to us white liberal women. There were three of us who were quite friendly, and I think in that context we were feminists. We really clashed with these guys and they said, "You're just naïve. You don't understand. These boys are animals. The only language they understand is the cane." And after I left I heard a story that these kids just cornered some of these teachers and beat them, and then the beatings stopped.

After Spes Bona I thought I'd get another job in a private school or something but there weren't jobs. It was hard to get jobs in white schools. It seemed to be a closed shop and I didn't realize that by teaching in a Coloured school it was really going to close the doors on white schools. Because white school principals seemed to view with suspicion people who had taught in Coloured schools. So I ended up at Steenberg. It was a terrible mess. It was terribly corrupt. Then they got a new principal there who was a reborn person who just pulled the school up. It's now a showpiece. As to him, he got money from the private sector and we got computers there, a rose garden with trees, and all sorts of things. He turned the whole thing around. It was a ghetto area and this school became the showpiece. I liked it because of the freedom. I like to get to know the kids and do my curriculum around the kids and I was able to do that there. It was "English for the Rejected."

Then I applied to Livingstone because I wanted a job nearer to home and I got it. Mr. Evans fell asleep during the interview, so I spoke to Dudley and Dudley was absolutely enchanting. I remember he said, "We have a policy of non-racialism in this school." He made it absolutely explicit. I stayed at Livingstone in '84 and '85 through the boycott. There was a benign Dudley spirit. It was kind of benign, open, and there was quite a lot of freedom to teach what you wanted to teach although there were inspectors. He was Livingstone. The kids were responsive. I remember in '84 there was the Tri Cameral thing. And the kids actually wanted to come out and boycott. But Dudley, I remember him giving them quite an impassioned speech to dissuade them from doing that. And he invoked examples of history from Nazi Germany and said don't be misled by demagogues. It was get your heads down, go back to work, get your education. It was my first contact with "education for liberation."

Even though Dudley left, the legacy lived on in '85. Eighty-four was like you had died and gone to heaven. It was like being back in England in a completely nonracial situation. Once you stepped into that school, it was as if race didn't exist. But in '85 I began to feel a little uncomfortable. I didn't feel as welcome. My contract wasn't renewed. Most of the white teachers' weren't renewed. But I mean we were discriminated against in a way. I don't know if I'm simplifying it, but if you belonged to WECTU, I think this could have influenced renewing your contract. In the department's eyes you were persona non grata. Ja. And yet, also, when I used to try and apply at a white school I felt discriminated against because I had been teaching at a Coloured school. I don't know whether it was paranoia, it was "Catch 22."

Rose Jackson moved to a private multiracial school in 1986. She taught for a term in an alternative program at Cape Town High School, a white school. Then she taught for a year at a white girls' school. She addressed the difference of awareness of the students at Coloured schools and white schools.

In '88 I got a job because they desperately needed somebody at Wynberg Girls, which is quite a traditional girls' school with an English tradition. It was very much like the school I taught in in Johannesburg. But I didn't mind it much. It was nice to be in a school where everything worked and was organized. The staff was awful. The enlightened ones were on leave. I found the girls politically totally uninformed. Not just politics but current events that were going on. They seemed to be ghettoized in a way. Once again there was a class of school leavers and I got on well with them. They were sort of school rejects. It was almost a replay of Waverly, the Johannesburg school. I felt I had to do stuff to boost their esteem. I taught in a very informal way. I liked the kids a lot, but they seemed to be living in an unreal world. Just the contrast with Livingstone in 1985 and the boycotts when the kids used to meet every day and plan strategy. They just knew what was going on and had a handle on political events and history. And these kids lived in an unreal world. If I'd had the choice I would have gone back to a Coloured school, which in fact I did when I went into black education. Because I felt it was very unreal. At one point I messed up at something not really serious. I didn't get my marks in on time or something. And the Head of Department said, "It's because you've been teaching at one of those schools."

She returned to SACHED the following year.

I got a job at Khanya College, which was for disadvantaged students. It was a project of SACHED. I was sort of language academic support with students who didn't have matric exemption. They couldn't get into university through normal channels. They were mostly African and some Coloured students. It was elite in a way. It was accredited by an American university. They would do two university subjects and the rest of the time they would do skills. That's where I came in— reading and writing, academic skills, life skills, organizing themselves. But it was mainly language. And if they passed those courses, they had an agreement with various mainline universities which were by that stage opening up. They would have two first-year credits and they could go into first year and do some second-year subjects as well. So I worked alongside the tutors. The learning curve for me was being part of a democratic organization where everybody had to do everything and everybody was part of every decision. I was cynical after a couple of years. The people who taught there were young black academics who were using it, that's a cynical way of seeing it, who were using it as a transit to study overseas. If they did okay there it gave them political credibility and they would get Fulbrights or EOC scholarships. So they weren't very interested in brushing up on their teaching. But I tried. I was supposed to work through them, not so much to work with students. To get them to take on board more effective teaching methodology. But I learned a lot about NGOs. It was riddled with conflicts and it actually fell apart at the end of '89. I learned a lot about politics and working in a democratic way, ja, it is very frustrating.

Rose Jackson concluded by discussing her move to a black teacher training college just before the 1994 election of President Mandela.

So I decided the only way I was going to get anywhere in teaching was to get an-other degree. So I went and got a B.Ed. in 1991. Then I was going to stay on and do my masters because one of the guys was going to take leave and he offered me his teaching. But the college in Khayelitsha, Good Hope College, offered me a job. The rector told me that within a year it would be permanent. By that stage all I wanted was a permanent job. In '93 Azapo and PAC were very active in the townships and whites were getting shot at. We had to go in under escort. I was a member of SADTU and there were a lot of quite conservative Afrikans people, and some of them held me personally responsible for Amy Biehl[3] being shot and various incidents. And there were times we couldn't actually get out of the college because they were burning tires. You couldn't actually go out. Quite a few people were shot at. For a while we came in a bus. And there was another shooting and people said they wanted to come in armored cars with police escort. We had a rector who, even though he must have been ex-Broederbond, was pretty enlightened. He worked with the community and he brought them in to advise us. And they said, "Don't be seen to have anything to do with the police because then you will really attract violence. We will escort you in." So we used to have to go and meet at the off ramp every morning and get into a convoy.

I think there was a tremendous feeling of solidarity. In '93 there were very few whites taking part in strike action. We got such support from our black colleagues. We were kind of ostracized by all the white staff. No, the white liberals were quite friendly but they said, "It's not for us. You go and be noble." I think that after the marches and being shot at that everyone felt quite close. I didn't seriously look for alternatives. I think for me it was real. I didn't want to go back to a Wynberg situation. I think I was hooked on what was for me to be in touch with some kind of reality teaching black students. I know one of my colleagues said, "Why do you get so starry eyed about your students?" I think I just really like teaching those students because I think it's kind of counterculture ideas following me. There seemed to be a place for them in Khayelitsha and the students seemed to respond. The way that I teach is to try to tap into where the students are, and I'm just very fascinated by their world. And maybe I feel that I understand Xhosa tradition. So I can design materials that are where the students are at and they seem to like what I do. I don't know. But they've always responded extremely warmly and enthusiastically. I'd like to feel that I make a difference.

Notes

1. The Broederbond was a powerful group of Afrikaner leaders.
2. Lovedale was a black teacher training school in the Eastern Cape.
3. Amy Biehl was an American Fulbright student who was killed in a Cape Town township by young people who had just left a black power meeting. The killing occurred just before the first democratic election in 1994.

Kevin Wildschut

I met with Kevin Wildschut at my flat in the City Bowl of Cape Town. Subsequently, we met at Garlandale High School. Wildschut had taught at Garlandale in the eighties and was an active member of the Western Cape Teachers' Union. He left teaching in the early nineties to take a scholarship at Leeds in the United Kingdom. In 1993, he returned to the staff of Garlandale. When I asked Wildschut why he became a teacher, his response was not atypical. "I come from a long line of teachers. My mother's a teacher. My brother's a teacher, my sister, my cousins. So it's a family thing. I have always wanted to be involved in teaching."

I attended Harold Cressy High. The reputation of the school is that it was one of the better schools around the Coloured community. The school's main focus was academic. So students weren't encouraged as learners to be involved in politics. We were kept away from student demonstrations; we were kept away from discussing serious political issues in class. But the irony is that many learners became student leaders, became political leaders. So I don't know if it's an indictment of the school, or whether it's a plus for the learners.

I worked for a year at a company called Juta, which is one of the big publishing houses in this country. A job was arranged for me by my English teacher. Which is really where my heightened sense of apartheid's wrongs began. I worked with a man who was a friend of my English teacher. And I saw him very much as someone who didn't want to rock the boat. Someone who was very compliant, who was very servile, very subservient. And he took a lot of abuse from his white superiors. And he, being my boss, put pressure on me to be equally subservient and equally servile. I was eighteen years old. Those days every company had to keep a place for white South African men coming out of the army. And someone came there, we shared the same musical interests, we used to listen to Neil Young. His pay was double what I received. He seemed to have longer tea breaks. His work was much easier. We were appointed in the same class, you know. I knew what was happening outside in the country. And I just rebelled. Actually they gave me a choice: "You leave or we fire you. And if we fire you, you're not going to get work because we're going to write a report." So I left.

And then I went to UWC in 1980 to do my teacher's training. Just as a student I remember many of the characters who became public leaders of marches and of rallies and so on who were students with me at the time. UWC was much smaller then, so you knew everybody and there was a sense of cohesion amongst the learners. Most of them came from a Coloured community. People who were ultra-conservatives, not actively involved in resistance politics, became more conscientized by what they saw on campus. By that I mean they experienced the beatings. They experienced the attacks by the security forces. They experienced the exposing of spies. They experienced the tear gas in the corridors. In fact, UWC was a radicalizing place. If you weren't an activist before you got there, by the time you left you sure were an activist!

After graduating from the University of the Western Cape, Wildschut was appointed as a teacher at Garlandale High School in 1984. He viewed his work as supporting and encouraging students academically in their studies and politically in the struggle against apartheid. He reflected on faculty political tensions and the controversy over the 1985 year-end examinations.

When I started teaching I actually knew quite a few of the teachers through our contacts in the Civics[1] in Athlone. These people were teaching there and they were names in our community. They were activists. So I felt quite at home, you know, going to the school. But when I started teaching it was a time of really heightened political activity. In fact 1985 was the year of the big riots—the boycotts. So, in 1984 the school was very young. It had only started the previous year in '83. Many teachers were still finding their feet, and this in terms of their jobs and so on, and the school was busy establishing an identity. And one of the things that we did was to encourage learners in the arts.

We also took learners to the student protest meetings. We were instrumental in forcing home the establishment of an SRC. And the SRC was highly politicized. The students were highly politicized and making contact with students from other schools in the Athlone area. But we discovered that there was a strong opposition from the management of the school, from the principal and from his two senior deputy vice-principals. And staff meetings were often war zones, battle grounds, between the "thems" who want to destroy education, who are playing with the children's futures, who are undermining authority, who are destroying what we're trying to build. We were the "thems"—the outsiders. The rest of the teachers were interested in teaching and going to class and marking scripts and doing what teachers are supposed to be doing. Obviously this kind of polarization went out of the staff room and into the student body because learners are very perceptive. They see what is happening. When they call meetings they see who's there to help them organize. They see who's there out in the streets where they live. When there's a protest meeting or when there's a march, they see who's there. And they began to sense this kind of tension.

And, in fact, this exploded on the school campus in 1985 when the matric final examination had to be written. And we had learners who said, "We're not writing because we haven't been taught for six months. How can we write?" Schools like Harold Cressy and Livingstone didn't write. And our management said to the learners, "You will write your final exam." And so learners who didn't write and learners who wrote came into conflict. There was tearing up of exam papers, there were mild forms of intimidation. There were the learners who were questioning educators and saying, "How can you force us to write when you know for a fact there's been no school because schools were closed?" The state closed the schools.

Where was I? I was firmly rooted in politics for change. I was part of the process that gave birth to the Western Cape Teachers' Union. And I was part of the local executive in Athlone. So that's where I positioned myself. It was a very difficult time because we all hold education very dear. I think there's no teacher who will say education is not important. What we were doing, our process was some of the slogans of the day like "liberation before education." And we were saying, we're teaching liberation education. So it was a mixture of classroom academic work as well as teaching and informing learners about the need to radicalize, to change what was happening in our country and to be part of the process of change. So when learners came to me and said to me, "Sir, should I study for my exams?" My response would always be twofold. "Yes, you should because it's going to be necessary in the future. But at the same time you cannot neglect to study the real history of today, the history that you're learning today."

He spoke with me about both the horrors and the joys of involvement in the struggle. He stressed the relationships, camaraderie, and trust.

I know of colleagues of mine who were threatened publicly and not only with their jobs but with their security. And in fact it happened. Basil would have told you. And I don't know if he told you, but as part of his interrogation the police repeated to him things that he had said in a staff meeting. I remember the morning that Basil was arrested along with some other colleagues of mine. I was woken up at about 4:30 a.m. with a phone call from another colleague and we agreed to meet somewhere quickly. And we met at 5:00 because Basil had been arrested and obviously people were fearing for their own safety. And we took the position that we're not going to run and hide. If the police want to arrest us, let them find us where we are. But there was no cause to point up, lift our hands, and say, "Here we are. Come and get us." So people were fairly cautious. We traveled around with a change of underwear and toothbrushes in our bags and in our cars all the time, because you never knew who was going to be next.

It was exciting times. We were discussing it around dinner the other night and we were saying that struggle relationships, friendships or romantic relationships, whatever, that have formed from that time have lasted. My wife and I, for example, met working on a union newsletter in someone's garage. Of course it was banned at the time, so we were doing subversive activities. And there are many other stories of people who met during the struggle, who lived on the run together and became romantically involved, who have married, who have kids today.

I think the atmosphere around the table was of such a nature that we remembered most of the good things. You know, the bad things we recall less often, fortunately. I think if ever a history is written or whatever about that time, for me, certainly one of the most important things is that spirit of camaraderie. That spirit of unity that like a mushroom cloud just enveloped people. As I said to you earlier, the bonds that come out of the struggle at times were really amazing and last still today. I was in London living with a South African woman who had been there for eighteen years and there was a knock on the door. I opened the door and there was a comrade of mine from Athlone. He'd heard via the grapevine that I was there and he looked me up. And that's the kind of thing that happens. It's wonderful. I think it's the whole question of like-mindedness. Sure there are disagreements. I mean, we don't necessarily agree today on the way it falls and what we should be doing within SADTU or within our Civic movements. There's a lot of disagreement about things, generally. But at least you know where the person's coming from. They're coming from a position that has been formed by struggle politics. Where they have learned to understand other people's points of view. Where they've learned how to practice democracy. You know what I'm saying? That kind of thing. It's not a question of, "Who are you? What are your credentials?"

I also think it's a question of having a sense of commonality, a common purpose. We had a common enemy and that was apartheid. That was the state. We were going to destroy this. We were going to crush it. We were going to establish democracy, one person, one vote. We were going to release Nelson Mandela. The whole agenda was understood and accepted by everybody, and how we went about it was we were going to do everything subversive. We were going to pamphleteer. We were going to go door to door. We were going to radicalize our churches, our mosques, our youth groups, our sports clubs. We were going to join the United Democratic Movement. We were going to campaign for the release of political prisoners. We were going to join civic organizations and NGOs who did the same thing. We were going to support all sorts of movements financially and otherwise. We were going to do whatever it took. And everybody knew that we would march, that we would boycott, that we would strike, that we would demonstrate, whether we were beaten or not. And everybody understood that. And everybody did it.

I told you the Western Cape Teachers' Union was banned along with all the other organizations, but we had to meet, you see. Those were some of the exciting stories. We would get in touch at school and say, "There's a meeting this afternoon in Newlands Forest, okay." So we would have 150-200, maybe more, teachers up in the forest with guitars, beer, meat for the *brais,* you know, and the first of it would be a party. But some serious meeting and planning strategies and discussion would be happening.

Kevin Wildschut discussed 1986 and his relationships with students.

So the next year these kids had made sacrifices in the sense that they had to come back to school, right, because they hadn't taken their exams. Obviously there was still tension in the air. It has taken a long time, in fact, the tensions are still there, because the level of distrust never disappears. I cannot fully trust people who I know ten years ago couldn't be trusted. It's such a serious situation. So those things are still there under the surface. But we're busy rebuilding the school. In '86 those learners had to come back. They repeated the year, very few of them with a sense of anger. The learners that I taught, certainly, came back to school with open eyes, with a sense that they needed to learn more than just the history in the textbook or the geography in the textbook. And we decided to use the arts—our culture, our music, plays, drama. We decided to use that vehicle and sports to build the school again. To get a sense of unity among the learners and teachers, you know. So we could begin to move forward as a school. And it worked. We produced some amazing plays, *Jesus Christ Superstar* being one of them.

It's funny because when you're a teacher you're up there and the learners understand in their own minds that there's this unbridgeable gap, even if it's just in terms of age. But when they see you outside the class and they remembered what they saw in '85 and they saw a different side to the teachers. There was a close bond between us. It did help the process of learning and teaching in my classes because I wasn't just "Sir." I was more than that. I was someone with whom they could communicate. It's almost as if the doors were opened. They had been opened. And, you know, I still have links with those learners today. In fact, just a couple of weeks ago we were at a party for one of their birthdays. So that's the kind of thing that bound us. It made the process of teaching easier for me and I'm sure it made the process of learning much more pleasurable for them.

The learners in the different regions had what they called Action Committees. There was, for example, the Noble Park Action Committee, the Athlone Action Committee, and so on. And these cells, if you like, of learners often came to people like myself, like Basil and so on, for advice and for a bit of leadership I suppose. Yes, so it did happen. There were actually quite a few. One very tragic story—I am sure Basil must have told you about Robbie. Now, Robbie was a learner when I first got to know him, and he was involved in the youth Civic and the Athlone Action Committee. Obviously, from there, his involvement deepened, and so on. So that's the kind of thing. Robbie was one of the learners who would approach us.

Fortunately in terms of our learners, none of them suffered unduly under detention or that kind of thing. None of them lost their lives as student leaders. So student leadership flourished amazingly. The whole political situation allowed learners' leadership potential to come out. Our learners were very dynamic learners. All of those learners became not only leaders at school, but outside in the communities they took very strong leadership positions. One that I remember in particular became the president of COSAS, Elaine Sacko. She was also the SRC President at UCT. Hewat Training College had a big hall, and we used to have a lot of meetings there and our learners were part of the leadership on that stage, speaking in public. It was really amazing.

Kevin Wildschut spoke briefly about the union, government harassment, and his own burnout, which caused him to leave the country.

As I said to you, the primary out-of-school activity for us was the Western Cape Teachers' Union. So, yes, a lot of our activity went around the establishment of our teachers' union in our community. Recruiting, pamphleteering, I was very involved in the newsletter. We also started a band and we were known as the WECTU Band. So whenever there was a rally or a function or fundraiser, or whatever, we would play. We have a very strong union link still today.

The same people who were victimized at school and harassed by police for what they did on school premises, we were the same people who were being victimized and harassed for starting a teachers' collective. So, it was all one and the same. I didn't want to resign. I had reached a stage where I wanted to get out. I thought that I had made my contribution in six-and-a-half years. Maybe it was time for me to look somewhere else. I wanted to explore other possibilities. So that's why I left. I went to England for a while. I sold my house; sold my car; cashed in my insurance policies; the whole thing. I left. In fact, there was a very strong feeling that I wouldn't come back, that I didn't want to come back. I was thinking that I needed to get away from the depressing and oppressive situation in education. You know, at that stage we had worked for so long. I know six-and-a-half years is not a long time, but when you're constantly up against authoritarianism and reactionaries and you're constantly undermined. I suppose you begin to feel a bit frustrated. And I was very frustrated actually. I just thought, I don't see any sun coming over this horizon. Let me just pack it in. I stayed away until the end of '91.

Wildschut returned to Cape Town and was able to return to Garlandale. He spoke of a different spirit—a spirit of victory and excitement. He also reflected on non-racialism.

I was fortunate to be given a temporary job because there were no teaching jobs. I was soldering little computer plugs and so on. And then I got a post for two months out in Retreat, then I taught for six months at Alexander Sinton, a school you probably know. Then the principal organized a job for me back at Garlandale. He always said to me that he thought I was a very good teacher. In fact, he bent over backwards to get me back. He really manipulated things to get me back. I didn't have a hate relationship with him. And he knew that I knew where he stood. And he knew where I stood. But on a personal level I could talk to him and I would never be disrespectful, even though we disagreed violently. I think that he was a very shrewd man. He and Basil had an outright hate/hate relationship.

When I got back it was a time where teachers were losing their jobs. In '93 people were being offered the voluntary severance package for the first time. What was happening, also, was that the school's management was undergoing change as well. People like Basil were being promoted up the ladder. So there was a different ethos in the school—a different climate. It was very exciting because the kinds of programs that we had envisioned in the eighties, the kind of teaching that we wanted to happen, and the kind of syllabi and the curriculum, all those things were suddenly changing. And the establishment of SADTU really accelerated that process. And I could get involved again, you know.

All those unions, all those little splinter groups, became SADTU while I was gone. So when I came back there was this sense of "Wow" we're 150,000 strong nationally. We're the biggest teachers' union, and we are going to drive the process for change in this country, whether they like it or not. And we will use our muscle, our numbers, and we will use it to get what we want on the table. We were fighting from a position of weakness. We were banned. We couldn't organize. Suddenly we were this, "Wow." It was wonderful. And everything we could say: What kind of philosophy do we want to underpin educational change in this country? Let's change the textbooks we've always been using. Some of us even wrote our own textbooks. And the union gave us that sense of belonging. That sense of accomplishment. The things that we struggled for in the eighties are realizable and are achievable and are in the process of coming to fruition. It was really exciting times.

But what I wanted to say is that we didn't know white people generally. And I'm sure they didn't know us either. So when we were in this wonderful union, suddenly we get to meet people from UCT. White lecturers, white teachers from other schools, one or two white teachers who were teaching in so-called Coloured schools in Mitchells Plain, and Athlone and so on. And they shared their experiences and you discover that it's not entirely different from what you're experiencing. Both as a person in a home and as a teacher at school. And then you just realize how similar people are—the same fears, the same desires, the same needs, you know. And not only white teachers, of course, teachers from the townships as well. The union is non-racial so you get to meet everybody and just realize that you're so strengthened as a teacher by the fact that your daily struggle is the same struggle as another teacher in the townships and another teacher in a white school. There's a line we can draw.

Wildschut did express reservations about a lack of student awareness, both just before and after the 1994 election of President Mandela. He spoke with depth about students not wanting to study or reflect on apartheid.

I didn't know any of the students when I got back to Garlandale. I didn't know them at all. So it was very much a sense of newness for me. I was a stranger to them as well. I discovered that for many learners it was a sense of, "Thank God that was over now. We can get back with our lives." Like it was for me as well. They didn't want to know. And still, many of them prefer not to know. In fact, the less said about the struggles that people waged the better. Because I think it jarred their consciences. Students were able to write knowledgeably about what happened to their elder brothers and sisters and their cousins in the late eighties. They were able to relate to the boycotts because their parents boycotted companies. They were able to relate to the deaths of some of the learners in their neighborhoods. The Trojan Horse incident, for example, in Athlone. The death of Ashley Kriel, of Robbie Waterwitch, and Colene Williams, and that kind of thing. They knew, for example, that Mr. Snayer's house was attacked by the Special Forces and they killed the man next door, and so on. So they knew all that. But that was knowledge. It wasn't experience for them. So the learners we had in '94 didn't experience. They were in primary school. All they knew was the fear of the Casspirs and teargas and the bullets and so on. But they couldn't understand it. They couldn't understand why it was happening. Okay?

So it was a completely different view. And, in fact, today many of the learners will not want to write about the eighties. They don't want to know the history of our country in the last fifteen years. "Why must we always talk about apartheid? Why must we do poems written by people who are talking about apartheid? Why can't we do something else?" It's almost like a sense of thank God it's over. It's done. It's past. Let's forget it and move on with our lives. And it's up to their older brothers and sisters, their parents, teachers like myself, who've lived through that time, who experienced it firsthand. It's up to us to keep that memory alive for them. And maybe present it in a different way, not in a preaching, teaching way. But maybe bring them on board in an experiential way. Maybe they can experience some of the things. Show them a film, let them listen to a tape, take them to the District Six Museum, maybe. Let's walk in Athlone in the streets and show them where things happened.

And then the German "*Nicht Zieder*"—"Never Again." It's so difficult to get that idea rooted at home because "Let's move on. Let's forget. Bury the past." I had this experience. I went to Auschwitz when I was in Europe. And when you approach that place it's amazing. There's no sign of life at all—birds or butterflies? There's just this pervading sense of death in that place. I couldn't take it. After two hours of walking around the perimeter and inside I left. I came back the next year. One of the things that the TRC is saying is, "Let's have monuments like that. Let's have some kind of public thing where people can go and remember." I don't know whether that's necessarily what people want. People don't want to.

Kevin Wildschut concluded with an experience that needs to be remembered.

I want to tell you about one of the more dangerous things that happened. My friend Basil came to me one day and he said to me, "There's a very, very important thing we have to do." So I said to him, "Sure, what do we have to do?" He said, "You've got to bring your car, and we've got to go somewhere." And so I said, "Fine, let's go." I got into my car, he got into his, and we drove to the school. And he said to me, "Just wait here in the parking lot, I'm going to go inside quickly." He went inside. He came out and he said to me, "Fine, everything's organized. You've just got to open the boot quickly." And I said to him, "What's happening? Are we moving newsletters, membership forms, or what?" He said to me, "No, I'm going to put some weapons, we're going to take some weapons home." I just went cold all over. I thought, "Oh my God. I've never held even as much as a little pistol in my hand."

Anyway so we moved the shipment of arms from our school. The weapons we loaded in our boots and I followed. And we took the guns and we drove them to his mother-in-law's house where Robbie lived. And then we moved the stuff, the weapons, from our cars into the house and we put them up in the ceiling through the trap-door. And that was a scary experience because if we had been found by accident or by design, I mean, we could have been shot on the spot. I've never been so scared in my life.

Note

1. Civics were neighborhood political organizations that opposed the government.

Vivienne Carelse

I interviewed Vivienne Carelse in her office at the Western Cape Department of Educa-
tion. Carelse taught art and was a leader of WECTU and SADTU, the latter at both the
provincial and national levels. She gives credit to both her family and her high school teach-
ers at Alexander Sinton for shaping her educational and political ideas. Her story is diverse
and provides insights into both classrooms and unions in the late eighties.

I started in 1985. I was twenty-two. It was Baptism of Fire because that was the
year when things took quite a major turn at schools, and especially the school I
was at. Yes. In fact, I was at the same school that I started at Alexander Sinton
in Athlone. I went straight to the University of Cape Town because the course I
wanted to do wasn't being offered at UWC. I did a Fine Arts Degree. And at the
time we still had to apply for a permit. I finished my Fine Arts Degree in '83 and
then I did my Teacher's Diploma in '84. I come from a family of teachers and I grew
up in the milieu of discussions about education and the need for transformation. My
grandfather was a school principal in a small village. Ja, it's quite a long, I suppose,
dynasty of teachers. My grandfather was one of the early members of the Teachers'
League of South Africa, and my parents, too, when they started teaching, joined
that. So I have that background. And that, in a sense, shaped the kind of opinions
that I adopted as my own, I suppose. We were, as children, always made aware of
certain things, and the fact that as a family we were displaced from our original
place where I grew up, which was on the coast at a place called Kleinmond. As a result of the Group Areas Act we needed to relocate and my parents decided to move
to Cape Town. And I switched from Afrikaans-medium education, which was my
first two years of schooling, to English-medium, which was fine, because I grew up
in a fairly bilingual house. And, being aware of that dislocation and the reasons for

it, and entering, you know, a school which was very, very politically conscious. It had teachers who made me aware of certain things. And it enhanced my understanding. And also at the same time my own involvement in youth organizations and building SRC's at the school, those were quite important influences. And having very good teachers and some of the worst! But I think, predominantly, some of the best teachers who certainly followed a hidden curriculum more diligently than conforming to what was expected of them. And I think that certainly created a context within which I made my decision.

Well, my art teacher was incredible. We had two art teachers. Randolph Hartzenberg, who's now a practicing artist and lecturing at the Cape Technikon. The other one was Roland Allen. And we would have poetry readings. It wasn't just visual art. It was about being exposed to films, plays, participating in mural-painting exercises. As a fourteen year old I got involved with the launch of the Community Arts Project. And we did murals there and joined Women's Self Defense clubs and the works. And then also English teachers. But also people like Basil Swart. He was my biology teacher in high school. Very, very politically active in a range of political organizations. He just had a general kind of militant streak in him, and he was very clear that one needed to resist what was going on. And he demonstrated that actively in what he wore to school, how he challenged the authorities, and how he conducted himself. I think as a kind of role model for pupils. I certainly think he was somebody who presented you with a whole range of contradictions which would make you question. Then there were people like the "Old Guard" who came from the Teachers' League.

Carelse returned to Sinton as a teacher. She was much more confident when she returned after completing her university degree.

I must be such an anomaly amongst teachers because I have had no other experience of any other high school. I mean my experience of other high schools have come through my activism and my teacher unionism, where I've gone in and organized and built a union. But I did both my teaching pracs at the same school. So I went to school there, did my two teaching pracs there, ended up teaching there. It's a bit weird because I think I probably limited my experience. But 1985 was quite a critical year in shaping that.

It was a bit odd. I was no longer the—not submissive, but fairly unproblematic student. Well disciplined, was one of the prefects and member of the SRC, but not a troublemaker, not a very vocal person. I was incredibly shy as a teenager. And having gone to varsity and becoming more politically conscious, and becoming more confident with speaking, I was now back there and I was articulate, confident, and exposed to far more things in the world. And I was able to work under the tutelage of my own two teachers, now as colleagues, Roland Allen and Randy Hartzenberg. And we were in the unique position of having three art teachers, so I was shaped and assisted and supported by them. I eventually became head of that subject at the school.

She reflected on launching WECTU and her relationships with students in 1985, her first year as a teacher.

The principal encountered me as a very different person. At the time it was the launch of WECTU. Teachers were largely being propelled out of their chairs to take some kind of action in support of what students were doing, and in support of their own demands, which had been brewing and stewing for decades. And I was one of its founding members in my first year of teaching. I worked at grassroots level in our branch. There wasn't much of an academic year, because by mid-year there was complete upheaval. The pupils came out and supported the national provincial boycott. We had a young core at the school from the 1980 period who had been part of TAC. The chairperson at the time, Vincent Farrell, was banned from teaching. In fact, he was sent to Coventry to go teach in a place called Sutherland, which was a godforsaken place, and eventually he left teaching. A number of those teachers were still at the school when I got there and became involved in the building of WECTU. In that year we spent a lot time assisting with Awareness Programmes at the school with students. Ja, working with the SRC in getting these programs structured around key historical dates. Building those Awareness Programmes into our general teaching programs, especially around history and language. We were also responsible for the extramurals at the school, so we would have plays and poetry readings and take children to film festivals. Exposing them, largely, to an awareness of a world beyond Athlone.

That meant that as a young teacher I was obviously up against some of the more conservative "old guard" at the school. I was seen to come in there as a young turk, just wanting to railroad a particular agenda through staff meetings. But there was a very strong base of teachers identifying with that left political profile within the teaching community. So there was no great difficulty in capitalizing on people's sense of social commitment and awareness. And so we would always strive towards getting a staff position on things, rather than a group of mavericks leading everyone else. There was a kind of consensus. We were striving towards consensus, and the staff always assessing very carefully how much they could stretch, you know, the leniency of the department in terms of coming out very clearly in support of students and teacher demands. And we traded on the fact that we were all members of the same staff and needed to take a staff position.

The staff meetings were very tough. They were, in fact, a real debating forum. I remember when we decided at the end of the year that because there had only been, in real terms, five months of academic work done, that the entire school could not conduct final examinations. The staff took a position. We consulted our lawyers and everything else. We met off the school premises in September of that year. The schools had been closed and there was a re-opening of schools. At the time the Coloured Education Minister decided to close schools for a period. In that year we were all in agreement that we could not have a final examination because it would be just a complete fallacy that kids could write an exam on work that they had not been prepared for. And there was no way that you could foist a kind of sense of normality on an abnormal situation. There were a couple of people who, due to all kinds of pressures, backed out. And the entire school population, all the pupils, repeated that entire year the next year voluntarily. We had an entire school repeating the year, which was phenomenal because it was with total backing of the parent community and the students themselves, who saw that there was no way that they would cope with the new standard, having been unprepared for it. Those pupils who didn't agree, because there were a small fraction of the student population who didn't, they left the school.

During the 1985 boycotts the government officially closed non-white schools. Carelse spoke about students, parents, and teachers reclaiming Alexander Sinton.

Often the kids had meetings at different schools and our school was often a site because we had a school hall. So you moved to get students onto the premises safely. And once we had a helicopter landing slap bang in the middle of our school yard and I had to disguise the SRC Chairperson as one of the cleaners, got a coat and stuff for him, and got him out. We had to get him off the premises in somebody's car boot, because he was going to be detained, probably indefinitely, if they had caught him. He's now one of the Provincial Directors for Police.

In fact, in '85 we had the re-opening of schools on September 17. We had a re-opening where the community, parents, teachers, and students, re-opened. We reclaimed our school because it had been closed by the Education Minister. We went there in the morning, we were going to unlock the school, the principal and the staff. We were going to enter and occupy the school, and try to have a normal day. The minute we got onto the premises the police came. They used to park on this field opposite our school. These huge yellow trucks, those huge Casspirs. They kept them there almost permanently during that period, and they just came onto the premises and started loading up. They arrested people. They filled about four of those normal standard police vans with parents and teachers. And they sat there baking in the sun because the community, the parents outside, decided they were going to barricade the school. They parked in the road on the pavements all around. Our school is on a corner on a suburban block. And on all the surrounding roads they had blocked it off so that no additional police vans could get onto the premises or get off. So there was a state of siege for a good few hours at that school until they mowed down a fence and drove through to take the people away. We were all arrested that day. About 197 of us were arrested for opening our school. We were held in Mannenberg Police Station for the whole day until the lawyers negotiated our release.

She spoke about her relationships with students, parents, and the community as well as the role of WECTU in both politics and pedagogy.

People saw me as being a very young teacher and very influential among students. Students confided in me because some of the pupils I taught were about three years, four years, younger than me. So I had access to them on a range of levels that the other teachers didn't. And I wasn't the only one. There were other teachers like me at the school who also had that same kind of relationship with the students. But I was able to offer the kind of perspective, I think, to parents that came with a kind of professional tag of being "the teacher." And therefore what I said made a little bit more sense because I was informed about the staff position.

We were all part of writing the constitution and organizing public campaigns in support of this union. Because the union was built largely in resistance to the apartheid education departments as employer, but also around the need for teachers to become organized around better service conditions. The other equally important arm of it was around professional development. And the fact that for professional reasons teachers in their daily tasks challenged the fact that there was an apartheid curriculum. That they were being expected to teach a differentiated one which was done on racial terms. And the fact that there was not a common education system. And as professionals you couldn't be seen to be working in a system that was unjust and hopelessly irrelevant. In many instances you knew that your syllabus was expecting you to teach children that their history started in 1652 and you know that it didn't. And it was that kind of thing. So the union had a two-pronged kind of role around the curriculum and demands for radical transformation and around service conditions.

Ja, we organized things for pupils and for teachers. There were campaigns around literacy and numeracy, and we ran workshops for students and induction programs into high school for primary school children, all of that. The work was multifaceted. It wasn't just around campaigns and placard-waving. It was around a whole range of things. So a lot of my time was spent doing that too. Site-based kind of issues where we worked with building organizations. With students in that area, forging links between students and teachers at the school. And consciously linking them with African townships with other schools. So that we could, in fact, begin to forge an understanding of the need for change.

People felt it was time to get out of their armchairs. They couldn't just be part of the kind of bleating from the periphery where you adopted a boycott-stance where you say nothing: "I will not be tainted by contact and talks with the department." "We will not be tainted with contact with other teachers who are less pure." But then also a very conscious choice to form an organizational alternative to the conservative teaching. And we actively sought links with the Democratic Teachers' Union, which was based in the African townships in Cape Town. And

SADTU's first president came from the ranks of DETU. So we looked at forging those kinds of links between those kinds of organizations. We posed ourselves as non-racial, non-sexist, democratic in our organizational form and structure. And opened ourselves to a range of democratic processes to ensure that accountability was in fact practicalized.

It was quite hectic because we needed to really do lots of institutional organization. We had to learn to timetable and do all kinds of things that, you know, were collective kinds of things. There was a lot of consultation on how we were going to structure our school day. How we were going to actively build Awareness Programmes into our timetable. Organizations like WECTU, for instance, were banned and had to operate underground. We had to meet in the forest around *brais*, pretending that we were going on mountain walks. I probably saw more of Cape Town during that period of repression that anytime else because we met in Newlands Forest and we would hatch our plans there. But we were creative, and that's what kept the organization dynamic. And it kept the school staff rooms lively areas of discussion and debate. I wouldn't have left teaching for anything at that point, because you were contributing to making change a reality.

Carelse spoke about both the difficulties and the energy at the school in the years following the 1985 school boycotts.

But '86, particularly, was difficult because you had students who had made that decision, but were struggling with having to repeat the year. It was comforting to know that everyone else was doing it too. But we had to face a lot of flack from the administration for having chosen not to administer the exams. Some of our members were suspended from teaching. We had to go on a whole campaign to get them reinstated. Because I was part of permanent staff I didn't get suspended, but there was the threat of an extended probation period, which they unofficially did. Others were summarily suspended, but we managed to get them reinstated. At our school we had twelve people out of fifty-four. It was an arbitrary choice. They just selected a random selection of people.

But the spirit of the school was generally very, very dynamic. It was really one of my most exciting periods as a teacher. Because as an art teacher, I saw the raw, kind of, blood and guts and gore of the whole process. Children came and unburdened themselves on paper. They just churned out artwork after artwork of the scenes that they saw around them—especially the younger children. They were really just, you know, expressing themselves on paper. Ja. Tires burning. Shootings. We had the Trojan Horse shootings on the street where the school is. Some of those pupils were at primary school when it happened and then came to our school—relatives of those children. Two of the boys at the school had got shot as well, but they were just injured, they weren't killed. But we had lots of detentions amongst students at the time as well. Many of our SRC pupils would periodically just be harassed and picked up. I would play music in my room. It was a therapy zone, I think, in school. I often had non-art students coming to work there as well. That was also the "Media Factory" of the school. We got the school newsletter going via the Art Department and some of my comrades in the Languages, English and Afrikaans. We got a school magazine going. The students themselves ran it and wrote articles. And we assisted mainly with layout and technical things. But I also taught my students silk screening and we did t-shirts and posters. So we produced some of the most exciting work coming from young children. It was exciting because we could produce them around key events.

One of Vivienne Carelse's favorite memories was of a three-week interdisciplinary remembrance of Sharpeville Day at Alexander Sinton in 1987.

It was March 21st of that year for Sharpeville Day. We planned a school Awareness Programme which lasted for about three weeks. History teachers, English teachers, I mean the whole school got involved. We photocopied one of the children's mother's passbooks, because at that stage Sinton had also become quite a non-racial school. We had non-racial admission policy. So, even though it wasn't written into the law books, we were admitting children from the townships. We had this copy of the passbook which we issued to every pupil at the school and to teachers. The SRC members and teachers had the right to stop anybody, teacher or pupil, to ask them to produce their passbook in that three-week period—the build up to March 21st. And the frustration that built up because you could also work out your own punishment. Because there was no real law and, like the lawlessness in the past, you could actually determine whether that child needed to go to detention or come and do some extra work or do something, you know, to pay for not having their passbook on them, at the time. So we built up a real frustration with having to carry this pass.

I was one of the drama people at the time for extramurals, and a group of us then worked with a small group of students and told them that they were going to be the militant organized group that would lead the demonstrations on March 21st. Another group had to be the police. We got uniforms for them. We got gunfire soundtracks and speakers and things set up on the *stoep* and we had rigged up the whole school the day before. It was like mass guerrilla theatre. We got these students to lead this kind of resistance to the pass.

There was a structured program. We had a guest speaker and everything at the school that day. Almost the whole school day would be devoted to our Awareness Programme. And then we had this kind of spontaneous demonstration and, on cue, the police came—the real police! A helicopter came. The kids just scattered and fell down and ran into classes. And one of the neighboring schools saw this chaos at the school and ran off and got the school marching to join us, not knowing it was all just mass theatre. But it was exciting because there was a real sense of history and commemoration of that history. But also, because of the nature of the period of State of Emergency, the police arrived, and they gave it a sense of authenticity even though it wasn't intended.

It was very powerful because I think those pupils afterwards said that, "You couldn't have made us realize the impact of this historical event more than by the way you did this." So, for me, that was quite significant. It didn't end too tragically though, because the police had to soon realize that they were being a bit over-dramatic about it, then left, and we were left to continue our program, to complete it. And that was it.

Beginning in 1988, Carelse was involved in national meetings to form a non-racial, unitary teachers' union. She traveled to Johannesburg meetings and hosted Cape Town meetings that culminated in the launching of SADTU in 1991. During that year she represented South African teachers at the Pan African Conference on Education for the Year 2000 in Ghana.

The other established organizations who could afford to send their own members, they sent along four people to accompany me, to chaperone me, or to make sure that I was going to say the right things and not be too radical. But we went and that's when I met Ivy Matsepe-Casaburri, who's now become Premier for the Free State. She was then one of the ANC education reps based in Tanzania. And she was, at that stage, my first encounter with ANC In Exile education people up front. South Africa was like the new kid on the block, in that conference. And I was able to make reports to the rest of the continent and other international guests about what had been happening, about Mandela's release, and about our vision for education. So that was, for me, quite an exciting event. And that, I think in a sense, threw me into an understanding that the teacher union was not just about being organized in South Africa, but also being organized internationally.

Chitra Narshi

Chitra Narshi finished her Teaching Diploma in 1983 at the University of Cape Town and begin teaching in 1984 at Alexander Sinton High School. She was the youngest teacher at the school, and she became involved in WECTU the year after she arrived. Narshi left to study in England in 1989 and then returned to the school and taught until 1992 when she became pregnant with her first child. She subsequently lived in California while her husband earned his Ph.D. She spoke about the changes that she experienced as a teacher in the context of pre- and post-1985. She also spoke of the influence of her professors at UCT. "Peter Kallaway was our Political Economy of Education teacher. I think he broadened a lot of my own perspective about education. Our history methods teacher, her name was Melanie Walker, tried to make us understand that our teaching had to be politically aware and we needed to make our kids think about certain things. Help them to be critical."

I was only twenty-one then and I was new on that staff. I was the youngest and that really intimidated me, and I was in this English Department, where everybody was much older than me. They had fifteen or twenty years of experience and I was really intimidated by that. No one was interested in saying we should do something interesting in class. Let's introduce the kids to an interesting comprehension or something that deals with apartheid or something that deals with educational segregation or something. So I was very intimidated by that and as a result my teaching was very dry. I felt it was dry because I became like a pedantic teacher, you know. I learned all the rules and I made sure that they understood the rules. And I would give them pages and pages of sentences to do and stuff like that. It was the way I was taught. And sometimes it just didn't make sense to me, but I was too scared to do anything about it and I always felt that nobody else on the staff was thinking like me. I don't know if I was scared or young or I just felt that I didn't have the experience. I became close to certain people in that year and those people were very active in the seventies and the eighties also. There were teachers that were dismissed in the early 1980s or they were threatened with dismissal. Some of those teachers were still there, but some of them were really scared about what had happened in the early 'eighties and they weren't prepared to say anything that rocked the boat. And so I just kept very quiet.

Nineteen eighty-four was also quite an important year because the Tri-Cameral Parliament was introduced. People who were classified Indian and classified Coloured could go and vote. But there was no vote for people who were classified black or African. So obviously that event had an effect on what was happening in the schools because the Department of Education tried to make everybody aware of what was happening and they wanted teachers to go and vote. Teachers decided they were not going to participate in this vote. I think kids boycotted school for the day and we came to school for just a few hours. And there was some backlash from the department. The department tried to victimize three of our teachers. We wrote this defiant letter to them explaining our position towards the election and our support of these three colleagues. And there was a response from them. But at the end of it all I think it was a victory for us.[1]

Occasionally I used to go to some of these resource centers outside of school and look at the kinds of material that they were using. And I came across interesting comprehension exercises and things that I could use in my classroom and then I started doing that. There was one article that I remember that came from *Grass-roots Magazine*. *Grassroots Magazine* dealt with problems of people living in the townships. Well there would be all kinds of articles, but there was a particular article about people complaining about their conditions in the flats. Living in the flats, you know, the broken washing lines and the damp in the flats, and the lack of electricity, lack of warm water, and Council not seeing to their needs and so forth. So I would use that as a comprehension exercise. And I found that the children just responded wonderfully because it was something that they could relate to. I taught fourteen year olds and most of them were very wise to the situation. They knew what was happening. And so they could relate to this article and that's when teaching became something interesting for me as well. And yet when I said to one or two of my colleagues, "Look, I tried this comprehension, why don't you do this? Why don't you try it?" They would just resist it, they weren't interested in any of it.

Narshi reflected on the 1985 year and the school boycotts.

So it was more just trying to adjust to a new job. You know, a new job, being young and trying to adjust to so many kids, getting used to them, just getting used to the environment. It was completely different at the start of 1985. Vivienne came along. I think we taught English together so we used to share ideas. I said to her, "You know I just want this year to be different, because I'm just tired of the way I'm teaching. I'm tired of what I'm doing in class." And we also didn't like the way certain teachers set their papers, you know with no kind of awareness content or social content to their papers, and we said well we're going to do something about it. And we started working together on the literature. But we were doing something like *The Day of the Trippers,* and it was very hard to actually put some political content to some of the literature that we were dealing with. There were short stories about space travel. You know, I mean that was the nature of the children's education. They had literature or texts that had no relevance to their lives whatsoever.

I think it was in March or just after March, I can't remember. I saw all these kids just streaming out onto the field and we knew there's something going on. Anyway the children were so angry. They said they're not going to come to school. They're going to boycott. So fine, the days went by like that where they would just stay away or a hundred kids would come to school and the rest of them just stayed away. And for months it went on like that. So that was a very, very important year. There were certain days that rallies were held at different schools. There were rallies that were held at our school and so all the children would gather in the hall and get speakers and they would organize this on their own with no help from teachers. Yet we were seen as some of the younger ones as more sympathetic teachers and we would help them or give them advice, you know. Whereas most of the teachers weren't interested, there were few of us. Every morning there'd be a meeting about what the day was going to be like. What are we going to do if this happens? What are we going to do if that happens? Are we going to teach if the children come to school? But our school belonged to a broader forum of SRC's. So this one day we just saw buses and busloads of children streaming in from other schools. We didn't know from where. Previously we'd be informed that this school was going to come to our school and they're going to have a rally. So at the rally they would have one or two speakers from organizations, they would have one or two student speakers, and sing. They'd chant a bit and then go home. But there's always this threat of the police. A couple of times they shot tear gas and they'd lock the school gates. And we'd be stuck in the school for two hours until they'd leave and they'd come there under some pretext—you know, looking for a teacher, looking for a student. And the days would go by like that. You'd just have to accept the situation.

Like Vivienne Carelse, she spoke about students, parents, and teachers trying to reclaim their school after it had been closed by the Department. She had great fear.

Then the Minister of Education decided he was going to close the schools. And we decided that in defiance we were going to go and reopen our school to show that the schools belonged to us and belonged to the people. It belonged to the parents, to the teachers, to the students. We gathered in the quad. There were probably about sixty people. Sixty or seventy people and they consisted of some parents, some students, and some teachers. Vivienne and I were walking towards the gates to see who else was coming in, and suddenly the police cars just skidded into the school grounds. One of the policemen left his car and closed the school gates. And a teacher and her husband had just pulled up at that moment and they stopped them. Her husband had just dropped her at school and they didn't allow him to leave. And they ran around and closed all the gates. And we started panicking! Then there were some teachers who were in that area that became really scared because they remembered what had happened in 1980 and 1976. And one or two of them had managed to hide with the help of the caretaker. But there were still policemen looking around, checking all the classrooms.

So they ordered us to gather in the quad. We stood there but we weren't aware of what was happening outside. And somehow or other there were people outside the gates, students outside the gates were trying to enter the school and they had seen all the cop cars there and they started gathering all their forces outside of the school. So the cops inside had to try to deal with us and deal with the growing crowds outside. And they realized that our group was small, they could handle us. They were going to see to this lot outside because even their police vans couldn't come through. They had to wait for more police vans to come and fetch us. They were using our school as an example to other schools, you know, and this crowd was just growing by the hundreds. They had blockaded the school. They set up rubber tires everywhere, burning rubber tires and this is what the kids did, hey. In the meantime, we were left to our own devices. We didn't know what was going to happen to us. So we used the phone in the office to phone our relatives and friends to say, "Look, we're stuck in school. We don't know what's going to happen. They're probably going to take us to the police station." We didn't have any food. Some students raided the tuck shop and we filled ourselves with chocolates and anything we could. They would throw a tear gas canister from the police van and we just rubbed ourselves with oil. Some of them managed to get fish oil from somewhere and we had to rub our faces with oil and our hair. I don't know how that was going to help, but that's what we did.

So we were outside for probably two to three hours because the cops were trying to disperse the crowds. They were shooting tear gas into the crowds but it wasn't affecting us because we were in the building. So after a few hours they managed to disperse them and we waited for the trucks to come along. I think in that group there were probably about ten to fifteen teachers, about twenty or thirty parents, and the rest of them were students. So they loaded us onto the vans, but the spirit was so wonderful. There was singing and the Muslim parents were praying and they wanted to pray for us for our protection. Even our principal was with us and these cops didn't care about whether he was a principal. They just treated him the way they treated everybody else, and loaded us onto the vans. But I was very scared, I was really, really scared. In fact, a lot of that time I was just in fear, I was in fear all the time. I knew that the events that were taking place were inevitable.

They were inevitable because of the kind of system that we were living under. And the children were the ones that were almost making the teachers more aware. They were rousing us to action. We also belonged to a teacher's organization. It was WECTU at the time. But they just seemed so much more spirited and they were ready to die for change. You know that's how strong they were. And we were still holding onto our jobs and security!

For me it wasn't a great issue, I mean not so much the job and security. I found it more with the teachers who had been there for a longer time. They had families and I didn't have a family at that time. It wasn't a major issue for me. I just wanted to protect myself. I didn't want any harm to come to me. Physical harm, that's what I just feared the most. I mean I was really scared. Sometimes you would try to drive through or drive past burning tires or drive through cop cars and my heart was just frozen. I couldn't deal with that situation, I just couldn't. And other people around me were just stronger, you know. They took us to Mannenburg Police Station. The nearest police station to us was Athlone, but they took us to Mannenburg because the cells were probably bigger. They had more accommodation for us. So they drove us there and they fingerprinted all of us and separated us into males and females. They left us on the side and we were getting hungry. But by that time they had gathered lawyers, and all the people and students were just gathering outside of the prison. Lawyers had come to see us and they had collected bail. They said they would charge us with trespassing, which wasn't serious. We could get away with maybe R60 or R80 and I had the money with me. I just gave it to the lawyer. I said, "Here take it. Get me out here."

Then the Department wanted us to go back and teach. Our view was: How can we go and teach if the kids were not ready to come to school? They were trying to put pressure on teachers so we would put pressure on students, but most of the students were not ready to come to school. They said that their demands are not being met and there's still all this segregation in schools and they're still having to deal with "gutter education."

Chitra Narshi was transformed as a teacher in 1985. She spoke about the years that followed the student boycotts.

After that in 1986 I just started with this new confidence I think, confidence in myself. And also with new ammunition and also wanting to do something positive for the students. And I had a very good relationship with them. And so we started the year with their talking about their experiences. And a lot of my classes spoke about how they felt. And they wrote poetry and they wrote stories and we had those stories and poems published in the school magazine. That was a very important part of their healing after going through that very traumatic time. They needed to talk about what they learned about that experience. And they were fourteen years old and they were forced to grow up almost overnight.

So I think a lot of the content of my teaching had changed. I wasn't so intimidated by other teachers or trying to force people into doing what they're not interested in doing. And there were other teachers who were very keen on what I was doing. So we'd share materials, you know, and drew up materials. I used to attend lots of workshops outside of school and look at racism textbooks. You know, how to make our lessons more politically aware, social. And I used to buy a lot of books and I tried to use some material on domestic labor, apartheid, and education. I'd give them magazines to read—*Upbeat* magazine. And we'd read articles from that and they were just so much more responsive. There was a book that I had that was actually for history teachers, but I used it in my English class and it looked at 1976. And I think that particular lesson was on looking at different people or people's versions of what had happened. And this was in 1986 or 1987. They had already gone through that, and if they hadn't been through it, then their brothers or their sisters had been through something, or their parents, you know. And it dealt with different accounts of 1976—students' accounts, teachers' accounts, workers', parents'. And there was an inspector who came and who wanted to evaluate my lessons because I needed to be promoted to a permanent teacher. And I did this lesson. I had this wonderful class and they were very bright and really responsive to whatever I did. And I did this lesson on 1976. I mean just thinking about it now, I just realized that I'd probably grown so much from 1984. I wouldn't have done that in my first year of teaching. And I did that and they responded well. I think what he was looking for or what evaluations looked for is how the students respond to you and whether you're interacting with them. And most of them they interacted with me. He was very impressed with this lesson, and he said to me, "No, it was very good and the children responded very well, and, please don't dwell on the past too much."

Yes, 1985 changed my way of thinking. After that I just needed to look at material and I knew that this is not relevant for students and that is relevant. I think that was an important change for me and I learned it in 1985. The years after that I would just try to expose my students to a lot of the anti-apartheid literature. Like the poetry of Faizel Azfat; he's a poet from Johannesburg and he had written a collection of poems. He came to the school and read some of those poems and the students could relate to that. Vivienne and I did a lot of work together. We'd set up exams together. Set up worksheets together. We'd go to workshops on anything to do with alternative education. I was also involved with WECTU and they gathered students from five or six different schools and we worked on productions. But it dealt with issues like hunger and segregation and what happened in the eighties and it was creative—not morbid and grim. Through dance and singing and a lot of music and it was really great, you know. The children really enjoyed it.

Narshi talked about Nelson Mandela visiting Alexander Sinton High School in 1992 just before she left the school

Mandela came to visit the school for an inauguration of an indigenous garden at the school. So we were going to use it as a showcase for our school. We invited important people from the community and we had ballet and drama. We worked with the kids. Obviously the environmental issue was related to poverty and the socioeconomic issues that we had. It was a major event. The children were so excited about this and some of them managed to shake his hand. It was just amazing. They wrote compositions and stories afterwards about how beautiful this day was for them because this man is so important in their lives.

Note

1. The teachers whose stories are told in this book viewed the creation of the Tri-Cameral Parliament as a government ploy to divide non-white South Africans.

Jean September

I met with Jean September in her home in Cape Town. September was both an elementary and a secondary teacher. She began her career as an activist and spoke of broadening her students' horizons. She was also a principled believer in non-racialism, which was nurtured by her parents through the non-racist sports organizations. Interestingly, September was not a teacher during the 1985 school boycotts. She was a full-time student that year at the University of Cape Town. In the late eighties and early nineties she became very active in teachers' union work. More recently, she has edited the union magazine and newspaper.

I started teaching in 1981 and I did my training at Hewat Training College in Athlone. I think I must have been about twenty when I started teaching. There was one thing at school that I knew that I never ever wanted to become, and that was a teacher. I don't think I was politically active in any of the structures, but the link was that I was quite active in the sport movement. And both my parents as well were sports people. So being schooled in non-racial sport was part of our upbringing at home. We were never allowed to go to any of the racial sports clubs. I think that molded the way one was going to think. So when anything educational came up, it somehow fit into that picture and although one was schooled at home in terms of a sport environment, it started permeating most of one's way of thinking of what was happening in South Africa.

So, at the time there were only two options, going to university or going to one of the colleges. And there was a problem with my matriculation results where one or two of my papers were marked incorrectly, which meant that that year I couldn't go to university. I was still having them re-marked and fighting the Department about it. And they sorted that out in June 1978, and then it was too late to enroll at any of the universities. So in the meantime I then said, "Okay, I will go to Hewat Training College and the following year I will decide what I was going to do." And once I was there I started getting into it and I really enjoyed the place and I enjoyed the people who were working there. And also the 1980s then came along and it was that whole education uprising once again, and I played a more active part during that time in terms of what was happening.

September graduated from Hewat and began her first job as a teacher in a working-class Mitchells Plain primary school. She spent a great deal of time working on extramural student activities and spoke about the faculty conflicts.

It was a school that had been running for about four or five years and when I started there were about five new teachers who had come into the school. There was a clear distinction between those new ones who would come in and the established staff. I realized that we had a little bit more to give than just being at the school. So we started involving students in all sorts of activities. I started a hiking club. We also started taking the students out, especially the Standard Fours and Fives, on an outing once a year. We would go by bus, let's say, to Knysna or to Port Elizabeth. Just the social-economic situation in Westridge, Mitchells Plain. It's very much working class. And the kids living there, most of them had never been to Cape Town before. They've never been to Table Mountain. So it's to give those kids an opportunity. For some of them it was a lifetime opportunity to go. And I then also started organizing some sport as well—swimming and tennis. And with that we started to think. Because I think we came mainly from a middle-class kind of background, and now to be really engaged with students who come to school hungry; who come to school abused. And I think it started moving on the kind of foundation that we had in terms of our own lives, although most of us were middle class, most could recognize that these are the real issues that one needs to deal with.

I think as soon as we started tackling those issues it became a problem for the rest of the staff. Which meant that you couldn't just go into your class and teach anymore. It went beyond that. And as soon as the students started enjoying what we were doing, they started looking at the others and saying, "But how come you're not doing anything?" Although they're primary school kids, we started putting pressure on the teaching staff. It also started putting pressure on the principal in terms of getting parents more involved in the school. And the principal, who was quite liberal, but also not wanting to change too much because it would eat into his time. So I think in 1982, or so, or '83, the tension started mounting in terms of what you are doing as a teacher.

Others started feeling threatened by that. So I think that's when it started building up and I was called into the office. And he said that some people were using the students and using sport to politicize others and to make people question what is happening. So I said, "Well, if people start doing that, I think they have a right to, and if there's something wrong, then we need to start to address it." So we were beginning to be seen as troublemakers at the school for changing how the school as an organization operated. And I think it wasn't with some kind of overt political agenda that we had at the school, it was just making things a little bit better at the school for the students as well as the teaching staff. But they weren't going to see it because it would tap into a lot of their time; and packing a lot of uncomfortable issues that should be raised. It also packed on the principal's authority as well because now it's being challenged in terms of saying, "But, you know, we want more say in what happens at the school," and that, indirectly, challenged him. I don't even think we sat down at any point to think about this is our strategy that we need to employ. I think it happened, rather than being planned. And once we were placed on the other side, we realized that the way we see education is very different from others. And then we began to sit down and say, "These are the things that we hold dear and, irrespective of what happens, we will stick to these principles."

She spoke about the importance of non-racialism.

In the four years we put on three plays at school which were quite big productions. Because it was the first school in Mitchells Plain to put on a dramatic production, we were asked to have it staged at the Nico Malan. Now the Nico Malan Theatre is the theatre where only on certain days were "people of colour" allowed to go. For the rest of the time, only whites were allowed to go to the theatre. And it was also one of those symbols of apartheid that I've never ever gone to. The other one was the Joseph Stone Auditorium in Athlone, where so-called "Coloured" people practiced the arts and only Coloureds were allowed to go there. And it's a place that I've never ever gone to either. It was a principled decision not to go to places where people were excluded.

So we were faced at school with putting on this production at the Nico Malan, and because myself and Felicia were instrumental in putting the production together, we refused. And I think that was one of the first things that came out into the open. "We want to give exposure to the children at those kinds of places. And, therefore, it's a good thing for the school to actually go." [*school's position*] I refused to do it. I said on the basis of my own principles and what I think is correct that we shouldn't be going. The two of us pulled out and we said that the rest of the staff was very welcome to take them and to put it on, but we're not going to be part of it. So it was the whole thing of being insubordinate and we were going to be taken to the department, and we were going to have little black marks made against our names. It was a principled position and in the end we knew they wouldn't be able to pull it off, so they declined the offer.

Jean September went back to school full-time at UCT after the 1984 school year. She talked of the irony of not being in the schools during the 1985 boycotts. She did at-

tend nightly political meetings and worked on alternative, anti-apartheid education at the
university.

I knew after '84 there was no way that I would be able to stay at the school and
get any kind of satisfaction out of it. Ja, I was also studying part-time at the University of Cape Town. I was doing my Bachelor of Arts Degree. So in the afternoon from about half-past-four till about half-past-eight on two evenings a week I
would attend classes. I realized that was the only way to get out of a primary
school. For some strange reason in this country you weren't allowed to have a degree and be teaching at a primary school. So in 1985 I took the year off from
teaching to do the final year of my degree. And so in '85 when the next peak came
in terms of education struggles in this country, I was once again a student and in
an institution where the population was largely white. And at the time only 20%
black students were allowed at the University of Cape Town, and it was only if you
did a course that they didn't offer at the University of the Western Cape. To me
that wasn't an issue because it was the only university that ran part-time degree
courses. So I didn't have to find any obscure subject that the University of the
Western Cape wasn't offering.

So I was involved in looking at some of the issues, because it was the first time
that teachers had come together to look at their own conditions. I think people
were quite isolated before. And I think what '85 did was show that it doesn't matter whether your school is in a working-class area or in a middle-class area, conditions are pretty much the same and it just varies in the level of how involved people are at the school and what kind of resources that they have. And it was also the
first time that people went into the African townships as well to see what conditions were like there. So I think it was that kind of coming together of teachers to
realize that if you're not part of the white system conditions were pretty bad at the
schools. But some people were comfortable because they had a little bit more resources than somebody else, than the other schools.

I went mainly to a lot of the meetings in the evening. So I spent quite a lot of
time in the evening as a participant in the process, not as part of the leadership at
all. So it's once again starting to do some of the propaganda work and putting out
the pamphlets whenever it was needed. Which were difficult to distribute at the
time because all organizations were banned. So, where to meet and how to meet,
you'd have to do it in secret.

*September joined the faculty of Westridge Secondary School in 1986. She was teaching alternative, anti-apartheid, history. She also spoke about her experiences with subject
advisors (inspectors).*

It was the first time that anybody or any group of people had challenged the Education Department. And I think it was that break in terms of really challenging the authorities now instead of challenging people only at a school level. I think up till that point I had been challenging at a school level and not going beyond that. The new element was actually directly challenging the education authorities. And as soon as you challenge the education authorities, you're actually challenging the government.

It was a time when I taught history and I taught it mainly to Standard Six, Seven, and Eight. I was doing alternative history with students. There was no way I was going to teach apartheid history. And I was fortunate that the person I worked with had a similar understanding of what we should be teaching and how we should be teaching. The head of the history department was also very sympathetic, so he would just let us teach whatever we wanted to teach. Now the problem was when the subject advisor came to sit in on our classes, he would want to see our students' books and then at the end of the year he would have to moderate our exam paper. So he would come in and we didn't care because we believed in what we were doing, that it was the correct thing to do and you don't teach history that is slanted to favor any particular group and particularly not apartheid history. So he would come in and he would sit at the back of the class and page through one student's book, and he would also see the posters up on the wall, and it's not your normal kind of posters that you have up. It's a lot of "Down with Gutter Education," "The Apartheid History Curriculum Should Be Abolished." So there were a lot of those kinds of posters in the class. People were against conscription where young white boys refused to go into the army. There were a lot of those kinds of posters up also. And the Cradock Seven who had been killed. So there was a lot of political stuff on the walls. The students also worked in groups. I did a lot of group work. After the lesson he called me downstairs and said, "That kind of cooperative learning is just not on. You know all the facts and you must tell the students what they need to know." And we got into a whole lot of debates. I said, "I'm convinced that my students are learning a lot more and a lot more skills in terms of the methods that we are employing in class, and I'm not convinced that rote learning is the best kind of learning."

So there was a lot of tension and I wasn't prepared to change and I wasn't prepared to listen to what he had to say. And then at the end of the year the paper was a lot different; it wasn't just testing whether students knew all the facts; it was testing skill as well as historical analysis. It was looking at cartoons and a whole lot of other stuff for comprehension. He didn't approve my question papers. They came back saying that "This is not the way that a history paper should be set. It's testing a whole lot of skills that shouldn't be tested. You have not stuck to the syllabus." Now, given that method of teaching, there's no way that you could get through this wad of work that you are expected to do in the syllabus. So I may have only touched about two-thirds of the knowledge that students should be tested on. And to him that was unacceptable. So it was the end of the year. There's very little you can do about that. To me it wasn't a problem because the kids were just going to write it, whether it had that approval or not. And even our head of the history department had the same attitude: "This is what the kids learned during the year. This is what they're going to be tested on." But the principal was put in a bit of a fix because he's the first line of management in terms of the "departmental chain." So he called me in and tried to "reason" with me. "Now, can't you just make one or two changes here and there and the other?" I told the principal, "If you want to change it, you go ahead and change it, but I will make it known that this is not the paper that I submitted." And then he just turned a blind eye to it.

Jean September became involved in progressive study groups that worked on anti-apartheid curriculum and materials. She found it a very exciting time to be a teacher in South Africa.

I think those were probably the most exciting times in terms of just developing as a teacher, looking at the different kinds of methodologies, looking at changing content and how it gets taught in the classroom. There wasn't a whole lot of alternative stuff, so I was part of a group that met once every three weeks where we actively looked at alternative history, for example. I worked quite closely with Melanie Walker; she was the history methods lecturer at the University of Cape Town with Peter Kallaway, and she taught the group of us. She taught us a different methodology, a more kind of radical methodology and every three months we would bring materials together. We'd decide on a theme and put materials together that teachers could use in their classroom depicting the struggles, the education struggles. So from '86 to about '89 I was engaged in that kind of materials development work. And then also looking at different themes that were more South African in terms of language study, instead of looking at a lot of these British, English textbooks that students were expected to use. We started making use of the African Writers Series and started putting that into our classrooms as well. We produced a whole lot of resource materials at the time. And so I think I developed on a different kind of level where we were running workshops and we were drawing people in who wanted to improve their classroom practice. So we did a lot of that kind of developmental work.

You were constantly challenging the system at the school as well, which made one, in a sense, almost unpopular with the majority of teachers who didn't see that as their role. All they were there to do was to teach. And then also changing the kind of content and the methodology. So it was challenging the people that you taught with at the school, because if your methods are different and you're teaching different content, at the end of the year you have to write one single exam. So my students would have a different kind of perspective in terms of what's going to happen and how they're going to write that exam than somebody who's just going through the motions and the traditional way of doing it. So that tension was always there between colleagues as well because you wanted to change what they were doing and they didn't like it. Some of them had been teaching the same things in the same classes for fifteen years, you know.

The student movement was beginning to grow and, although they weren't structured, we started working on student programs at the school. Setting up SRCs to give students a better voice, mobilizing the parents as well. And at the school there was a clear break between those who were activists and those who just sat on the sideline. So there was a very clear distinction in the staff room between the two camps and there was very little compromise. To organize teachers at that stage wasn't really a major issue for us. You either, in a sense, had the faith or you didn't. And there were no in-betweens. There was no room for fence sitters.

September was involved in the union as well as anti-apartheid protests. She spoke about dealing with the police during this time.

You see, at that time, it was very much linked to setting up a teachers' union as well as challenging the government more politically. And I think from '86 to '89 I got involved in the politics a lot more than I had in the past. So it was playing a whole lot of different roles at the same time. At the school we would develop the students. Take students on camps and develop that kind of student leadership, not only at the school, but we took all the schools in Mitchells Plain, all the high schools, and we had identified students who had leadership potential. And we would train them. So they were the leaders of the student movement in Mitchells Plain, which not only put them under threat, but it put us under threat as well. Phones were tapped and people were followed at school. The police would come and visit you at the school and just walk around your classroom. Yes, they would come in and they would say, "No, we just want to walk around and see what's happening." You can either allow them to do it or you could give them a whole lot of lip, which is precisely what we did, we just gave them a whole lot of lip. But there was also very little you could do, because there was a State of Emergency at the time and the police had "extra-ordinary" powers to do that kind of thing. So you ran the risk of being locked up.

It happened at our school fairly often. There were mass meetings at the school, and the police would surround the school, and we intervened protecting students from being picked up and arrested. If the police really got angry with you, they'd just throw you in the police van also. So that happened fairly often. You'd sit in the jail cell or sit in the back of the van for a couple of hours and then they would just release you because they didn't have anything on you. Ja, but there was a whole lot of pressure also. As soon as you were thrown into jail, it snowballed once again. Students would come to the police station and before long there would be one, two thousand kids outside and their parents. So there was a lot of that kind of support.

Jean September concluded by talking about working with students.

Ja, there was a lot of working outside of school time with students, especially student leaders. There was that bond of trust that built up between us, and there are a few of them that I still see today. There are also those one or two students who became student leaders in the Western Cape. The police were looking for them, so we would provide accommodation for them. We had to keep them moving all the time. There were students who took a principled position not to write their exams at the end of '85 and there were two girls who were extremely bright. And in '86 when I went to Westridge, they had taken the position that they were going to repeat their last year at school. But because they were student activists, it cut into a lot of their academic time. So although they were bright enough to get a matriculation exemption, which would allow them to study at university, the one wanted to study medicine, and for that you really need A's in almost all your subjects. So I knew somebody at the University of Cape Town. There was this bridging course for students in the science field. And I wrote them saying that she was a very good student, but because of her community and student involvement she has this potential but she needs an opportunity. So it went to the Council at UCT and they gave her a chance.

And then we also started identifying schools where students were disadvantaged in the townships and we wrote a whole list of schools and said that one needs to view students coming from these schools differently and not just use academic criteria at the end of the day. So I think in the late eighties we managed to make that kind of inroads at UCT. But I think it's also because we knew one or two people in the faculty who knew what was happening in the townships.

Glen van Harte

I interviewed Dianne Gordon and Glen van Harte in their home in Woodstock, an inner city residential area of Cape Town. We sat around the kitchen table and their four-year-old son, Simon, was ever present. For some reason their home elicited memories of the sixties in the United States. Glen spoke much more than Dianne and his story is told below. As the evening ended we sat and looked at photographs from meetings and parties of the Western Cape Teachers' Union. Dianne and Glen were both members of WECTU's first executive and later held offices in both WECTU and SADTU. Glen van Harte's story touches a wide range of issues and events.

I started in 1984 but can I go back a little bit and just give you a little about who I am and where I come from. I come from a peri-urban town called Bellville. It's predominantly Afrikaans-speaking, which is the language of the oppressor. An Afrikaans town and the divide between the white side and the black side is a big highway and you never cross that road. And I think that's quite important, because that characterizes quite a lot of one's interactions with people. My mother is a teacher who comes from a highly critical family. She belonged to the TLSA and at that time the TLSA was a banned organization, as you know.

My memories are about my mother trying to hide magazines because security police might be coming to knock on our door, okay, and they in fact did do that. And so I have quite a good memory of getting up in the middle of the night and somebody knocking on the door. It's a classical scene but it did happen. And so I went to Athlone to the Christian Brothers, which is a Catholic institution. We're not Catholic, incidentally. And this school was a private school, but it was a private school really in name only because we paid something like R10 a month (in 1999 this was less than $2 a month, in 2002 less than $1) school fees. That's what we paid in school fees and we had to travel there every day. And they were all Irish-Catholic. And that's quite important because in 1976 I was in Standard Eight, which is Grade 10. It was a time of heightened detentions in the country. I remember we as students at the time feeling that we needed to be supportive of what was happening in the townships and elsewhere. And I remember making a point at the assembly that we needed to go out because there was going to be a march somewhere and we decided we wanted to join the march. And the Christian Brothers came to us and said that there was no way we could participate in the march for three reasons. The one reason being that the authorities would close down the school because they were white Christian brothers in a Coloured area and they had to get a permit to stay in the area. And the second reason was that they had parents who fought in the wars in Ireland. The principal, in fact, had lost a brother and lost a father in the war, you know the IRA kind of stuff. He had lost family members in that, and there was no way that he was going to be sacrificing students in this particular battle. So it's heavy stuff. And the third reason was, of course, that our parents would never allow us to participate in these sorts of things. But anyway that was the first time when you're confronted with authority. We said, "Well to hell with you. We're actually going to go." And we went out and, of course, we got absolutely clobbered by the cops and ran back to school. And I think that was three or four times in 1976 when we actually participated in action of that kind.

van Harte started university at the University of Cape Town but ended up graduating from the University of the Western Cape. He was allowed to enroll at UCT because his major was chemical engineering and the degree wasn't offered at UWC. After his first year he decided to study general science so he was forced to transfer. After completing his studies he began his teaching career at Gronvlei Secondary School in Landsdowne. It was his only school.

So my friend was teaching at Groenvlei and he'd said, "Why don't you come to Groenvlei." And I think the school started on the Tuesday. On the Monday I decided, "Well, I need to get a job somewhere." So I went to the school and I said, "Look, I need a job." And my hair was long. I mean you can imagine hair and jeans and all of that. The principal said that he was looking for a physical science teacher but I must cut my hair and I must wear a tie. Which is exactly what I did.

So for two years I taught for a good autocratic principal. Being the head of the school, when he said, "Jump!" we all asked "How high?" And that was fine. We did a lot of exciting things in that time. One of the things we were all very interested in was drama and music. We used to put on plays and so on. I love it, still do it. Put on plays. And I think it was great because the students always used to be thrown by that. I was particularly old fashioned in the way that I dealt with students. They would have to stand for me. And I wasn't much older than they were, but that's the kind of tradition that you come from. They would have to stand for me and we would greet and they would greet me and then they would sit down.

So there was a flurry of activity and work. We always believed that we needed to not only work with students in a classroom context, but also we needed to work with them outside of the classroom and away from the subject. We're not talking about tutorials. I was responsible for chess and a colleague was responsible for, I think, table tennis. And we used to take them music; and we used to put on productions or cabarets or revues, we used to call them. So we'd have a focus on poverty, or we'd have a focus on hopelessness or whatever, and then you'd do a whole kind of revue thing around that. It was great. That was '83, '84 and so on.

van Harte's perception of 1985 was that students radicalized teachers.

Then in 1985, of course, things became quite heated and hectic. At our school, at Groenvlei, we were hit particularly hard because the police felt that we were one of the centers where things were happening. So we got the brunt of police action at our school. Groenvlei is an interesting place because it is situated on the edge of a working-class area called Hanover Park and the middle-class area which Dianne's parents come from called Lansdowne. So you've got this school, Groenvlei, which draws its population from both sides because it's an excellent school. So it had an excellent reputation because our matric results were among the top in the country. So that was always a source of pride for the principal and for the teachers because we were in a working-class area.

And then, of course, '85 comes around, and the kids decide that this is rubbish and they start aligning themselves with schools where things are less than perfect. And then deciding on certain days to go to rallies and just staying away from school. At the time we were still teaching. And then it became more and more ridiculous because some days you would end up with two or three kids in your class and our view was always, "Well, if you have two or three people in the class, then you've got to teach." And the principal supported that. Then we became a bit skeptical about that. We said, "But this is ridiculous. We need to respond as teachers to what was happening as well, because it doesn't make sense for the kids to get beaten to a pulp on the other side and we're sitting at school teaching two or three students English and physics, you know."

And then we started to become involved, and we set up SRC structures. So what happened was you would meet with the students. I remember one particular incident which stands out very clearly in my own head. The students had been to another rally and they had said that the next rally would be at Groenvlei. They volunteered, which they told us two days before the time. We responded and we said, "Well the first thing we need to do is make sure that you have good microphones." That was our point because we were not going to have chaos, but we were going to have the rally and we were going to have it in the quad and they were going to be seated and the thing was going to happen. And that's what happened. The students arrived and we said they needed to have marshals, and they got marshals and organized themselves. And then you can see our own politicization coming through as a response to what students were doing. I think that's very, very important. You tend to forget that we were responding at that initial stage to what students were doing.

I remember getting a phone call from a parent and a parent saying, "The kids are trapped in the school." They had gone to a nighttime rally at the school. And so we got into our cars and went. And we didn't think about danger or anything. Because you were a teacher. That was your job. You needed to ensure the safety of the kids because that's what parents expected us to do. And that was a different approach. You weren't only the teacher in the classroom. You were somebody in the community. You saw yourself as a community person. So we went there and I remember trying to ferret kids out of the place and then we got trapped by the police. I remember running into a house, five of us and seven kids. We ran into a house. The door was open. And there were two people watching television—classic scene. And we ran in, they didn't bat an eyelid. They just pointed to a room and we ran into the room. And I think that attests to how the community itself, while they may not have been out in the street, their role was one which said, "The door will always be open."

The principal was getting more and more upset with us. And then when that particular rally did happen, the police attacked the school violently and a lot of our students got beaten up, got shot with tear gas. The whole school was enveloped in tear gas on more than one occasion. And then the students developed these ingenious systems of counteracting the tear gas. They came to me, as a physics person, "What do you do?" And I said, "Look people, the only thing that we really can do, but don't quote me on this, is we need to have buckets of water sitting in place." Which is what they did and it worked. Buckets of water and sand. And I was totally proud of these kids because they were using science in a far more practical way than in the lab.

He spoke about Awareness Programmes.

We were not teaching anymore but what we were doing was developing Awareness Programmes at school and that was a big thing. The Awareness Programmes were basically an attempt to bring structure into not teaching. Now I think very often it is where the whole notion of People's Education came into being. So what happened was you would have students crying out for their history of the country. Crying out for where they had come from. Why is it that they find themselves in a school like this, whereas in Westerford or the other side the schools were like that? And the students were beginning to ask those questions, and it was our job to respond to that and say, "Well let's look at that in a far more coherent way." And then what would happen is we would develop these programs with a core grouping and then there would be questionnaires flying around and there would be sessions of discussion; there would be open forums in the playground for students. And we would never participate. We would just make sure we were on the perimeter. But the students ran the show. All that we did was ensure that they weren't going to be brutalized. So that if a cop did pitch up, then it would seem as though this was part of the school program. So in some instances we were also window dressing for the outside.

van Harte reflected on a threatening parent when he did not administrate exams at the end of the 1985 school year.

They had done a total of three months' work instead of nine or ten months. So the question at the end of 1985 was: Should they write an examination or not and what was the substance of that exam going to be? Because exams were for promotion purposes to the next standard, we felt that the only decision that could be made was that there must be no exam and that the students would need to repeat the year. And we met with parents and they supported it. The parents supported it. It was wonderful. Because we also established the Parent Forums, and the PTSA structures began to be formed as a result of these meetings we held with parents to keep them informed. But there was a group of parents who wanted their students to write the examinations, as you can imagine, because they wanted their kids to progress to the next year.

Just one story about that year which I think indicates the kind of abuse that we had to face. I remember going into the classroom in October, the physics students, they'd all huddled in the lab. The lab was always a haven for things. It was a great place. I remember going to the lab and the place was surrounded by cops. Every day there were policemen. And there used to be parents' cars parked all around the school. This was the atmosphere. That's the other reason why we said we couldn't write the exam. The atmosphere wasn't right. We had police on the premises all the time. Sometimes you had a policeman at every single teacher's door. And I remember going to this classroom and saying to my class, "Look people. I think that you need to know that there's no way that I'm going to administer the examination." And, of course, there were a lot of Vivas and support for that. But there was one little girl who decided that this was it. She ran out of the lab. The lab was upstairs and she ran down and went out the gates and she went to a car. And the next minute I saw a man get out of the car with a gun in his hand, her father, and he came and I heard him say, "Who the fuck is going to stop my daughter from writing an examination?" He was coming for me. And I saw him walking and I realized what was happening. I said: "Kids you're going to be fine. I'm just going down to the principal's office." I ran down the stairs and the principal's door was locked and I barged in and there was a sergeant major from the police standing there. I thought I was safe. And so I said to the principal and sergeant, "Look, there's a parent out here who's about to come in and shoot me." And the principal and the sergeant major said, "Look sir, we are not here to protect you, we are here to protect the learners!"

van Harte stressed student-teacher relationships after the boycotts. He also explained the depth of education at the school.

I think what did change was the relationships with students. And what had happened was that the students knew who supported them during the time of 1985. And so they were always drawn to those teachers for support. So we continued with our dramas and all of those sorts of things in a heightened way. But what was also interesting was that the students themselves had said, "We at Groenvlei can't continue to be producing these dramas. We must work with other schools where these things are not happening." So what happened is we used to cluster up to six or seven schools and then we'd put on these massive drama things. So we would have these huge festivals and we would put on plays, not plays, it was always revues, because a play was far too structured.

In the classroom itself, I think, for me personally there was a far more relaxed atmosphere because I was beginning to break down the barrier between the student and the teacher. And I think the power relationship changed somewhat in class. And that had changed fundamentally for me. And I think that affected the way in which you interacted with students. You never hid your politics from the students, never. I think for us that was very important. You used every opportunity to inform them about where you stood on certain things. I think we all believed that this thing of neutrality was nonsense. I mean, we had a position; we had a perspective. And we were never scared to tell our students what the perspective was, but we also said that they were at liberty to disagree with our perspective. So I would make the point that I supported the ANC to my students. And some of them supported the National Party. And that was a source of great tension and conflict. But I think it was very healthy because they needed to know where I stood on everything.

And when it came to education we spoke clearly about "gutter education" and our understanding and our contextualization of "gutter education." We said that the education that you were getting at this institution from me is the best education that I can offer you. The system itself is "gutter education," but that doesn't mean that you can't hold your head up high and speak to any student about physical science at any other institution. Even if we can only do 50% of the experiments. That was a very important point for us to make.

When I see the word "gutter education" today I still flinch slightly, because I still think how many misunderstand the context of that word because it's not about bad teaching. It's about a systemic approach to education. I think that at

Groenvlei I taught with the best colleagues in education. Still to this very day the best colleagues imaginable. I'm not saying I'm the hottest physical science teacher around, but I love the subject and hopefully that rubbed off. And students came to the school to do physical science. And they came to the school to do English because Brian and Celeste were in those things. And they came to the school to do math because Noel was in the Math Department.

He spoke about WECTU and SADTU.

WECTU became very important. I think at one level it was, let's be honest about it, at the very least, all my friends were members. That was important because the people you socialized with were members of that organization. But that wasn't the only reason. In a hierarchy that's the lowest one. But it is one. It is there. Freire was the bible at the time. I think also it was for me a sense of safety. I never felt as though I was alone at the school or that we were only sixteen or seventeen, but that we were part of a far broader group. So when we spoke about "us," that "us" was not just the Groenvlei staff. That was about other schools. And there was also a sense of power that was given to us because we always knew more about what was happening in other schools than our principal or the management structures of the schools. And what that meant was that when principals said all other schools are this now, we could say, "No, but you're talking nonsense. They're not doing this. At Mountview they're doing that. At Crystal they're doing that. At Livingstone they're doing that, and so on." So it gave us the edge in the debate and discussion in the staff room. You're a member of WECTU so you know what's happening. And so what happened was our numbers grew because of what was perceived as that power of knowing what was happening at other schools.

I think at that time we felt it was important to begin to look at what the problems are in education, okay. Why is it that our students are not doing well when compared to white kids? And that process was an important one and there was a lot of discussion. But I think also what was important was that we would begin to ask the other questions. And the other question for me was: Where were our colleagues in the townships? They were not with us. They had established their own organization, called DETU (Democratic Teachers' Union). So you had WECTU and you had DETU. And DETU operated within the black township schools, whereas we operated in a kind of Coloured township situation. So we felt it was important that we needed to talk to them, so we began to meet in the late eighties. We began to say that we needed to talk with one voice. We needed to begin to get together. And so it was the start of establishing SADTU. It was the beginning of being SADTU.

Both Dianne Gordon and Glen van Harte became more involved with SADTU in the nineties preceding the 1994 democratic election. van Harte concluded with a story that connects the past and the present.

I think it's important to realize where we all are now. I'm an advisory in the Education Department for physical science. But I always remember during that time in '85 one of my functions was to tell advisors that they were not welcome at the school. And in fact, I remember the person whose job I now have came to the school. And they would always send me to talk to them. My job was to say, "You're not welcome at this institution because we don't believe that what you're doing is of any benefit to education." And I remember one inspector I had to escort off the school premises. I was walking with my hands behind my back and he was walking with his hands behind his back. I said, "Look, I have to kick you off the school premises because the staff has asked me to do this and that's exactly what we're doing now. No hard feelings." And the man walked silently off. I went into the department in 1996. It was my first big meeting with the rest of the team, and he was there. He almost fell off his chair.

Mandy Sanger

Mandy Sanger has quite a reputation in Cape Town as a "radical" teacher. Although she has taught at Vista High School since the early nineties, she remains active in community and union organizing. Meetings with Sanger included stops at Don Pedro's, a pub that was/ is quite popular with progressive Capetonians. Sanger began her teaching as an unqualified teacher in 1983. She returned to the University of the Western Cape after that year and re-started her teaching career in 1988. Her recollections and reflections provide a chronology of radical political thought and action in Cape Town.

Well, I come from a very anti-teaching family, my father hated teachers. I grew up with these kinds of stories and anecdotes that teachers were basically lazy drinkers who didn't really work and were basically carrying out orders of the government. It was the only protected job for your kind of Coloured elitist world. Ja, my father's an artisan. He had difficulties getting jobs, because at that point I think the only thing that black people could do, if they wanted to be professional, was become a teacher or nurse. Everything else was closed. So he couldn't get into university to do art, and he basically had to go and work in factories. But interestingly, he had great respect for many of his own teachers. He's not a resentful person. So, I mean, in the Western Cape you had this motley group of middle-class, mainly teachers, and anybody who wants to fight apartheid and who was not a teacher didn't quite feel at home.

I went to South Peninsula, which is relatively one of the few stable kind of black schools in the Western Cape; its one of the oldest schools. It's in Diep River, which is in the southern part of Cape Town, the southern suburbs. And it's a relatively middle-class high school. And people who went to South Peninsula knew they'd come out relatively successful. So a stable school, also quite political, as were all the more middle-class schools at that point. I started 1976 and I ended 1980. And I think that's where a lot of my political activism grew from. The second year of high school, 1977, brought about heavy politicization of young people in the Western Cape. It was the forceful removal of squatters, and that's when they started Khayelitsha, and they tried to force Xhosa-speaking people from the more kind of settled Cape Flats further out. It created quite an important mobilizing point for students.

We kind of launched a SRC. SRCs were illegal, any form of political action or political debate was outlawed. I think in '76 we started out, because we were quite a middle-class type school, with environmental type action, you know. I remember when I was in Standard six, that's Grade 8, through our environmental type programs, we were able to meet students from other schools. And five years later those were the student leaders in the Western Cape. And then we launched things like history societies. So history societies in that whole period, '76 to '80, took on a very political feel about it. I mean the moment you were associated with a history society, you were known as a political student. Well, I think slowly but surely, from '76 onwards, schools started networking. We launched in '78, '79 what was called the *Interschool Magazine*. It involved the kind of maturing group of people who started out writing about environment type programs, the ozone layer. And it developed more of a class consciousness about the environment being destroyed. It lasted throughout 1980, which was the big year that everything blew in the Western Cape, the school boycotts. We launched the Committee of 81. Eventually it gained momentum. It included schools from the rural areas, the outlying areas, so it wasn't just your kind of urban Cape Town. And the entire complexion of the Committee of 81 was different from *Interschool Magazine*, which was just a group of students who liked writing. It became more community political. The character of Western Cape politics has always been to get small groups of people together to talk about politics. And they spend a lot of time in the lounges talking about what they think. In the 1980s, the whole notion of mass rallies began, rather than us getting together, developing a magazine, and getting people to read it. I think the Committee of 81 started leading rallies, kind of more broad-based community type action. So they started talking about linking student action to rent boycotts, the whole civic movement started in 1980. Largely, I wouldn't say the students started it, but students went around the community after school and got parents together to start talking about the rising cost of living, so it had spawned that kind of movement in the Western Cape.

Sanger spoke about her high school teachers.

They were largely Unity Movement teachers; they were largely opposed to what we were doing. They wanted us to behave very nicely and not spoil our chance of becoming doctors, lawyers, teachers. Their whole point was that you go to school and the best way to fight apartheid is if you are qualified. They were extremely anti-mass popular organizations. But they were role models in the sense that they were political. Yes, the fortunate thing about our school was that they would never be seen to be expelling or suspending students for being involved in politics; it was seen as a good thing. A lot of teachers were members of the Unity Movement, so they'd invite us to the discussion groups on Saturdays and Sundays, and we'd go. They had an education foundation, but they essentially saw political action as being outside of school time. Despite my dislike and criticism of the Unity Movement, many of my teachers were inspiring classroom practitioners. They made school enjoyable and were committed teachers. Our opposition to the Unity Movement at school was not adversarial. It was more of a situation where as young students we resisted being politically adopted by them and developed our own independent political networks.

Sanger's decision to attend the University of the Western Cape was political. She spoke about the reaction of her high school teachers, organizing at the university, and her racist professors.

And they were very disappointed with me for going to the University of the Western Cape. Because it was considered to be a bush college, and was considered to be a product of apartheid, and Afrikaner masters, whereas UCT had more respectability. That was largely why a lot of us resisted being part of that kind of way of looking at things. And we became an opposition to them at school, because we felt that we needed to link up with more working-class students, students from rural areas, and you'd get those students at UWC, not at UCT. We went straight from the Committee of 81 to university. I mean, I had no idea of what I was going to do. We did teaching because it was easy in terms of getting a bursary, because the government at that point encouraged black people to become teachers or nurses, so in terms of the bursary, you got financial backing.

The whole idea was that we would launch SRCs because SRCs became a form of mobilizing. It was Afrikaner lecturers, they only spoke Afrikaans. They were incredibly hostile, so it was a very hostile environment in '81. Yes, that was one of the reasons why we went there. Because we felt that it was an important way to organize students, that you'd get your political students, or you'd get students who'd take the spark in a sense. The whole emotional spark was important, you know, all very romantic about it. In fact, we had a kind of group called Spark.

Well then I did a normal B.A. So I did the kind of things I enjoyed at high school, which was English, sociology. I did anthropology but then eventually we had to drop out. We dropped out because what they taught was racist anthropology. I mean the moment you came with anything different, you were literally alienated or kicked out, it was very hostile lecturing. When we launched the History Society at UWC it was banned from campus. It was a fight, it was a struggle to actually get it to operate. So even though I didn't do history, we all became part of the History Society, because it was the alternative to the SRC which we could not have.

Mandy Sanger left UWC after one year and became an unqualified teacher. She spoke about the politics of the ocean community south of Cape Town where she first taught.

Well, I did to a certain extent want to be in education. Because from high school a lot of the political debates were sort of about education, or about the lack of access for the great majority of people. So in a sense, I was interested in education. And then I was able to go and teach. At that point most teachers were unqualified in black schools. Your few middle-class schools had qualified teachers. I taught for a year in Hout Bay in a junior primary school, kind of physical education, health, and English. When I look back it was a very important year because I had the luxury of practicing, battling with my own ideas of teaching. Because my teaching experience was about organizing the community, organizing youth groups, and a lot of it was teaching people in the Paulo Freire way. So even though I didn't learn about Paulo Freire at the university, by the time I went to the university we had kind of an idea of Paulo Freire. How we had to teach people literacy. So we taught in the civic organizations, the community organizations. We used to have political debates and pass literature around and translate literature from its academic language. So for me a lot of that was teaching. And when I went to teach for that first year, I basically implemented my community teaching experience. It was a hell of a challenge. The interesting thing for me was that all the parents of the children were very militant unionists. They all belonged to the Food and Allied Workers Union, which was one of the radical unions in the Western Cape. And every single parent, because they lived in the fishing village and they worked in the fishing factory, every single parent belonged to that union. Parents' meetings were very political meetings. And you could actually go to parents who weren't necessarily formally educated and you could talk to them about their child's education.

After one year she returned to complete her degree. She reflected on the progressive changes at the school and talked about her community organizing.

I was only there one year because at that point I think most people were called temporary teachers; teachers weren't protected in any way. And depending on your relationship, largely with the principal, or somebody in authority, you'd get permanent status. So it was common for teachers to be temporary. And then I completed my degree, and I continued to be part of student organizations. I mean every single year was a boycott at UWC. So for a month or two months we'd have student uprisings. No, I wasn't at that point specifically working on them, because

I think when I left university the first time, a lot of my focus shifted more to youth organization and community organization. In a place called Steenberg, which just borders on Retreat, where you have largely sub-economic housing and mainly workers. I volunteered for the Plastic and Allied Workers Union; we worked for the General and Allied Workers Union, they were all fledgling COSATU unions at that point. And we volunteered for them, so we largely organized youth civics and youth organization, young workers.

Well, the way our degrees work is that you only spend one year in education, that's your final year. Things began to change and you began to get people like Jakes Gerwel, who were a lot more vocal. And the lecturers at UWC, the progressive ones, began to show and rear their heads. That whole '84/'86 period was a very militant period in South Africa's history, and particularly in the Western Cape. People basically had a choice: They could either bury their head in the sand and be collaborative with the system by their non-action, or they would have to rear their head and take a stand. So if you were a lecturer, you identified yourself as an education worker, if you were a doctor and you wanted to be progressive, you'd identify yourself as a health worker. So teachers began to form fledgling unions. You had the lecturers who were progressive belonging to the WECTU.

Because she was very political Sanger held six temporary teaching positions between 1988 and 1991, when she was hired as a permanent teacher at Vista High School. She spoke about her temporary jobs, political issues, challenging the curriculum, school inspectors, scared principals, and teacher schisms.

Well then, yes, I got a job. But, I spent my first three years in about six schools. I was a temporary teacher. The first year I managed to teach for the entire year. It was in 1988 and it was quite a heavy period in South Africa. Because that's when they were marching for the release of Mandela. Talk of negotiation was in the air, so I think the authorities became more intransigent as well. And so a lot of us, at my school, I taught in Mitchells Plain, about five of us lost our posts. And they had to employ new teachers in those posts afterwards. So it wasn't as if we lost our posts because there weren't jobs, they actually got rid of us because of politics, because we were trying to launch a union and because we were organizing students. We used to take our teaching quite seriously in terms of the subject matter. So a bit of our high school experience to become middle class rubbed off on us. We didn't reject it entirely, so teaching was very important. I was teaching English and physical education. We'd have afternoon classes, sporting activities would be very important. So it would be your progressive teachers who'd come early to school and organize students in sport, who'd stay very late after school and be part of education programs.

We had at that point a very rigid kind of curriculum. You got what was called a syllabus, and it had very clearly written points that you had to teach at particular times of the year. And you had to spend a lot of time going through that syllabus and ticking off that you'd completed it. An inspector would come and check up whether you'd done the lesson. So they'd check that you were teaching the correct topics, no political topics, nothing that would allow students to be very critical. Obviously, as a teacher it would be like shifting the deck chairs, but you had a very rigid syllabus that you had to complete. And a lot of it was about teaching memory, not understanding. It wasn't about whether the teacher was being creative or getting the kids involved in education. It was quite a policing thing. Yes, most of my teaching life was that kind of thing. But we resisted it largely. And that's largely why I had to go from school to school. Because we'd inevitably link up with groups of teachers and say that we refused to be policed. And we'd try to teach alternative lessons; we wouldn't stick to the syllabus.

I think the great majority of teachers in that whole period would just be quiet; they didn't want to be bothered with any kind of activity. They were the ones who went into teaching because they had no alternative. They never went into teaching because they wanted to teach or they had a vision for transforming education. They were just basically there to earn a salary. As activists the thing that made us different from the people who taught us was that we felt it was important to organize the unorganized. So we always wanted to reach out to people. So through sport, if it wasn't through politics, it would be through sport that we would link up with them. And we tried to create a situation where they would feel the need to defend us, even if it just meant keeping us at the school.

Well, I taught at Cedar, which was a Mitchells Plain school and then we were kicked out of the school. Ja, and then I managed to get a post nearer to home, nearer to where I was organizing youth at a school called Lavender Hill. Ja, at that point it was one of the most depressed communities in the Western Cape. Incredibly poor, high levels of unemployment, but the principal there was a relatively progressive principal. He was progressive in the sense that he belonged to the progressive sports movement. So in that sense he was able to give me a post. And he had quite a few teachers at his school who were progressive teachers. And he allowed for that. Of course, he had to walk the tightrope. But the post that he had available was only a temporary post and only for a short period. So when I lost my post there, it wasn't because I was kicked out, it was because I was only in the post for three months.

There was one other person who was expelled from the previous school at Mitchells Plain and we worked closely together at Grassy Park High. We worked quite closely together with students. At that time a lot of the work with students, apart from work with the SRC, involved sport. One period of that year was a major campaign to release Mandela. So there wasn't a major boycott in the same way that we spoke about the 1980 boycotts and 1976 boycotts or the '84-to-'86 period. But there were still school disruptions and a lot of tensions on the staff. The difference was that when schools were disrupted they were disrupted for a day or two. So right through 1993 that characterized schooling.

I'm a bit ambivalent about Grassy Park. I'd reached a point where I felt "just let me get out of here." Partly because of the principal, but also the dynamics on the staff. Grassy Park was one of the more established schools at the time. It had staff who had been there for a very long time. Many of the teachers were also ex-students. So, on one hand there was a lot of openness about the staff, but on another level they were quite close-minded, wanting to maintain certain traditions that they considered to be Grassy Park. But I think a lot of the conflict around our union was because a lot of the teachers were members of the Teachers' League of South Africa. Whether they were active or not or whether they were merely a legacy, I'm not sure. But the point is there was an ethos of the Teachers' League of South Africa there and we were considered to be trying to bring in a new union that was too closely in line with the ANC. So, towards the end of the year I felt my energy could be much better spent elsewhere.

Sanger then went to teach at a one-year job at Garlandale which is where both Basil Snayer and Kevin Wildschut teach. Her memories are of faculty cooperation to teach against the system.

We said we'll go and do our normal teaching that the government wanted us to do. So we taught the prescribed syllabus and ticked off that we'd done certain work. But what we'd do is we'd throw in extra. If you were a history teacher you'd teach a bit about alternative history, so you'd teach the history of the ANC. So in other words it involved doing a normal class lesson but changing the content. And in the process of teaching English skills like reading, listening, comprehending, writing skills, you'd also impart a particular alternative content. So it involved that. The kids were a lot more motivated than most of the schools I've been to. The kids were sort of a mixture of your more middle-class and your working-class student. I didn't have as many disciplinary kind of problems as I'd had at other schools. So I enjoyed teaching at Garlandale. The one thing about Garlandale that I really enjoyed was the way in which teachers tended to work together. So in terms of setting joint exam papers, talking about what they were going to teach, there were some very interesting people on that staff.

Mandy Sanger joined the staff at Vista High School at the beginning of great transition in South African society. She spoke about desegregation at the school just before the election of President Mandela.

Then I was appointed at Vista High School in a permanent position. It was a time in which people were becoming very enthusiastic about being unionized and having rights. I think it's the first time in South Africa's history where teachers have very real rights. The first time where there's a lot of talk going around in staff rooms about the principal not being allowed to victimize teachers. So it was a period in which teachers were beginning to gain confidence, not your selected few teachers who were prepared to stick their necks out, but teachers in a kind of rank-and-file sense. There was a groundswell. So my teaching at Vista was in that context. There were a lot of conflicts and fights around the right of a principal to appoint his friends. And I came into the school in an official kind of way and I got the support of the bulk of the teachers who at that point were staunch union members. And it wasn't a kind of union appointment, but it signaled the fact that more than just the principal agreed with the appointment of somebody.

Well, at the time schools began to open up. This was before '94 and our school was affected. A lot of the students from the community who would normally come to our school had an opportunity to go to white schools. And a lot of students from the townships, the so-called African townships, had a right to go to our school. So it created a whole different dynamic in the sense that for the first time you had formal apartheid being broken down. In a sense that people are sharing the same desks, the same space. So all the anger, the hatred, the fear of the unknown came out. And I remember spending a lot of time intervening in vicious racial fights between students.

In that period, a lot of the fears of the Coloured people were being exploited by the previous oppressors, and our community was affected. All the notions that blacks were going to come and take your homes. All those fears about black people getting the best jobs, getting the best education, all those fears were exploited. I mean there was a lot of National Party sentiment in our school. Well, my role was to teach students my position and to contest their positions. But I allowed them to fight very openly. So in the class that I taught there were always a lot of National Party students who were very vocal. And the classrooms became battlegrounds, in a sense, for people to debate and shout about it sometimes in a very chaotic way. I don't believe in suppressing people's racial ideas. So when people shout slogans at each other I won't tell them, "Don't do that." I would rather begin to talk about the bad effect of those racial slurs. A lot of the classrooms were about racial fights. But I think it was all part of the healing, where people who have never had a chance to be together get together for the first time. And my first year at Vista basically was about seeing those things happen in the classroom. And seeing how difficult it was with teachers to begin to oversee that because you don't have teachers who think about race. And the way those of us in the mass democratic movement had to think about it. You have ordinary teachers confronted by people being racist for the first time and they were sometimes themselves racist. So they use racial terms like "kaffir." And, you know, because a lot of the township students could not speak Afrikaans, they were perceived to be stupid by teachers. So the language thing became quite a serious thing. But for me it was a useful period.

Sanger concluded with thoughts about 1994 at Vista High School.

I think it was different—very energized. I felt, and maybe I'm being a bit biased, but my kids wrote essays that were far more interesting than I ever got from them before. There was a general increased awareness about everything. People were far more open to discussion because that was the method of the time. So whether we were talking about issues related to the elections or any other issue, people were just geared towards debating and talking and fighting. As an English teacher, that's the best atmosphere to have because you're basically wanting people to get out their ideas. And it's a very difficult thing to do under normal, calm situations, because to ask kids to just brainstorm, they sit and they look brain-dead. And in that period, people were just a lot more lively. I felt, as an English teacher, the school was quite open to new ideas.

Jeff Cohen

I inteviewed Jeff Cohen in his office at Herzlia Secondary School, which is a Jewish day school in Vredehoek, an inner city suburb that is at the foot of Table Mountain looking out over the bay. Cohen went to Herzlia in 1992 as a math teacher and he is currently the principal of the school. In the eighties he taught at Crestway, returned to school at the University of Cape Town and then Columbia University. He came back to teaching at Heathfield and then taught adult education in Langa. It is almost as if he has had four different teaching careers.

I graduated my Honours degree in philosophy at UCT at the end of 1980. I'd been working in restaurants and stuff, although I didn't really see that as a long-term career selling pizzas and things like that. I had a lot of mathematics in my degree, and math has always been my particular love and passion. So I'd heard from a friend about a job teaching mathmematics. My girlfriend at the time was teaching at the school at which the big boycott in 1980 started. The school is called Crystal High School in Hanover Park. She was there at the time and so I really had a day-by-day account of what was going on there. My friend taught at a school called Crestway. It was a very ordinary working-class school. It's in an area called Steenberg in Concert Boulevard, which is the main road passing through the center. In fact, Concert Boulevard divides the suburbs of Steenberg and Retreat. Of the two areas, Steenberg was the more depressed of the two. Retreat was lower middle class and I would say Steenberg was lower class. I don't use that pejoratively but in terms of incomes. Steenberg tended to have higher unemployment, poorer people.

Anyway, he told me that he'd taught at the school and the principal of the school was a guy called Yusuf da Costa, who was an ex-Unity Movement guy, and himself was highly politicized. And he was an anomaly in the old Coloured Affairs schools, because you had to really be a brown noser. And this was a complete anomaly. How da Costa had been appointed was one of these freaks. Anyway, he had been appointed and he was a brilliant principal and my friend spoke very highly of him. So I called the school, you see. Anyway, the long and the short of it is that I got a job there, teaching mathematics. And that started me on my teaching career, working with a fantastic man like da Costa. There were some wonderful colleagues there.

I started in 1981, the year after the boycotts, but it was still a time of considerable ferment. There were boycotts during that time but nothing like the 1980 boycott. That was the big one. I was there from 1981 to 1983. I was the most junior member of staff, obviously, and it was an exciting place to be. The kids were exciting kids. They were highly, highly politicized. Of course, now, looking back, I realize that it was mostly just radical chic except for a few pupils, most of them were really just enjoying the fun of making loud noises and getting hurt. And colleagues—I met some remarkable people there. People who were politically involved. Some were perhaps less politically involved, but were fine teachers. So I learned a lot from them in that respect.

My head of department in mathematics in my second and third years there was a guy called Yusuf Gabru. He and Yusuf da Costa were fairly typical of the caliber of some of the people at Crestway High School. Which in the miserable, dreadful, depressed scene in Coloured education in those days, it was quite a beacon. da Costa, he was the shining light of that school, and he held it together brilliantly and he recruited fantastic teachers. Great people. So, it was exciting times and the school had been built for eight hundred pupils. We had eleven hundred and fifty. And the nearby school, which I won't name, had been built for a thousand pupils and they had about five hundred. So the contrast was the principals. Principals (*als* at the end) but also the principles (*les* at the end). When da Costa left the school fell apart.

Cohen spoke about the spirit of the school and the commitment of teachers to students.

There were lots of events that stand out vividly for me. School began at 8:00 a.m. or 8:15 a.m. I can't remember. And the pupils' level of mathematics was very low. I used to come to school at seven in the morning. I gave classes every morning and I was not the only person, by the way. And the kids would come and many of them were so keen. They would come at seven in morning and then we'd give tutorials again after school till 4:00 p.m. or 5:00 p.m. They'd stay. No problem. I'll give you two little anecdotes. We had one pupil. He was in the eleventh grade. We called it Standard Nine in those days. At junior year he was a bright lad and he was in my mathematics class. And one of the teachers who was an extraordinary woman, called Cas Abrahams, she was his sort of class teacher, his homeroom teacher. And she noticed that he was not doing as well as he should be. He was doing poorly in all of his subjects, and she picked up that he was really a bright lad. So she went to check out what the home circumstances were and she found him living in a two-room apartment. So there would be a bathroom and a kitchenette and two rooms. Okay. Not two bedrooms. A two-roomed apartment with twenty-seven other human beings. Okay. That was Malcolm. And she made arrangements and took him out of that to another home of one of his friends and the results were remarkable. Now he'd never spoken about it. He never complained. He wasn't a winger or a whiner. He came to school every day. He did his best. But when you're living in two rooms, and they were not big rooms, with twenty-seven other human beings! Anyway, that was Malcolm.

A youngster called Randall. I taught him mathematics. He was my top student in the eleventh grade that year. He wasn't the top in the whole year group, but in my class he was the top and he was getting grades which would be regarded as pretty good in those circumstances. And then the year ended, and the following year we came back to school and he wasn't there. Where was he? Well, his father had passed away and that was the end of it. He had to go out to work. And that was the last I ever saw of Randall. Fine young man; very committed Christian; he was planning to go to the ministry.

Cohen spoke about the Awareness Club and a somewhat contentious event.

At Crestway we formed a thing called the Cultural Club. Now most Coloured schools had them. It was a cover for the Political Awareness Club. You had to call it Cultural. And I was one of the teachers involved, Yusuf Gabru was another. The ones who all ended up getting detained and, of course, the kids. And one day, one of the kids who happened to be in my homeroom class came to me and he said he's got access to this movie for the Cultural Club. He can get it for free and it's called *The Holocaust,* or something like that. It was a Hollywood story, though it was also a novel, based on the Holocaust. Now, obviously, the Holocaust deals with issues of human rights. Now, there's me, a very assimilationist Jew making no issue of my Jewishness at all. I know my history. I was brought up Jewish and I read widely and that, and I thought, "Well hey, this is a good idea. We live in South Africa apartheid." So I said, "Yes, great, let's get it for the Cultural Club." At our next meeting I tell them, "Wayne got us this movie on 'The Holocaust.'" And there's a silence. I said, "What's the problem?" Yusuf Gabru says, "But isn't the Holocaust used as a justification for the existence of the State of Israel?" Now I wasn't a Zionist at that time. And I said, "Well, it may be that it is used for that, but that's not the point. This is not about Israel, this is about human rights." Anyway there were strong misgivings but in the end we did show the movie. It's a dreadful movie. It's appalling. I'm sorry we showed it, it's so horrendous. But anyway, that's another matter.

Cohen briefly discussed States of Emergency and government oppression.

I can't recall if the Emergency had been lifted or if it kind of drifted into oblivion. Ja, one never really knew. My best Emergency story is the day it was declared. It was declared and it was in the newspapers and over the radio. This was in 1985. I was about to leave for the States, but I ambled down the street to some friends of mine. So I said, "You know, guys, there's been an Emergency declared." So they said, "Oh, well what does that mean?" So I said, "Well, they can detain people without trial. They can search homes without a warrant. They can do this, they can do that." And I listed all the things and my friend just sat and looked at me, and he said, "So nothing's changed." And of course he was right because the Emergency really was the Emergency in name only, because all of those laws were already on the statute. Of course people were dying left, right, and center. They were shooting people in the streets. They could already do whatever they wanted, and they did! So when the Emergency ended I don't know that it made a difference, really.

Jeff Cohen liked teaching and he returned to UCT in 1985 to earn his teaching degree. He received a scholarship to study at Columbia University in 1986, and then returned to South Africa and took a post at Heathfield, a Coloured high school not far from Crestway. He spoke about teaching in a Coloured school and two unhappy years at Heathfield.

I never considered going anywhere else. In the first instance, when I first went to Crestway, I didn't have a teaching qualification. I couldn't have taught at a white school. By this time I was in fact pretty highly qualified, ridiculously qualified by South African standards. And I don't know, I guess that was my place, that was where I wanted to be. It was nothing kind of fancy and I'm going to save the world or anything. I never had that. It was just that was where I wanted to be. It was right. I had a number of friends in the Coloured community. I felt at home there. I felt I was doing work that was worth doing, so it was fulfilling for me. It's hard to say. It wasn't something I thought about. It never occurred to me to apply to any of the white schools. It's one of those things that happened. No great force or anything like that. No great decision. It just happened.

I joined WECTU, which was the left-wing union. There were very, very strong WECTU people at the school. And I joined WECTU and I belonged to WECTU and I supported WECTU. And then WECTU called a strike. I can't even remember now what the issue was, whether it was a political issue or a wage issue or both. I don't even remember now. But I just remember that I felt very strongly that we should not strike. We were not workers in a sense like industrial workers where the strike is aimed at capital and by striking you hit capital because their profits are hit. We were teachers and if we strike the kids lose out. The government doesn't give a damn; in fact, it actually suits the government to have Coloured kids not in school. It was playing right into their hands. The only people who lost were the kids. Well, that was my way of thinking. It still is. I still hold the same views I did then. So what happened was each school's WECTU members were asked to vote on whether to strike or not. We had our meeting and the leading folks were very keen that we should strike and they made it quite clear. But then I spoke at the meeting and I urged us not to. And I think there may have been a couple of others who also spoke. Anyway, the long and the short of it is the vote in our school was against the strike. And the leading folks were very angry, and they made it clear to me that they were angry. They said, "Well, this is only our school, you know. This is not the national decision yet. You realize that we'll have to abide by the national decision." In any event they came back the next day very triumphant and saying, "Well, the vote is to strike, and now we have to." And I thought about it and I felt I couldn't. I just decided in the end, "Yes, I want to support my union but my first priority is to the children I teach." I'm sorry if it sounds self-righteous. Anyway, that's how I felt, and I resigned from WECTU on that day and they never spoke to me again. Literally. If I went to the table, they would turn away. And that really made me feel very unhappy, of course it was meant to. But it's not nice to feel that you're regarded as a scab and whatnot. I didn't strike. I went to work that day. And that was that.

Cohen left his job at Heathfield because of a dispute with the department and took a job at a private non-racial school.

Ja, so I had a friend, Harold Idesis, who had started one of these colleges, Rosebank College. I had taught there part-time during my year that I was getting my Teacher's Diploma and then I stayed there for the following year until August when I left for the States. So I had been at Rosebank. And they had a position for me, so I went back for a year to Rosebank. We call it a college. It's a different use of the word from your use in North America. It's high school level, but the kids are treated as if they are at college. So they don't wear a uniform, which is unusual for here. They're given a lot more freedom. The classes are very small and there is very little in the way of extramural activity. It's very academically focused. One goes there in order to concentrate purely on one's academia and get good grades to get into a university or college.

This was the eighties and school was still segregated by law, but Rosebank College and the other colleges were not. It was blind-eye stuff. So it really was non-racial in the best possible sense of the word. And in fact, 1984 when I was part-time there, I took one matric level class and in that class there were maybe fifteen kids, tops. And I had a Greek kid, two black kids, two Muslim kids, a Chinese girl, a couple of white South African kids, a Portuguese kid, and a Jewish kid. It was like the real United Nations. You either had to have money yourself or you had to be sponsored by someone.

Rosebank College was sold and Cohen left to teach at a black school in Langa.

Ja, I immediately got another job in black education at St. Francis Adult Education Centre. It was started by the Catholic Church and subsequently sort of half taken over by the Department of Education and Training, as they were known, Bantu Education, as they've been called before. And it was for black adults who had themselves taken their matric exams but had failed and who wished to come back and complete it on a part-time basis. So they would come during the day. There was also a night school but I taught in the day school. And they would take two or three subjects per year.

And that was great for a while and then I think I just ran out of idealism, eventually. There were incidents there that really made me think, "This is not for me." I mean you do know that there are nice people and not so nice people like normal, but the overall approach to education was just one that I couldn't feel comfortable with. It was a diploma-oriented approach, a lack of inquiry. And the political I think just outweighed the educational to such an extent that I just felt stifled. I just felt I couldn't stay anymore. So I really felt like I'd run dry, and I consulted my wife and then I decided I wanted to get out of teaching and I applied to medical school and I wasn't accepted. Unsurprisingly!

The ANC was unbanned and Nelson Mandela was released from prison when Jeff Cohen was a teacher in Langa.

I began January 1990 in Langa. I had been there a month and there was this announcement that there was going to be this speech in Parliament on the 2nd February. We suspended classes for the day. We all gathered in the staff room. Somebody brought a T.V. in and we watched it. So there I was sitting in Langa. The Langa march in 1960 and Sharpeville Day, and all that. Ja, two people shot dead in Langa. I mean, Langa was the center. And there I was sitting in Langa on 2nd February with all my colleagues. It was a non-racial staff, and there's De Klerk saying the ban on the ANC is lifted with immediate effect. And we all just leapt and cheered. And he said that Mandela's going to be released and I can't describe the feeling. I can picture it. I can live it. I can smell it. The atmosphere, the summer day, the dust in the air. And driving home that day, I just remember I had the windows of my car open and I put my hand out the window because I felt the air must feel different! It's like the world has changed. Mandela's coming out. The ANC is legal. What's happened here is a miracle, a miracle.

Cohen spoke about his move to Herzlia in 1992.

And then I got a call from the guy who was the principal of this school. He'd heard that there's a Jewish math teacher who's not working. And he had a position and he phoned me and I said, "Absolutely not. I'm not interested." First of all, to go to a white school was just not what I wanted. Secondly, to go to a Jewish school, I mean I'm a Jew through and through, but I'd always been very assimilationist. The thing is that I didn't see myself as part of the Jewish people or anything like that. I saw myself as a human being and a South African.

Anyway, he was a shrewd guy, Solly Kaplinski. I'd heard quite a lot about him as an educationist, so I said to him, "Look, I'm not interested in the job. Forget about it. But I am interested in meeting you and just talk as one teacher to another." He said, "Sure, come up here on Friday afternoon." Very clever guy, he knew exactly what would happen. So, anyway, I walked into this school and within five minutes I knew I'd come home. So I called him back a couple of days later, and I said, "Well, is the position still going?" And he just said, "Great. Come on in." And that was that!

So January '92 I began here. I just felt so comfortable. I still revel in that fact. So that's the first thing. The second thing is that I do feel a sense of home after the journey that I have taken. I taught for seven years in black and Coloured schools and for three years in non-racial private colleges, and I just felt no one could point a finger and say I don't know what's going on out there. I've never done anything. I felt I really have tried and I've really put my money where my mouth is in that respect. I don't expect great Nobel prizes for it, but I just feel I haven't gone an easy route, and if I feel comfortable now I've earned it.

During the eighties, this school was well known for its political involvement and its anti-apartheid stance. The kids here were politically aware and active. The Jewish heritage and the Jewish emphasis on freedom and justice and what is right. The school certainly embodied that through those years. Solly Kaplinski certainly encouraged it and fostered it, and I can't speak about his predecessors but I'm sure they did too. By the time I came here, although Solly was still here, it had already begun to turn into more of a "me" generation, and that's where we are now. We try hard. I try hard. I'm still passionate about righteousness and justice and freedom. And as one who was fairly close to the action in the apartheid years, I try and instill that in the kids. And I try and encourage them to know and not to forget what happened here in South Africa not long ago.

But it's not easy now. We're in a comfortable time. We've got a constitution, which, I mean no disrespect, but I think it's even better than the U.S. Constitution. I keep a copy here. Because I think it's one of the finest documents I've ever read. It says things which even the American Constitution's too scared to say. And it doesn't include the right to bear arms, I'm glad to say. We're the possessors of a system which for all its flaws and failings we have a democracy here. We have a functioning democracy and ten years ago we never thought we would have that. It's a fantastic thing.

June Bam

I interviewed June Bam in her office at the University of Stellenbosch, a once exclusively white Afrikaner-only university. During the struggle years June Bam taught in Grassy Park, a Cape Town southern suburb that is predominantly Coloured. Bam provides a chronology that weds the personal and the political. She was involved in numerous political organizations but she is also an extremely committed educator. Bam is unique in that during her career as a teacher at Grassy Park High School she had conflicts with both conservative and radical teachers. In fact, there was a time in the early nineties when she was threatened on the phone and she didn't know if the threats were from the right or left.

June Bam graduated from high school in 1979 and began teaching in 1980—a year of school boycotts.

The period was one of chaos. The principal expressed a confidence in me and I had nothing to do. I just thought, "Okay, let's take up the challenge." And, of course, I had already been through sort of political training with Brian Dublin. Now, Brian Dublin was the math teacher who was at the school, and he was a Unity Movement guy. So his mission was not to teach us math, but to teach us politics. He taught us that whatever we do must be transformative and we had to be revolutionary. So if an opportunity arises, you must make it a revolutionary opportunity. And when the principal sort of dangled his keys and he said Old Room 1, I didn't think of science. I didn't think of Standard Sixes. I didn't think of youth my age who were still there. I didn't think of the ethics. I didn't think of qualifications. I just thought this was the revolutionary opportunity.

I started on 15 March and the kids were shocked. They said, "But you were just in school, you were in matric the other day." And they knew my boyfriend, and they'd just seen me in my school uniform just a few weeks earlier. It was rowdy and the girls didn't know how to handle me because there's always competition with girls at schools and many of them were my age. But soon after that they settled down. I knew my matric science very well and I was trained by another teacher. Every afternoon she would train me in experiments. And I'm sure I was probably the lousiest teacher. So the staff had to gather every afternoon. The staff were shocked to see me. The older men were in their fifties and sixties and they told me, "What do you have to offer?" And then, of course, when this whole thing came out about qualifications and unqualified teachers, because that was what the protest was all about in 1980, their qualifications were revealed and I was one of the higher qualified people at the school. And then they were very uncomfortable. They would just not include me, you know. I was still a child and they had been at the school for twenty years. Of course, I became closer to Brian Dublin, my mentor. He was just too happy to have me there, because now I was no longer his student, but also his colleague.

She spoke about the school during the boycott. Included in her reflections are the different political perspectives of the teachers and a short commentary on the principal.

There was nothing. You used to sit every day and wait for the students to determine the day. And then if the students don't determine the day by 10 o'clock, the principal very hurriedly called a staff meeting to keep the staff in check because most of them ran off. We would talk to the SRC. We would gather at the library with the SRC and just talk to them about leadership. Brian would talk about the possible spies on the staff. And he told the students that they must conduct themselves in a revolutionary situation. I was their age so it seems ridiculous. They were also seventeen and eighteen and I was sort of the teacher person whose identity was completely confused at the time—mentor and child and student. And my role would be to talk to them, take them through reading; doing drawings. I did drawings and got them to draw posters. We read the 1943 Programme of the Unity Movement. That was Brian's thing. He'd give us something like Arnold Kettle's *Introduction to Marxism* or he would photocopy something out of Trotsky. So we would read hard-core kind of stuff, okay. I would be in the reading group with the students. The reading group first took place on weekends and then eventually it took place during the boycott time. There were demonstrations. Other schools would come. And there would be all kinds of protests, and schools from the area would just march into our school from all over. Mandy Sanger was the leader and she was on the Committee of 81. So all of them would gather there and Brian did play a very important role in speaking with them. Brian was very respected and many students spoke to him. He was young. He was twenty-one. And I think it's probably because he's also very relaxed and he had the look of Fidel Castro or Che Guevara.

They would have their uniforms on and went to jail with their uniforms on. They would have their ties on. Even if you went to the townships you'd see uniforms. So they would come to the school and it wasn't like in 1985 where they just marched in. It was slightly different. It wasn't as intense. In 1980, as far as I can remember, the principal could go and negotiate with police at the gate. And he cried one day. There's a photograph of him standing by the fence crying, "Please leave my children alone." I can remember they would beat the kids up the minute they're out of the school, yes. But not on the school, as far as I can remember, not on the school.

People didn't like the principal politically because he was seen as a collaborator. As a principal he was very humane in the sense that he knew all his students, he knew their names. He took a lot of interest in protecting the students from police or any other interference. Very, very humane but his politics were just completely screwed up. He came and broke up our meetings and he tore all the pictures that I'd got the students to sketch. Ja, he said that I must get out of that relationship with the communists. But I didn't. I wouldn't.

The other teachers were silent. The majority of teachers were trained at places like Hewat Training College and they only had to have Standard Eight or Standard Ten if they wanted to be a senior teacher. And it was like school. They wore uniforms at the college like children, with stockings and everything. And they would have a siren and they had to queue up as teachers. So that their college training, their teacher training, was like kids. So they came to school as if they were still kids. And they'd never had the kind of exposure to Brian's kind of analysis and in a way, I felt, even if I have to be arrogant about it, I felt a bit superior to them. I was young but I could see they didn't have a clue about understanding education in South Africa and apartheid. Students didn't listen to them because the students gained a sharper understanding of society through the activities and discussions and exposure to political leadership, reading groups. And the students soon realized that these people knew nothing and they lost respect.

The boycott came to an end towards the end of 1980. I remember there were exams and the kids wrote. So Grassy Park High did come to a settlement and there were exams and there was some normality. We went on a tour during the summer. Brian and I and Doreen Musson decided to educate the students about southern Africa. We went to Lesotho and Swaziland and the rest of South Africa. We went on a six-week tour, and I was the organizer with Brian. So at the end of the year when everything came to a close we took the matrics on this tour, a bus tour. And we just went on forever. And we had the worst experiences in Pretoria when we slept and cooked meals on the pavement. It was an education. So we had this whole apartheid experience on the road. This was a political tour and I took it very, very seriously.

June Bam enrolled at UCT in 1981. She spoke about the university, leaving her fam-
ily, living in a hostel for women on the street, and a teacher who became her mentor.

As the year was ending all the matriculants were getting vocational guidance.
People from UCT would come and talk to the students even during the chaos. So
I would go in and just listen. I wanted to teach. I really enjoyed the year. I enjoyed
the students. I enjoyed being part of teaching and learning. I liked the school situation. And, of course, I was taking my role that Brian had cut out for me so clearly
very, very seriously. And I said, "I want to go and study education and become a
very qualified teacher."

I went to UCT but I had a commitment. I wanted to go back to Grassy Park
High when I was a qualified teacher and do serious work. And then when I got to
UCT I was exposed to other people and traditions—to the ANC people. I was
going to Brian Dublin's reading group. I was going to the Worker's Reading Group.
I was going to the ANC Reading Group. But as I read I became more critical of
Brian and I was sort of drawn closer to the Worker's Tradition. And that's how I
got into the Youth Movement—Athlone Youth Movement. It was the leftist
youth movement. So I was with them. I was exposed to all this reading about family and I suddenly saw my father as an extreme reactionary man. And I just wanted
to break away and become this real educational revolutionary, whatever that is.
And then I left home. I didn't know where I was going to, but I just wanted to
break away, to develop. I went to UCT because I was studying at UCT, and I didn't
know what the heck I was going to do that night, but I didn't want to see my family again. I didn't see them for two years. And then I met with one of the students,
and she knew a place in Athlone where they have all these girls who have left
home. It's called Baker House in Athlone, in the streets, you know. So I went
there and that's when my whole world opened up to another world. It just broadened my vision from the narrow Grassy Park Unity Movement experience to one
that was more critical. I got closer to people who were real activists.

Ja, the one moment they would be sleeping, you know, I would share a room
with one, and the next day they would throw them out because they were found
prostituting the night before. So they would share their experiences with me
about living on the street and selling your body for money. And we would all talk
about where we were going to get our money, you know. And I would borrow
money from them too, from the prostitutes. They would help me and I would help
them. Oh, it was a terrible experience, but it was a very good experience because
it made me very tough. Yes. And then of course the Brian Dublin training of his,
"Make these prostitutes revolutionaries!" Completely bizarre. And I tried to take
them to the Athlone Youth Movement, you know, and give them reading. And,
of course, they thought I'm a nutcase. So I, still as stupid and stubborn as I was, I
would take them to the meetings. And then they end up doing the dishes. They

weren't interested in the discussion. Or they would end up just sleeping with one of the guys in the group, and then I would become completely devastated, you know, because it's not working out. I was young. I was naïve. And I would be so confused because how could this comrade use them. I would look at him the next morning. "How could you sleep with this woman. You were supposed to have made her a revolutionary?"

Then in my third year while at a reading group I met up with Jean Pease. And she tells me, "You can't live on the streets like that. You've got to come and live with me." And she was alone. She had just divorced. So I moved in with her. She was in Lansdowne. So I go and live with her and she was much older than me. She was a teacher. She was a science teacher, a very good teacher. And then she also got me to teach at Crestway. I became mature there as an educationist. I think there was the choice, you know. I could have become an activist or a serious, school-bound kind of educationist. And that's when I made the choice that I wanted to become a teacher.

June Bam graduated from UCT and reconciled with her family. In 1985, she returned to Grassy Park High School as a permanent teacher. This was a year of intense school boycotts; schools were closed by the government from April to September. Her memories are of political organizing and working with students from Grassy Park and nearby schools.

Then I only applied to one school, Grassy Park High. The principal was gone and there was a new principal. He was very organized, very ambitious. But that was a good thing for the school after the boycotts, because he wanted to make Grassy Park another Harold Cressy. Okay, so he had this mission. But this was also reactionary. In order to do that he had to get rid of all political activities, but do it in such a way that it sounds terribly progressive and legitimate, you know. So I go back into that situation. I got a permanent post. My first year and it was boycotts. And I thought, "Shit. I have just arrived." It was very militant and much harsher. And now the police were really stepping in, okay. By then I was married to Ghert. He was at the neighboring school. So, I walk into this classroom and it's the same room where I taught in 1980 and there are real working-class kids from Lavender Hill. And immediately we clicked. I clicked with the students. Yes, living in the hostel meant something, yes. And then I said, "Listen, we're to start a Youth Movement." I got Ghert into the idea and I got another activist into the idea. I then said, "But when we start this Youth Movement, we can't have it the way Brian Dublin had it, where you're completely separate from the youth and you just see them in reading groups. They've got to become part of your life and they've got to actually enter organizations." So I used some of the Athlone Youth Movement ideas at Grassy Park High.

We started this Youth Movement with forty people from the surrounding schools. This was during the boycott. So we'd call meetings and meetings. They stayed with me and some didn't have clothes and didn't have food. And then I got to know that some of them didn't even have parents. They would live with an older brother or sister. There was nothing to work for in South Africa. So I said that even if they are going into the working class, the important thing is that they are trained for the factory floor, to lead in a trade union. And that was my thing.

I became very unpopular at the school. The school was very organized. It wasn't the school as in 1980 where there was chaos, okay. It was very organized with a very set timetable, very strict discipline. The principal was trying to keep the school together at all costs as the model school that can even survive the boycott. And what I was doing was to make the kids aware and get them to break out of the boundaries of the discipline. I was alone. There were people who just didn't say anything, but they started to discuss me in the office as a threat to the school, to the school's discipline and ethos. And then they also couldn't understand what had happened to me because they just remembered me as a little girl and they couldn't control me.

I was called in and told I was an instigator and that the parents would be informed about my activities if I didn't stop. And then at a mass meeting one of the parents got up to say to the community, "If you want to find out who's really causing all this trouble with the kids, it's the Bams." So it was a battle. I think what protected me was the fact that the principal knew I was extremely hardworking. He also knew that there was a lot of respect for me. The students up till today still come to me. So he didn't know how to handle me.

June Bam took a leave to have a baby and spent her time helping to organize students against apartheid. She returned to Grassy Park in 1986. She spoke about politics at the school between 1986 and 1990 as well as teaching history.

I had my baby in January. I returned June 1986. When I came back there was antagonism. It was like, June's coming back school is going to be disrupted again. The Youth Movement was still in existence and we were still busy with our political work. And things now change dramatically because it's now a diverse group of intellectual people at the school. Yes, very, very different and very challenging. And the boycotts continued. Then it's disruptions. Then it's quiet. And that was right up to '88, I think. But Grassy Park was very quiet compared to the rest of the Western Cape because of the principal. It became one of the schools that started to be recognized as where you should send your kid if you want good education.

I was teaching history. Part of a mission! Students started to do history because many of them in the Youth Movement were exposed to the reading and discussions. History became a very established course at the school and we drew up our own curricula. But then I was called in and told I was teaching illegal stuff. And I'm going to be in trouble and I must remember the school is going to be in trouble.

So I said, "No, that's nonsense. You are allowed to teach what you want to teach and in any case the subject advisors cannot come to the school and what do they know?" I carried on with what I was teaching. They would take history with me and then what happened was all the bright kids started history. And that was the highlight of my career because working-class kids used history for leadership positions and to push their teachers.

In 1990, the school became intense as there were teacher schisms at the school. Although there was a critical mass of progressive teachers, they didn't always agree on tactics. Eventually, the progressive teachers came together as members of SADTU.

I took teaching extremely seriously. At the end of the day, I always thought that my weapon would be: I'm never absent, I'm never late, and I teach well. And teach, you know. That is how I saw myself as well as politically. They can be in whatever they're involved with, that's fine, as long as they also take their education seriously. And there would often be blow-ups at staff meetings.

So I was hated. And then there was a smear campaign. They said that I was a reactionary. I was a reactionary and I was playing into the hands of the conservatives. And the conservatives were saying I'm an instigator, I'm disruptive. Yes, they targeted me. "We'll burn you and your baby. You'll never see your child." On the telephone. It was very difficult for me because I didn't know who it was, but there were very definite attempts to intimidate me. We'd walk in the streets and they would shout. They would shout, "*Afbreeker! Afbreeker!*" The one who breaks down. They would intimidate the students in the Youth Movement.

Then we started to work together—the progressive teachers. We realized that we actually had a lot in common and the principal was gone, so he wasn't playing one against the other. So he caused a division, and as long as there was division on the staff it was fine for him because we were fighting so that we didn't stand together. So 1990 comes and we find that we actually share a hell of a lot in common. And this acting principal gives us a lot of space and then we start working together and we start teaching. They would give me their material. And they were also damn good teachers. That was really marvellous. And we even became more powerful, and our influence was more constructive. Mandela was released and we found a lot of common ground. They then became our comrades and we were all in SADTU. They had a lot of faith in me and I became one of the leaders within SADTU.

Oral History Craftsmanship as an Outsider

As I boarded the plane in South Carolina to travel to South Africa in January 1999, I was carrying Andre Brink's collection of essays, *Reinventing a Continent: Writing and Politics in South Africa*. The first essay in the book, "Speaking in Voices," begins, "You have no right, says my WASP acquaintance in New York a propos of my novel *A Chain of Voices*, no white writer has either the right or ability to appropriate black character's voice." Brink goes on to provide more examples of the same and to question the thesis. His examples are literary, such as, should Tolstoy not have written Anna Karenina? Is Fugard's work inauthentic? He argues that "unless one's public experience becomes fully integrated with one's most private awareness, writing about this experience can never transcend the level of the obvious or the propagandistic."

The question of the possibility of an "outsider" capturing the tone of a culture is asked often in fields like anthropology, sociology, and history. Corinne Glesne addresses the issue in her book *Becoming Qualitative Researchers*. Glesne presents arguments that support the position of Brink's WASP acquaintance, but she also presents the counter position of the "insider" being incapable of seeing past her own involvement. A precept that Brink appropriates from ethnographic methodology challenges the issue as either/or. The precept usually goes something like "The ethnographer's work is to make the strange familiar and the familiar strange." As I noted in the Introduction, there were colleagues at the University of the Western Cape who were convinced that people spoke to me because I was an "outsider." That they talked to me because I didn't represent any of the teacher or political groups in South Africa. I hadn't built distrust.

The late Barbara Myerhoff worked as both an outsider and an insider. She had completed her doctorate, which was a study of shamans in Mexico, and decided to visit a Mexican-American retirement center in Los Angeles, where she lived. After completing her degree she did library research on seniors and she wanted to do fieldwork. The Mexican-American link was because her prior research was with Shamans in Mexico. When Myerhoff made her contacts in Los Angeles, she was told in no uncertain terms to go study her own people. In her wonderful, whimsical way she thought about it and decided that one day she was going to be a little old Jewish woman (that never happened as she died from cancer when she was forty-eight years old), but she was never going to be an elder Mexican-American. She tells the story of the people at a Jewish retirement center in Venice Beach in her often-cited book, *Number Our Days*, which became a film of the same name.

A South African example of insider research that had a great effect on me was an essay Crain Soudien wrote as part of a commemorative volume in honor of Cape Town artist Peter Clarke and poet James Matthews. It is not so much specifics, as it is the tone Soudien creates that is so important to oral history. The richness of working-class life that Soudien portrays provides a picture of apartheid Cape Town that made me feel as if I was present. Soudien certainly was there. Interestingly, it made me question my own work in South Africa in spite of my knowing that the people whom I interviewed did tell me rich stories. But because Crain Soudien was so close to the life he portrayed, it also made me long for future oral history projects at home in South Carolina.

There are other questions regarding outsider/insider oral history work. In the United States Peter Friedlander addresses the issue in his theoretical work on interviewer-interviewee interaction. Friedlander explains how difficult interview communication can be, and he was interviewing someone from a similar background to his own. He discusses the huge communication gaps that are possible even when people share cultures. "Yet in spite of this common ground, we initially had considerable difficulty with language and meaning. . . a common language had to emerge out of our collaboration, one whose logic and terms of description would be clear and unambiguous to each of us. . . the actual emergence of our common language, and its verification, came after only months of 'practice'" (Friedlander, p. 134). In South Africa there are ongoing oral history debates because there are eleven official languages in the country. Marijke du Toit has discussed the issue in the context of both teaching oral history and doing oral history research. She argues that it is imperative that Xhosa-speaking people are interviewed in their first language. The day I listened to her presentation I taught my first class at the University of the Western Cape. There were sixteen students in the class and fourteen of them were first language Xhosa. All of the students spoke English, but they talked to each other in Xhosa and most of their daily conversations were in the language. We missed each other's point quite often during the semester. At some point we knew each other well enough and trusted one another so that misunderstandings were communicated at the moment. But communication was hard.

Although the issues that du Toit raises are important, they aren't directly relevant to the oral histories of apartheid-era teachers I interviewed. A few of the teachers I spoke with were first language Xhosa or Setho or Afrikaans. They had all spent their professional careers, however, in English-speaking settings and many of them received degrees from the University of Cape Town, which is definitely an English language institution. Du Toit's questions, though, do lead to other issues of culture and language about nuance, local terminology, and slang. Over time these barriers lessen, but initially there are statements that are not part of the outsider's vocabulary. For example, I didn't know what a "chalk-down" was and had never heard the word "casspirs." The former is a teacher's strike and the latter is a dreaded police vehicle that carried many policemen and also rammed fences and walls during apartheid.

Without denying cultural issues as an outsider, it might be that this particular oral history was meant for an outsider to research. And although it appears arrogant, it might open doors for South African oral historians to begin interviewing a broad spectrum of local teachers. That said, there are other issues that are important to this work. Oral history and memory have facilitated a great deal of debate, both in South Africa and internationally. Issues of class, race, ethnicity, and gender have been included in these discussions. In the United States insights into these issues are presented in Michael Frisch's book *A Shared Authority*. Frisch argues that oral historians must address the effect of the present on the past. In a review of the reviews of Studs Terkel's *Hard Times*, Frisch is astounded because reviewers did not address the fact that the people Terkel interviewed did not speak of the systemic issues of capitalism when they discussed the Depression. Frisch argues that the American dream and current ideology masked probing of the racism and class disparity that exist in the United States.

Sarah Nuttall and Carli Coetzee's book of essays, *Negotiating the Past: The Making of Memory in South Africa*, is rich for its diversity of critical essays. Discussions and debates on oral history and memory are especially important in South Africa as they revolve around the Truth and Reconciliation Commission. The South African discussions are relevant to my work with South African teachers. While the universal debates regarding oral history and memory are repeated in South Africa, there is also a new calling and questions of the uses of memories that become stories. Njabulo Ndebele stesses the importance of the "legitimacy and authority to previously silenced voices." He also stresses the possibilities of reflection that memory facilitates. "Isn't it that there is something inherently reflective about memory, as there is about narrative? If so, narratives of memory, in which real events are recalled, stand to guarantee us occasions for some serious moments of reflection" (Ndebele, 1998, p. 20). While Sean Field, the director of the Centre for Popular Memory, cautions oral historians about the constructive nature of memory, he too promotes oral history in a paper he presented at the TRC Conference. "The evocative power of the spoken voice needs to be heard, documented and interpreted. . . . Oral historians and oral history projects in South Africa and other African countries have a history of gathering the stories of oppressed, marginalised and economically poor people. This form of research, teaching and communication—with a range of potential outcomes—has profound value for South Africa's socio-political transformation" (Field, 1999, pp. 2, 3).

The teachers' oral histories presented in this book offer the same possibilities. They are stories of the effects apartheid had on these South African teachers, but also the teachers' human spirit that fought the apartheid regime. In that sense they are examples of some of the debate in South Africa regarding memory and apartheid. In an essay titled "Telling 'Free' Stories? Memory and Democracy in South African Autobiography Since 1994," Sarah Nuttall analyzes World Bank Vice-President Mamphela Ramphale's autobiography, A Life. Her analysis of Ramphale's book is illuminating for post-apartheid South Africa because it addresses both personal and collective freedom. Nuttall argues that Ramphale is "declaring herself free" in her writing and then says, "Memory apparently, loses its inhibitions and speaks of silences, restores a missing past, leading to what Nadine Gordimer has termed 'the liberation of openness'" (Nuttall, 1998, p. 81).

"Liberation of openness" is what comes to mind for many Americans when they consider the Truth and Reconciliation Commission. But the TRC also has a lot to do with "nation building" and provides us with the opportunity to examine the uses of memory. The people who testified were able to make public statements for the first time. In the new South Africa they had a voice. But how far does that voice go? How do South Africans react to Bishop Tutu's words after a particularly hard day of the hearings? "We should all be humbled by what we've heard, but we've got to finish quickly and really turn our backs on this awful past and say: Life is for the living" (Tobias, 1999, p. 6). But when do we do that? How much do we hear? How much do we say? How long do we listen?

It was important that South Africans were able to celebrate the victory over apartheid—celebrate collectively as a nation as well as celebrate anti-apartheid heroes. But I return to Bishop Tutu's words. A harsher representation of South Africans "remembering in order to forget" is presented by Ingrid De Kok. De Kok explains that National Party leader Danie Schutte voted in favor of implementing the TRC so that South African apartheid could be a finished issue. She quotes Schutte as saying that the TRC was a way of "getting the past out of the way" (De Kok, 1998, p. 59). De Kok's analysis is insightful. "The language of the 'clean break' turns into the apparently ethical consideration of 'forgive and forget' and 'life must go on.' It expresses a terror that, if we take one glimpse backwards, we may be dragged back into the apartheid underworld" (De Kok, 1998, p. 59).

Just as many Germans want to forget the Nazi past, there are many South Africans who want to forget apartheid. Steve Robins makes this point in a discussion about his father. "Like my father's silence about the Holocaust, it seems likely that millions of black parents are unable to express what they feel about the humiliations and pain of their everyday experiences of racism under apartheid" (Robins, 1998, p. 125). Kevin Wildschut, whose story is told in Section Three, spoke emotionally of the same issue in the context of his current students. Wildschut had visited Auschwitz and he contrasted the German *"Nicht Zieder"*—"Never Again," to an attitude of "Let's Move On"—"Let's Forget"—"Bury the Past." "They don't want to know the history of our country in the last fifteen years. 'Why must we always talk about apartheid?' It's almost like a sense of thank God it's over. It's done. It's past. Let's forget it and move on with our lives."

For me this brings even more questions about the continuing effects of apartheid. Bishop Tutu's words have been said in different ways by many South Africans. Danie Schutte and Kevin Wildschut's students have different perspectives and motivations. So why do they both want to forget? When one writes oral history there are almost always people whom you want to interview who scorn talking about the past. Interestingly, the teachers whom I met as I worked on this particular project were eager to tell their stories. But many of the people I spoke with told me that they rarely talk about the issues of the past. Yet, the teachers whose stories are told above were both open and forthcoming. And they remembered a lot of events that need to be passed on to the generations of their children and grandchildren.

The teachers who are the essence of this book wouldn't be included in the textbook definitions of heroes or victims. They are not heroic if people like President Mandela and Bishop Tutu are how we define heroes. They aren't victims either, though, if that is defined by the deaths of the Cradock Seven or Steve Biko. But they were greatly affected by apartheid and their lives as teachers include both bravery and horror. When Richard Dudley and Tom Hanmer sent the police away from their schools in the seventies, they were defying the apartheid state. As were Mandy Sanger and Glen van Harte and others who joined student protest marches in 1985. It was the case when Rose Jackson marched through the streets of Khayelitsha in the early nineties, and when Vivienne Carelse, Chitra Narshi, and Jean September taught their students lessons that were critical of apartheid ideology and legislation in the eighties. And it certainly was the case when police threatened teachers and students; or when Neville Alexander, Sedick Isaacs, and others were jailed. The horrors of apartheid were ever present in these teachers' lives, but it couldn't steal their souls.

All of this aside, these teachers were the people on the ground. Their stories are important because they are citizens who spent their lives working with South African children under apartheid conditions. Because of the government and because of the times, education and politics were never separate parts of their lives. So the people whose stories are told in this book offer both personal and collective windows to teaching and learning and school life during the apartheid years—and those stories are important. As I was leaving Polly Slingers' house he said, "Your research won't mean anything unless you are hard on Eiselen." I thought to myself that other people like Cynthia Kros have done critical work on Eiselen, and I said, "Mr. Slingers, my work will be worthwhile if your grandchildren read your story." Of course, I was talking about collective grandchildren. But even more than that, the stories of the teachers we have met are examples for teachers and future teachers and others, both in South Africa and around the world. They are important because they are stories of political and academic teachers who exude commitment and caring and love, for both their students and their country. They are *"teachers with the fighting spirit."* As an "outsider," I can only hope that I have done justice to their lives.

Bibliography

Adhikari, Mohamed. *Let Us Live for Our Children: The Teachers' League of South Africa, 1913-1940.* Cape Town, UCT Press, 1993.

Alexander, Neville. "Non-Collaboration in the Western Cape," in *The Angry Divide*, edited by Wilmot James and Mary Simons. Cape Town, David Philip, 1989, pp. 180-191.

Alexander, Neville. *Robben Island Dossier, 1964-1974.* Cape Town, UCT Press, 1994.

Ayers, William. "I Search, You Search," in *Writing Educational Biography*, edited by Craig Kridel. New York, Garland, 1998, pp. 235-244.

Bam, June, and Pippa Visser. *A New History for a New South Africa.* Cape Town, Kagiso Publishers, 1999.

Brink, Andre. *Reinventing a Contenent: Writing and Politics in South Africa.* Cambridge, MA, Zoland Books, 1998.

Chisholm, Linda. "Education, Politics and Organisation: The Educational Traditions and Legacies of the Non-European Unity Movement 1943-86." *Transformation* 15. 1991. pp. 1-25.

Daniels, Eddie. *There and Back: Robben Island 1964-1979.* Cape Town, Mayibuye, Books, 1998.

Deacon, Harriet. "Remembering Tragedy, Constructing Modernity: Robben Island as a National Museum," in *Negotiating the Past: The Making of Memory in South Africa.* Edited by Sarah Nuttall and Carli Coetzee. Cape Town, Oxford University Press, 1998. pp. 161-179.

De Kok, Ingrid. "Cracked Heirlooms: Memory on Exhibition," in *Negotiating the Past: The Making of Memory in South Africa.* Edited by Sarah Nuttall and Carli Coetzee. Cape Town, Oxford University Press, 1998, pp. 57-71.

DeVilliers, Elizabeth. *Walking the Tightrope: Recollections of a Schoolteacher in Soweto.* Johannesburg, Jonathan Ball, 1990.

Dudley, Richard. Jonas Fred Bosch Memorial Lecture, pamphlet printed by the New Unity Movement. Cape Town, 1992.

Fanon, Franz. *Black Skin/White Masks*. New York, Grove Press, 1967.

Field, Sean. "Memory, the TRC and the Significance of Oral History in Post-Apartheid South Africa," paper presented at The TRC: Commissioning the Past. University of Witwatersrand, June 1999

Finnegan, William. *Crossing the Line: A Year in the Land of Apartheid*. Berkeley, University of California Press, 1994.

Friedlander, Peter. "Theory, Method, and Oral History," in *Oral History: An Interdisciplinary Anthology*. Edited by David Dunaway and Willa Baum. Walnut Creek, Altamira Press, 1996, pp. 150–160.

Frisch, Michael. *A Shared Authority: Essays on the Craft and Meaning of Oral and Public History*. Albany, NY, State University of New York Press, 1990.

Goldin, Ian. *Making Race: The Politics and Economics of Coloured Identity in South Africa*. London, Longman, 1987.

Goodson, Ivor. "The Life and Work of Teachers," in *South African Review of Education*. V2, N2, October 1996, pp. 1–19.

Jeppie, Shamil, and Crain Soudien. *The Struggle for District Six*. Cape Town, Buchu Books, 1990

Kallaway, Peter. *Apartheid and Education: The Education of Black South Africans*. Johannesburg, Raven Press, 1984.

Kallaway, Peter, Kruss, Glenda, Fataar, Aslam, Donn, Gari. *Education After Apartheid*. Cape Town, University of Cape Town Press, 1997.

Kallaway, Peter. *The History of Education Under Apartheid*. New York, Peter Lang, Publishers, 2002.

Kathrada, Ahmed. *Letters from Robben Island: A Selection of Ahmed Kathrada's Prison Correspondence*. Cape Town, Mayibuye Books, 1999.

Kihn, Paul. "Players or Pawns?: Professionalism and Teacher Disunity in the Western Cape, 1980–1990." MPHIL Dissertation, University of Cape Town, 1993.

Krog, Antjie. *Country of My Skull*. Johannesburg, Random House, 1998.

Lewis, Gavin. *Between the Wire and the Wall: A History of South African Coloured Politics*. Cape Town, Johannesburg, David Philip, 1987.

Mandela, Nelson. *Long Walk to Freedom*. South Africa, Macdonald Purnell, 1994.

Molteno, Frank. *Students Struggle for Their Schools*. Cape Town, The Centre for African Studies, 1987.

Nasson, Bill. "The Unity Movement: Its Legacy in Historical Consciousness," *Radical History Review*. 1990, pp. 189–211.

Ndebele, Njabulo. "Memory, Metaphor, and the Triumph of Narrative," in *Negotiating the Past: The Making of Memory in South Africa*. Edited by Sarah Nuttall and Carli Coetzee. Cape Town, Oxford University Press, 1998, pp. 19–28.

Nkomo, Mokubung. *Pedagogy of Domination*. Trenton, NJ, Africa World Press, 1990.

Nuttall, Sarah, and Carli Coetzee. *Negotiating the Past: The Making of Memory in South Africa*. Cape Town, Oxford University Press, 1998.

Nuttall, Sarah. "Telling 'Free' Stories? Memory, Democracy in South African Autobiography Since 1994," in *Negotiating the Past: The Making of Memory in South Africa*. Edited by Sarah Nuttall and Carli Coetzee. Cape Town, Oxford University Press, 1998, pp. 75–88.

Parker, Tony. *A Life in Words: Studs Terkel.* New York, Henry Holt and Company, 1996.

Robins, Steve. "Silence in My Father's House: Memory, Nationalism, and Narratives of the Body," in *Negotiating the Past: The Making of Memory in South Africa.* Edited by Sarah Nuttall and Carli Coetzee. Cape Town, Oxford University Press, 1998, pp. 120–140.

Soudien, Crain. "We Know Why We're Here," *Race Ethnicity and Education* vlnl 7–29 1998.

Soudien, Crain. "Social Conditions, Cultural and Political Life in Working-Class Cape Town, 1950 to 1980," in Willemse, Hein. *More than Brothers.* Cape Town, Kwela Books, 2000.

Tabata, Isaac Bangani. *Education for Barbarism: Bantu Education in South Africa.* London, Prometheus Books. 1959.

Tobias, Saul. "History, Memory and the Ethics of Writing: Antjie Krog's *Country of My Skull,*" paper presented at The TRC: Commissioning the Past. University of Witwatersrand, June 1999.

Tutu, Desmond. *No Future Without Forgiveness.* New York, Image/Doubleday, 1999.

Western, John. *Outcast Cape Town.* Berkeley, University of California Press, 1996.